Truman, Palestine, and the Press

Recent Titles in
Contributions in American History

The Fragmentation of New England: Comparative Perspectives on Economic,
Political, and Social Divisions in the Eighteenth Century
Bruce C. Daniels

The Frontiers, 1607-1860: The Agricultural Evolution of the Colonial and
Antebellum South
John Solomon Otto

Progressivism at Risk: Electing a President in 1912
Francis L. Broderick

The New Deal and Its Legacy: Critique and Reappraisal
Robert Eden

Campaigning in America: A History of Election Practices
Robert J. Dinkin

Looking South: Chapters in the Story of an American Region
Winfred B. Moore, Jr., and Joseph F. Tripp, editors

News in the Mail: The Press, Post Office, and Public Information, 1700-1860s
Richard B. Kielbowicz

North from Mexico: The Spanish-Speaking People of the United States. New
Edition, Updated by Matt S. Meier
Carey McWilliams

Reagan and the World
David E. Kyvig, editor

The American Consul: A History of the United States Consular Service,
1776-1914
Charles Stuart Kennedy

Reform and Reaction in Twentieth Century American Politics
John J. Broesamle

A Quest for Security: The Life of Samuel Parris, 1653-1720
Larry Gragg

Anti-Racism in U.S. History: The First Two Hundred Years
Herbert Aptheker

Truman, Palestine, and the Press

Shaping Conventional Wisdom at the Beginning of the Cold War

Bruce J. Evensen

Contributions in American History, Number 144
Jon L. Wakelyn, Series Editor

GREENWOOD PRESS
New York • Westport, Connecticut • London

Library of Congress Cataloging-in-Publication Data

Evensen, Bruce J.
    Truman, Palestine, and the press : shaping conventional wisdom at
the beginning of the Cold War / Bruce J. Evensen.
        p.   cm.—(Contributions in American history, ISSN 0742-6828
; no. 144)
    Includes bibliographical references and index.
    ISBN 0-313-27773-7
    1. Palestine—History—Partition, 1947. 2. United States—Foreign
relations—Palestine. 3. Palestine—Foreign relations—United
States. 4. United States—Foreign relations—1945-1953. 5. Israel—
Foreign public opinion, American. 6. Public opinion—United
States. I. Title. II. Series.
DS126.4.E86   1992
956.94—dc20   91-30604

British Library Cataloguing in Publication Data is available.

Library of Congress Catalog Card Number: 91-30604
ISBN: 0-313-27773-7
ISSN: 0742-6828

First published in 1992

Greenwood Press, 88 Post Road West, Westport, CT 06881
An imprint of Greenwood Publishing Group, Inc.

Printed in the United States of America

The paper used in this book complies with the
Permanent Paper Standard issued by the National
Information Standards Organization (Z39.48-1984).

10 9 8 7 6 5 4 3 2 1

To my loving wife and family

for the many years they patiently listened.

They bore my enthusiasm gracefully.

And to my brother, Steve, co-laborer in the faith,

who did not make it to this finish line.

Contents

My thanks to Stephen Vaughn of the University of Wisconsin-Madison, who has been an enormous help at every step in this research. His continuing counsel and encouragement made this study possible. Particular thanks as well to Professors James Baughman, William Hachten, John Cooper and Kemal Karpat of the University of Wisconsin-Madison for their assistance on specific chapters. Louis Liebovich of the University of Illinois at Champaign/Urbana and Doris Graber of the University of Illinois at Chicago kindly consented to review particular sections of the book, as did William David Sloan of the University of Alabama. Robert Farrell of Indiana University and Richard Kirkendall of the University of Washington were very helpful in assisting my research at the Truman Library in Independence, Missouri, as were Benedict Zobrist, Phil Lowderquist, Irwin Mueller, Liz Safly, Dennis Bilger and Neil Johnson of the Truman Library staff. Ida Cohen Selavan at Hebrew Union College in Cincinnati deserves special thanks for her assistance with the Zionist press. Bob Frykenberg at Wisconsin helped develop the battle plan on accessing British collections. My thanks to Margaret (Peggy) Blanchard of the University of North Carolina for suggesting in an elevator ride Greenwood as a publisher and to Cynthia Arnett, Tom Roser, Joe Baker and Sue Sublewski at DePaul University in Chicago for their very considera ble assistance with this project and to Paul Sublewski for his ingenious macro.

Preface: Reporter as Spectator and Participant in the Construction of Conventional Wisdom

My interest in the relationship of policymaking, the press and the public in the construction of the Truman administration's Cold War Palestine policy began in the spring of 1983. I was based in West Jerusalem working out of the Binyanei Haooma, the Israeli convention center, that served as headquarters for news bureaus serving much of the Western world. The West Germans, the French, the Dutch, the Swiss, the Japanese, and the Americans all shared cramped office space in a building designed to facilitate transmission of their stories home.

Western correspondents worked and relaxed as a community within a community enclosed in common experiences which led to a sharing and deepening of their conventional wisdom. Military patrols took reporters to the same stories at the same time, to interview the same people who told the same stories, which were cleared through the same censor and transmitted at the same time via satellite to editors, who may or may not have been aware of the sameness of the stuff they were getting. When the day's work was done, reporters often joined one another at the American Colony Hotel in East Jerusalem to trade drinks with the wire service guys and the network news bosses. Everyone watched and read everyone else's work and monitored the British Broadcasting Company repeater station in Cyprus as well as Kol Israel, the radio voice of Israel, the Israeli press and Jordan's English language newscast; and if they did not, their editors made sure that they did.

It soon became apparent that the demand from editors was not to report everything that one knew or could be known about the conflict in the Middle East, nor even something new. One was instead expected to report all or most of what everyone else did, and more or less at the same time. Efficiency, not enterprise, was behind professional advancement, if not survival. A reporter failed to meet the expectation of an editor at his or her own peril. Everyone remembered the case of the young reporter who asked if Israel was in Africa and the over eager correspondent who wrongly reported that American marines were about to storm Beirut. The novice was taken to a map and schooled in the fundamentals of conventional wisdom, while the veteran was reassigned for violating his. Editors abided ignorance better than error.

Being attentive to what others reported initiated newcomers into what passed for the "facts" about the Middle East. They obediently learned to file story after story that were but part of a larger story, hatched from a line of logic they had brought in on the plane with them and reified by colleagues who shared the same certainties. The logic underlying this conventional wisdom operated in a closed curve. Reporters invariably sought out sources who sustained the taken for granted and used the same sources who did not as mere foils. In this way, many of the reporters telling stories about the Middle East during the spring and summer of 1983 tended to define what they were seeing first and to see it only afterwards. When asked, they were often unaware that the "facts" they gathered were being made to fit a storyline that had been fashioned long before in the collective understanding that tends to guide the storytelling function of the press wherever its stories are told. Those who acknowledged that interpretation guided their "fact-finding" reckoned that reporting was impossible without it and that conventional wisdom was a better guide to getting stories accepted and read or viewed than wisdom of an unconventional sort.

The stories a reporter tells, particularly in foreign news, appear as much a product of organizational constraint as the culture-bound interpretations that inform that storytelling. To justify the cost of keeping a correspondent abroad, well over $100,000 annually at this writing, editors expect a certain number of stories filed, broadcast, or published, which pressures the reporter to produce regularly. Organizational expectations as well as personal rewards become tied to the reporter finding a formula that keeps the editor satisfied. The tendency is to work within a comfort zone that assures the production of stories within a conventional wisdom or prevailing logic shared by editor and audience alike. This domain of the routinely accepted serves as the wellspring for much Western reporting coming out of the Middle East.

What passed for conventional wisdom on the Middle East in 1983 and 1984 appeared rooted in some sense of the region's political history, even if individual correspondents seemed uncertain about the details of that history. It was commonplace, for instance, for them to speak of the West Bank or Gaza as Israeli-occupied territories. But between 1948 and 1967 when Jordanian armies controlled the West Bank that territory was not referred to as "Jordanian-occupied" in the Western press, despite the fact that Jordan had taken possession of the land through military action in 1948. More recently, the press has come to use the term "Palestinian" to refer to an Arab living in the West Bank or Gaza. But "Palestine" is a Roman term describing land extending eastward from the Mediterranean Sea beyond the Jordan River. After the nation of Jordan was created within the British mandate over Palestine, the term "Palestinian" did not immediately come to mean Arabs living west of the Jordan. So for the press now to refer only to Arabs living west of the Jordan as "Palestinians," is a political judgment of who has the right to rule Palestine.

Reporters defend themselves by saying they are not in the business of making political judgments but rather of reporting the judgments of others. In other words, they do not make things mean, but simply report the meanings others have assigned to things. Among themselves, reporters do not take such talk seriously. Their personal conversation and memoirs are filled with how necessary the "Fourth Estate" is to those who govern and those who are governed. They see themselves as mediators in the policymaking process, democracy's referees, whose vigilance assures the competition between policymakers and interested publics in policymaking is no unfair fight. Some journalists still hold to the Enlightenment notion of reporter as public servant, one who provides citizens with the information they need to make sound choices. Most reporters on the foreign beat, however, are not as confident the public is up to the job of making fine distinctions. These journalists see their social responsibility as making things mean, to put news into interpretative frameworks that aid the understanding of editors and audience.

Certain critical historians have seen a conspiracy in this and have suggested reporters are in business to facilitate those who exercise social control, whether they be presidents or publishers. But most reporters are far more parochial in their pursuits. Their ambition is to have their work printed or broadcast, with an occasional kind word said to them by constituencies with whom they are in most intimate contact---other reporters, editors, sources, and on rare occasions, readers or viewers. Theirs is not an epistemological struggle. They do not stay awake nights trying to separate fact from fact-based fiction or choosing from among several equally attractive alternative interpretations to guide their storytelling. Rather, reporters are guided by a latent sense of economy, an instinct for what will work, an understanding sharpened by a career in storytelling that has made them expert at making things mean. To be a good journalist is to make the stories that one tells go unchallenged, or if challenged, to have them hold up.

How the taken for granted in foreign policy gets taken for granted and the role the media play in that process interested the British journalist and Parliamentarian Richard Crossman, who was a leading member of the Anglo-American Committee in 1946. The committee's failed mission was to come up with a recommendation for the future status of Palestine that would be acceptable to British and American negotiators as well as the Jews and Arabs of Palestine. The committee's work collapsed, Crossman was certain, because leading politicians had little time to focus on the particular problems of Palestine and instead relied on bureaucratic interpretations of the committee's work. These government workers, he insisted, had a personal stake in perpetuating policies on Palestine with which they had become identified. These policies helped to sustain old ways of seeing, which worked to frustrate the initiative needed to bring various factions closer to settlement. It was perhaps for this reason that Chaim Weizmann, Israel's first president and a veteran observer of Western ways of seeing, remarked that fact-finding committees routinely passed through Palestine, often leaving more ignorant than when they had come. The reports committee members wrote, Weizmann noted, were hardly read and then quickly forgotten.

In the complicated world of foreign policymaking, U.S. State Department officials have often boasted their experience and training has taught them what is best for the country. But American diplomats involved in the Truman administration's consideration of Palestine's future often perpetuated old ways of seeing by relying on information as limited as reporters' accounts of the Palestine story. Perhaps the best example of this came on the eve of the formal ending of the British mandate over Palestine in May, 1948. At a stormy White House meeting called to consider American recognition of a new Jewish state, Secretary of State George C. Marshall angrily denied press reports that he had sent a secret message to David Ben-Gurion, the head of the Jewish Agency and the man who would in two days become Israel's first prime minister. "I did not know that such a person even existed," Marshall admitted.

Marshall's ignorance was matched by public indifference. In November of 1947, the month the United Nations voted to partition Palestine into separate Jewish and Arab states, twice as many Americans favored Jewish aspirations in Palestine over Arab interests, but two in three favored neither side or had no opinion. Although the press was daily filling with reports of Arab-Jewish violence in Palestine, by year's end most Americans listed the high cost of living, the growing Soviet-American conflict, the Marshall Plan and the Taft-Hartley Act as the issues that most concerned them. By the end of February, 1948, the problems of Palestine were further subordinated to fresh fears of war with the Soviet Union. Czechoslovakia's fall to a Communist coup prompted a major war scare. A network newscast warned that an imminent Soviet air attack was being planned over the North Pole. Before a joint session of the Congress, President Truman urged an immediate return to the military draft. More than one-half of all persons polled thought the United States would soon be at war, and seven of every ten so persuaded were certain the war would be with the Russians.

Walter Lippmann has observed that foreign policymaking proceeds along lines of interpretation, which are in part informed by the press. By defining first and seeing only afterwards the press provides a preoccupied public with "pictures" of the world that become the basis for action. Cognitive psychologists and political scientists point out that Lippmann's observations hold true only insofar as the public is paying attention and only to the degree that news reports appear to fit the public's storehouse of preconceptions. In 1948 these preconceptions ran in the direction of seeing Palestine as a field of competition involving the Great Powers and to a lesser extent, as a haven for Holocaust survivors. By 1983 and 1984, Western reporters still saw the Middle East as an East-West testing ground, as well as a place where Palestinian "rights of self-determination" continued to be violated.

Researchers in political communication suggest political learning appears guided by ways of seeing that commend themselves to us by virtue of convenience and economy. We see the world in the way that we do, and the political actors in it because it pays us to see the world in that way and not in some other way. The "pictures in our heads" of the way the world "really is," are replaced by other pictures, but less frequently than we would admit because thinking anew and afresh is difficult and time-consuming. This case is true for the public and policymakers just as it is for the press whose business it is to reproduce stories that can be swiftly assimilated into our storehouse of meanings. News, therefore, becomes not simply the reportable event, but the event that obtrudes into a reporter's reality in a place where he is looking and in a way that welcomes the interpretation he brings to the event.

Most reporters and policymakers quickly learn that they frustrate the expectations of their publics at their own peril. That is why a commonly held wisdom forms the boundaries within which reporter and policymaker comfortably operate. When either strays into an enterprise zone he or she is all alone and faces the fate of the reporter who saw marines assaulting Beirut. To be premature or late may be as deadly a sin as getting it wrong. That is why policymakers and the press in the West are conservative forces, whose reproduction of meaning is always attentive to a public, which votes or views, or chooses not to. The inattentive faces loss of professional life. Therefore, each becomes an excellent map reader, understanding the limits of reportable boundaries and predictably operating within those limits. This ritual of mutual consent can be seen in reporters and policymakers who projected themselves into developments in the Middle East in 1948, as well as those who did the same in 1983 and 1984. Few recognized how fragmentary was the information that served as the basis of their reports, how interest-bound their conclusions, or how Western ways of seeing shaped the content of what passed for the conventional wisdom on Palestine.

The purpose of this book, then, is to examine how conventional wisdom---or the taken for granted---came to be constructed in the American debate over Palestine that preceded and helped make possible Israeli independence. In this debate, the media, along with an array of interested publics and competing policymakers struggled to shape a Palestine policy that could command consensus at the coming of the Cold War. Each realized what President Truman conceded, that no foreign policy initiative, once begun, could be sustained indefinitely in the absence of public support. The efforts to win that support became enmeshed, particularly after March, 1948, in issues extending far beyond Palestine's borders. At risk was America's perceived postwar role and the place of the United Nations in that world. That these were the stakes, or so it appeared, owed much to the power of interpretation and the force of political imagination. And it was within this realm of the politically possible that reporters played their role as spectator and participant. This book is an unfolding of that dual role and its place in the historical process that led to the creation of Israel.

Introduction: Riding the Tiger

In his memoirs, Harry S. Truman observed that during his first six months in office in 1945 he discovered that "being President is like riding a tiger. A man has to keep riding or be swallowed." This realization was especially true in the Middle East where the new president had more than the problem of Palestine on his hands. Waning British influence in the region coincided with an intensification of the Jewish-Arab struggle at the close of World War II. The new administration viewed these conflicts in the broader context of East-West tensions and the crisis over rebuilding war-ravaged Europe. In Truman's view, the Russian military occupation of parts of Iran at the close of the war "threatened the peace of the world." The president and his secretary of state, George C. Marshall, became convinced the Iranian action was a prelude to the penetration by the Soviets of Turkey and the outright occupation of Greece. Truman wrote that whereas at Potsdam he had shown little appetite for becoming embroiled in the intractable problems of the Middle East, subsequent events outside his control forced his hand.[1]

In recent years, much of the literature analyzing these events has reflected each author's attitude on Zionism and the efficacy of creating a Jewish state in Palestine. Those opposing such a state criticized the Truman administration for caving in to the pressure that made it possible. Those sympathetic to Zionist objectives saw the president inevitably giving way to the force of informed public opinion.[2]

At issue in this debate over President Truman's Palestine policy is the relation between American diplomacy and the mass media. Historians have questioned the degree to which a mobilized public shaped President Truman's Cold War policy and the extent to which that opinion was shaped by him and members of his administration through the nation's press. Certain historians have claimed the Truman administration initiated the Cold War as a result of

economic and imperial considerations.[3] They suggest the public proved
"malleable, compliant and permissive" and set imprecise limits that hardly
inhibited the implementation of Truman's Cold War initiatives.[4] These
researchers reached this conclusion by relying on two kinds of evidence. The
first was a series of statements that Truman and his aides made concerning
their general disdain of public opinion as a guide to foreign policy.[5] The
second kind of evidence was mass media research that saw the public as
predominantly passive, inattentive to foreign policy issues, and failing to
actively engage political information. This formulation enables the researcher
to argue that neither the press nor public opinion played an important role in
constraining presidential foreign policy in the Cold War period.[6]

A competing school of scholars contends the Cold War cannot be
understood unless one recognizes how public opinion created a framework
which constrained the Truman administration. These researchers pay particular
attention to the policymaking environment, seeing it as a field that defines the
realm of the politically possible. Policymaking is seen as a two way street in
which political leaders initiate policies that are tested in the court of public
opinion. That opinion lends legitimacy to the actions of policymakers and
redefines the boundaries within which future decisions will be made.[7]

Much of this discussion assumes certain things about the formation of
public opinion and its influence over policymaking that is the subject of
widespread investigation by students of the mass media. These researchers
have conducted more than 200 studies into the agenda-setting function of the
press, attempting to better understand the relation of the press, the public, and
policymakers within the policymaking process.[8] The prevailing view of these
scholars has shifted significantly in recent years. Initial research in the field
suggested the press had a powerful hand in the formation of opinion and could
be used as an instrument in molding sentiment in support of specific
objectives.[9] That view was later challenged by scholars who argued that the
power of the press over opinion was greatly exaggerated, and that the press
tended to reflect public opinion more than it formed it.[10] In recent years, this
limited effects model of the press has been further modified. Researchers have
seen policymaking as a process in which the press, the public, and
policymakers act upon one another in reciprocal ways. Who is influencing
whom at any point in time is subject to change as circumstances change. These
researchers emphasize the essential fluidity of the policymaking process and
the latent power of the press, under certain circumstances, to affect the
outcome of that process.[11]

This study examines some of the larger questions diplomatic
historians, political scientists and mass media scholars have raised concerning
the relation of the press, the public and policymakers in the development of
American foreign policy. It analyzes media coverage of the Truman
administration's Palestine policy in the sixteen months leading up to the

creation of the state of Israel in May, 1948, and the efforts of various interested parties to influence that coverage. In the case of Palestine, American Zionists and senior officials within the State Department were two of the primary players who saw the media, and particularly the *New York Times*, as a site of persuasive activity distinct from yet linked to the broader strategies of mobilizing support for their positions. Through this competition, the media became more than the simple servant of the administration on Palestine. Instead, led by the *Times*, it played an increasingly active part in the policymaking environment, at first encouraging and later discouraging administration designs on Palestine at the beginning of the Cold War.

The expanding role of the media in reporting the conflict over Palestine passed through three distinct phases from the time the British turned the problem over to the United Nations in January, 1947, until the partitioning of Palestine in May, 1948. This period saw Palestine move progressively from the sidelines to the center of the world stage. During the first phase---from January, 1947, through November, 1947---the nation's daily press and its radio commentators primarily regarded Palestine as a place of competition between the Soviet Union and the United States. This outlook made the reporters and editors highly susceptible to arguments advanced by the State Department suggesting that partition would lead to chaos and Soviet penetration in the Eastern Mediterranean. A second phase in media attention to Palestine began on November 29, 1947, when a two-thirds majority of member states in the United Nations voted to partition Palestine into separate Arab and Jewish states. The *New York Times*, joined by elite dailies and network commentators, vigorously endorsed the action and concurred with President Truman's claim that the action supported the U.N.'s mission of preserving postwar peace.

It was not until March 19, 1948, however, when the Truman administration abruptly abandoned its support for partition and called for a U.N. trusteeship over Palestine that the third and most crucial phase of press coverage began. During this time, the *Times* saw itself as an active player in the Palestine controversy, not out of any great love for the Zionist cause but because it perceived the administration's switch on Palestine to be an act of moral cowardice in a time requiring firm resolve. The eight weeks that followed not only saw the Truman administration lose control over its Palestine policy but how that policy was interpreted in much of the media. This development produced a policymaking environment that played into Zionist hands because it redefined for President Truman the realm of the politically possible, leading eventually to his abandonment of the trusteeship scheme and his recognition of the Jewish state within minutes of its formal declaration on May 14, 1948.

The relationship of the press and policymakers in the case of Palestine is examined in this study at several levels. It includes the Truman administration's ongoing fear of premature disclosures; the press' ever-constant demand for news and the administration's sometimes hasty efforts to provide it; the administration's continuing anxiety over how it would be represented in the press; the press' perceived impact on public opinion; and the administration's effort to cultivate the press and thereby improve the image of its policy in the minds of the American people. Cultivation included leaking stories to the press that would be positive to that image, while stopping leaks perceived as damaging to it.[12] In this effort, the administration found certain segments of the press highly cooperative and others intensely combative.[13]

Also examined is the amount of attention governments paid to the press and how reports---some factual, some distorted---compelled the Truman administration to act both publicly and privately to dispel those reports. The result was a continuing series of contacts with foreign governments and agencies who needed to be calmed as a result of what they had read in the press.[14] Such was the case, as well, for factions within the Truman administration which attempted to use the press to combat one another and to speak directly to their constituencies. A notable example of this infighting was the conflict between the White House staff, headed by Clark Clifford and George Elsey, which was sympathetic to Zionist aspirations in Palestine, and the Near East division of the State Department, which was not.[15] Members of the media were aware of the conflict, that reached out to embrace the defense community, the Joint Chiefs of Staff and the American mission to the United Nations, and the media itself. The *New York Times*, in particular, was one of the sites of that struggle.[16]

Complicating this policy debate were the actions of Zionist groups and a Zionist press arrayed against the forces opposed to the creation of a Jewish state. The American Zionist Emergency Council, in particular, was well placed to lead the struggle for statehood. Through more than 400 local councils, it applied unceasing pressure at the grass roots level, hoping to mobilize opinion.[17] This effort helped to produce a groundswell of public pressure in behalf of Jewish statehood. And on November 29, 1947, thanks to the partition vote, Zionists could claim a new and powerful ally when the *New York Times* was won to their side.[18]

Particular attention is paid to the *New York Times* in this study because of its understanding of its role in molding opinion during the Cold War and because Truman apparently gave more attention to it than any other paper.[19] One veteran White House reporter and a Truman press aide suggested the President considered the *Times* his "Bible of informed opinion."[20] But the *Times* was not the only paper that Truman examined regularly. By his own estimation, he daily read each of the New York, Washington, and Pittsburgh papers, as well as the *Baltimore Sun*, the *Philadelphia Bulletin*, the *St. Louis Post-Dispatch*, the *Kansas City Star*, the

Chicago Times and the *Chicago Sun*. "I read them because I like to read them," he told reporters. "And I find out lots of things about myself I never heard of."[21]

Truman's humor did not extend to editors and publishers he considered antagonistic. He labelled their editorials part of the "sabotage press" and suggested that in other times and other places they would have been shot. Truman's derision extended to columnists like Drew Pearson, Walter Winchell, Joseph and Stewart Alsop and Walter Lippmann, men whose judgments Truman saw drawn from "ivory towers." Truman was equally contemptuous of network radio commentators who he felt failed to understand the purposes of his policies. Even in retirement he remained convinced too many of them engaged in a pack mentality and were "overly sensitive to criticism." Jack Bell of the Associated Press thought precisely the opposite was true. Bell claims that Truman's insistence on a bipartisan foreign policy "made him extremely hostile to his critics." Bells says it made Truman appear to have "a chip on his shoulder." The more Truman said that criticism did not bother him, Bell was convinced, the more apparent it was how much "it got under his skin."[22]

Bell's impression was shared by many reporters who covered the Truman White House. Richard L. Strout of the *Christian Science Monitor* thought a lot of reporters "decried and minimized" Truman because he had "the disadvantage of following a famous President." Robert Riggs of the *Louisville Courier-Journal* thought Truman would be capable of little more than "an earnest and inept presidency." What he lacked in experience would be all the more dangerous "through his lack of self-control." White House correspondent Raymond Brandt summed up the opinion of many when he lamented that he "couldn't believe that Truman was up to the job." Bell thought Truman's problems were a matter of style. Franklin Roosevelt had had the finesse that Truman appeared to so clearly lack. Joseph Alsop, a cousin to Roosevelt, admitted a "patronizing attitude" to Truman but could not help thinking of him as "bold, strong, and limited," a man "full of average virtues" overwhelmed by the "vast problems" of the postwar world. Alsop shared Riggs' conviction that Truman was "an overly fastidious man in a neat gray suit" without the faintest clue of how to guide American foreign policy. Veteran Washington reporter Robert S. Allen agreed. Truman's "cocky self-confidence," Allen observed, only intensified the impression in the press that Truman was essentially "insecure" in his new post and "inadequate to the tasks that beset him."[23]

The reservation of journalists to Truman seemed to be shared by members of the White House staff that Truman inherited from Roosevelt. Carleton Kent of the *Chicago Times* recounts that Truman's closest advisers wondered about his ability to lead the nation. Presidential aide Jonathan

Daniels wrote that as Truman waited to be sworn in as thirty-third President on April 12, 1945, the general impression one got "was of a very little man sitting in a very large leather chair." The President's point man on Palestine, Loy Henderson, had similar fears following his appointment as director of Near Eastern and African Affairs at the State Department. Henderson, who began his career at the State Department a quarter of a century before, was frankly disturbed by what he saw. His concern was that the new President would not be able to stand up to the problems of the postwar world because of his "limited international background." To Henderson, this was nowhere more true than in Truman's handling of Palestine. "Under pressure of the Zionist juggernaut," Henderson remembered, "the President, members of Congress, other leaders in American life, the press, and the radio found themselves entangled in the problems of Palestine. The pressure on the Department of State was terrific, and my office unfortunately was one of the centers of the storm."[24]

Controversy also swirled around the man in the White House. "There'd never been anything like it before," Truman told Merle Miller years after the events of the period, "and there wasn't anything like it after." Truman appears to have thought that he could use the press as an instrument to guide opinion and create a favorable climate for his policies. "We have established a going policy," he told reporters at a news conference on October 17, 1947, "and you are a part of that policy. It is a policy of this country, of the United States, and not simply this administration, and you are as just as much in it as I am." Truman reiterated his call for public and press support for his foreign policy initiatives in subsequent meetings with the nation's radio news editors and newspaper editors. But his mishandling of the controversy over Palestine seemed so acute that one of Truman's closest friends in the press, *New York Times* chief Washington correspondent Arthur Krock, publicly predicted that Truman was so unpopular he would fail to win the nomination of his party if he ran for another term.[25]

Complicating Truman's efforts to appear presidential on his Palestine policy was the President's failure to achieve consensus on the issue within his own administration.[26] This failure stemmed in part from the attitude of certain senior officers within the State Department, who saw the department as the sole legitimate author of American foreign policy. They often viewed the president and public opinion as necessary nuisances that stood in the way of policy initiatives department analysts thought best for the country.[27] It was precisely this sense of exclusivity and paternalism that eventually rankled Truman. He complained that "striped pants conspirators" in the middle echelons of the State Department were out to "cut my throat." Secretary of State James F. Byrnes defended his men. The only people in his department who wore striped pants, he pointed out, were presidential appointees.[28]

In January, 1947, when this book opens, Byrnes was leaving the State Department. He turned over to his successor, George C. Marshall, a military man with little experience in the art of diplomacy, a department publicly proclaiming itself the servant of "a people's foreign policy." What this meant was not that the department would be lead by public opinion on policy matters but that it would strengthen its public information activities designed to mobilize consent for its policies. The department's efforts were watched skeptically from Times Square, where *New York Times* Sunday editor Lester Markel complained the department was failing to take the American people and the press into its confidence. Markel urged the department to break down the wall separating policy-making and the public and to make the press and the public a full partner in defining the nation's foreign policy objectives.[29]

Markel's attitude toward the policymaking process highlights another of the subplots in the story of Palestine at the beginning of the Cold War. Markel was to be a vigorous spokesman for an increasing number of reporters and editors who saw Cold War conditions requiring something more than simply reporting facts. Interpretative reporting was seen as a way of alerting the public to the critical conditions of the Cold War and of bringing their participation in the decisions the crisis required.[30] This approach strongly assisted the department's interpretation of events in Europe and the Near East through 1947, when the administration was perceived as standing tall against a worldwide Communist menace that many in the nation's press considered quite real. But interpretative journalism also challenged department policy when, after March 1948, the administration was widely seen to have caved in to idle Arab threats, thereby exposing a lack of moral will needed to preserve postwar peace.

This book examines how it was that the media came to report events in Palestine within certain interpretative frameworks, or what Doris Graber has called "visions of reality."[31] It also probes the efforts of competing parties to win over the media to their frames of reference and the impact these forces had on the public and private debate over America's Palestine policy in the early days of the Cold War. An analysis of primary sources and the media itself during this period suggests that the American news media did not insist on any particular course of action on Palestine in the months leading up to Israeli independence. Nor is there evidence to conclude the media exerted a direct and powerful influence over the shapers of policy and the public at large. The media's influence after March, 1948, in particular, seems to stem from the way it mirrored public opposition to administration policies and gave voice to that opposition. In so doing, it provided the context for conventional wisdom over which contending parties fought. This was a wisdom not simply mirrored in the media, but a wisdom that the media had a hand in making. And it was in this way that the media, led by the *New York Times*, made its most significant contribution to the controversy over Palestine. For there were many ways that events in Palestine could have been interpreted in the months leading up to partition; whether one reported developments there as a civil war, in the context of Jewish rights, or Arab rights, or even the Great Power struggle, a certain power lay in the hands of who is doing the defining.

Research suggests that the power to define policy alternatives or to offer visions of reality that provide the context for policymaking, is not the exclusive province of policymakers but rather is a process in which both the media and interested publics participate. This study draws upon recent work in political science, diplomatic history and mass media research, which contends the public may not be as passive as previously supposed. Instead, several studies have found that audiences openly challenge the political information that they are given through the news media by national leaders.[32] Research has identified specific conditions in which the public's circumspection is greatest. Those conditions appear when an ethnic or minority group feels threatened, or when war seems imminent; when an issue has been before the public for an extended period, allowing the public to weigh alternatives and enabling the press to seek out sources that express those alternatives; and finally, when policymakers appear hesitant and disunited concerning which policy option to follow.[33]

Many of these conditions for doubt existed during the Truman administration's consideration of its Palestine policy in the sixteen months leading up to partition, and never more so than on March 19, 1948, when the administration abruptly challenged conventional wisdom by abandoning partition. Shaping that wisdom was a major goal of each of the primary players on Palestine---from a divided administration to the British government, from American Jews to the Jews and Arabs of Palestine. Each considered the media a powerful ally in defining the stakes in Palestine, which made the media an important part of those stakes. For each sought to influence the American media, and through it the American public, and as a consequence, was influenced by the voices of each. It was in this way that the media was permitted not only to report and comment upon, but also to subtly reshape, the events it covered.

NOTES

1. Harry S. Truman, *Memoirs: Year of Decisions* (Garden City: Doubleday, 1955), pp. 96 and 379. Harry S. Truman, *Memoirs: Years of Trial and Hope* (Garden City: Doubleday, 1956), p. 1.

2. See John Snetsinger, *Truman, The Jewish Vote and the Creation of Israel* (Stanford: Hoover Institution Press, 1974). Robert P. Stevens, *American Zionism and*

U.S. Foreign Policy (New York: Pageant Press, 1962). Evan M. Wilson, *Decision on Palestine—How the U.S. Came to Recognize Israel* (Stanford: Hoover Institution Press, 1979). Alfred Lilienthal, *The Zionist Connection: What Price Peace?* (New York: Middle East Perspectives, 1978). For background on these studies see Frank E. Manuel, *The Realities of American-Palestinian Relations* (Washington: Public Affairs Press, 1949). For works distinctly more sympathetic to the Truman administration's Palestine policy and its decision to recognize the Jewish state consider Samuel Halperin, *The Political World of American Zionism* (Detroit: Wayne State University, 1961). Bernard Postal and Henry W. Levy, *And the Hills Shouted for Joy: The Day Israel Was Born* (New York: David McKay, 1973). Zvi Ganin, Truman, *American Jewry and Israel, 1945-1948* (New York: Holmes and Meier, 1979). Michael J. Cohen, *Palestine and the Great Powers, 1945-1948* (Princeton: Princeton University).

For the broader context within which the Truman Presidency operated in considering the Palestinian question see Richard Crossman, *Palestine Mission: A Personal Record* (New York: Harper, 1947). Bartley C. Crum, *Behind the Silken Curtain: A Personal Account of Anglo-American Diplomacy in Palestine and the Middle East* (New York: Simon and Schuster, 1947). Moshe Davis, *Christian Protagonists for Jewish Restoration* (New York: Arno Press, 1977). Hertzel Fishman, American Protestantism and a Jewish State (Detroit: Wayne State University, 1973). Carl J. Friedrich, *American Policy Toward Palestine* (Washington: American Council on Public Affairs, 1944). John Higham, *Send These to Me: Jews and Other Immigrants in America* (New York: Antheneum, 1975). Bruce R. Kuniholm, *The Origins of the Cold War in the Near East: Great Power Conflict and Diplomacy in Iran, Turkey and Greece* (Princeton: Princeton University, 1980).

Also consider Gerald D. Nash, *United States Oil Policy, 1890-1964: Business and Government in 20th Century America* (Pittsburgh: University of Pittsburgh, 1968). Aaron David Miller, *Search for Security: Saudi Arabian Oil and American Foreign Policy, 1939-1949* (Chapel Hill: University of North Carolina, 1980). David S. Painter, *Oil and the American Century: The Political Economy of United States Foreign Oil Policy, 1941-1954* (Baltimore: Johns Hopkins University, 1973). Richard H. K. Vietor, *Energy Policy in America since 1945: A Study of Business-Government Relations* (Cambridge: Cambridge University, 1984).

3. See William A. Williams, *The Tragedy of American Diplomacy* (Cleveland: World Publishing, 1959). Gar Alperovitz, *Atomic Diplomacy: Hiroshima and Potsdam* (New York: Simon and Schuster, 1965). Walter LeFeber, *America, Russia, and the Cold War* (New York: John Wiley, 1976). See also, Gabriel Kolko, *The Politics of War: The World and United States Foreign Policy, 1943-1945* (New York: Random House, 1968). Joyce and Gabriel Kolko, *The Limits of Power: The World and United States Foreign Policy, 1945-1954* (New York: Harper and Row, 1972).

Lloyd C. Gardner, *Architects of Illusion: Men and Ideas in American Foreign Policy: 1941-1949* (Chicago: Quadrangle Press, 1970). Lloyd C. Gardner, *Imperial America: American Foreign Policy since 1898* (New York: Harcourt, Brace, 1976). Athan G. Theoharis, *The Truman Presidency: The Origins of the Imperial Presidency and the National Security State* (Stanfordville, N.Y.: Earl E. Coleman Publishers, 1979). Barton J. Bernstein, "American Foreign Policy and the Origins of the Cold War," in Barton J. Bernstein, ed., *Politics and Policies of the Truman Administration*

(Chicago: Quadrangle Press, 1970), pp. 15-77. Charles L. Mee, Jr., "Who Started the Cold War?" *American Heritage* 28, 1977, pp. 10-15 and 23.

A variation of this argument is that Truman deliberately exagerrated the Soviet threat to generate Congressional and public support for the Marshall Plan. See Gordon A. Craig and Alexander L. George, *Force and Statecraft: Diplomatic Problems of Our Time* (New York: Oxford University, 1983), pp. 115-116. Norman A. Graebner argues that Truman's Cold War campaign arose out of the "perception of danger" rather than Soviet acts of hostility. See Graebner, "Public Opinion and Foreign Policy: A Pragmatic View," in Frank B. Feigert, et. al., *Interaction: Foreign Policy and Public Policy* (Washington: American Enterprise Institute, 1983), pp. 20-21.

4. The citation is from Thomas G. Paterson, "Presidential Foreign Policy, Public Opinion, and Congress: The Truman Years," *Diplomatic History* 3, 1979, pp. 1-3 and 17-18. See also, Manfred Landecker, *The President and Public Opinion* (Washington: Public Affairs Press, 1968), pp. 63-70. Michael Leigh, *Mobilizing Consent: Public Opinion and American Foreign Policy* (Westport, Conn.: Greenwood Press, 1976), introduction and pp. 3-11. Also, Graebner, pp. 14-21. A variation on this argument is provided by Ole R. Holsti, who suggests that the public is generally inattentive to the "means" of foreign policy-making, but not the "ends." This gave the Truman administration considerable leeway, Holsti reasons, in constructing its Cold War policy against the Soviet Union. Holsti, "Public Opinion and Containment," in Terry L. Deibel and John Lewis Gaddis, eds., *Containing the Soviet Union: A Critique of U.S. Policy* (Washington: Pergamon-Brassey, 1987), pp. 20-58.

5. Paterson relies on oral history interviews from Truman staffers George Elsey and Francis Russell. Transcripts of these interviews are in the Harry S. Truman Library. Independence, Missouri. He also cites Margaret Truman, Harry S. Truman (New York: William Morrow, 1973), p. 356. Landecker cites Harry S. Truman, *Mr. Citizen* (New York: Bernard Geis Associates, 1953), pp. 261-264. He also cites an interview he conducted with Truman in 1962. Leigh cites Truman aide Richard E. Neustadt, *Presidential Power: The Politics of Leadership* (New York: John Wiley, 1960), pp. 99-100. Graebner cites Paterson.

6. The authors come to this conclusion by relying on Gabriel A. Almond, *The American People and Foreign Policy* (New York: Praeger, 1961), pp. 80, 99-106, and 136-143. Also, they use James N. Rosenau, *Public Opinion and Foreign Policy* (New York: Random House, 1961), pp. 35-37. Bernard C. Cohen, *The Public's Impact on Foreign Policy* (Boston: Little, Brown, 1973), pp. 106-113, 129-130, and 178-183. Also, Lee Benson, "An Approach to the Scientific Study of Past Public Opinion," *Public Opinion Quarterly* 31, 1967-1968, pp. 522-567.

7. John Lewis Gaddis, *The United States and the Origins of the Cold War* (New York: Columbia University, 1972), p. 360. See also, John Lewis Gaddis, "The Emerging Postwar Synthesis on the Origins of the Cold War," *Diplomatic History* 7, 1983, pp. 177-180. Charles S. Maier, "Revisionism and the Interpretation of Cold War Origins," *Perspectives in American History* 4, 1970, pp. 313-347. J. L. Richardson, "Cold War Revisionism: A Critique," *World Politics* 24, 1972, pp. 579-612. Richard A. Melanson, "Revisionism Subdued? Robert James Maddox and the Origins of the Cold War," *Political Science Reviewer* 7, 1977, pp. 229-271. Robert Browder, *The Origins of Soviet-American Diplomacy* (Princeton: Princeton University, 1953), pp.

119-120. George C. Edwards and Stephen J. Wayne, *Presidential Leadership: Politics and Policy Making* (New York: St. Martin's, 1985), pp. 103-104. See also, Benjamin I. Page and Robert Y. Shapiro, "Effects of Public Opinion on Policy," *American Political Science Review* 77, 1983, pp. 175-190. George H. Quester, "Origins of the Cold War: Some Clues from Public Opinion," *Political Science Quarterly* 93, 1978, pp. 647-663. Ralph B. Levering, "Public Opinion, Foreign Policy, and American Politics since the 1960's," *Diplomatic History* 13, 1989, pp. 383-385.

8. For a summary of this research see Everett M. Rogers and James W. Dearing, "Agenda-Setting Research: Where Has It Been, Where Is It Going?" in James A. Anderson, ed., *Communication Yearbook* (Beverly Hills: Sage, 1987). Agenda-setting studies analyze the degree to which the public agenda---or what kinds of things people discuss, think and worry about, including their attitudes on public policies---is shaped by what the news media choose to publicize. See Roger D. Wimmer and Joseph R. Dominick, eds., *Mass Media Research: An Introduction* (Belmont: Wadsworth, 1987), pp. 385-389.

9. Walter Lippmann initiated the discussion of the impact of the media on public opinion in *Public Opinion* (New York: Free Press, 1922). Subsequent research seemed to suggest the media had a powerful influence over men's minds and in the construction of their political opinions. See Harold D. Lasswell, *Propaganda Technique in the World War* (New York: Knopf, 1927).

10. Research since the 1920's has suggested a far more restricted role of the press in forming political opinions. See Paul Lazarsfeld and Frank Stanton, eds., *Radio Research*, 1943-1944 (New York: Duell, Sloan and Pearce, 1944). Paul Lazarsfeld, Bernard Berelson, and Hazel Gaudet, *The People's Choice* (New York: Columbia University, 1948). Kurt Lang and Gladys Engel Lang, "The Mass Media in Voting," in Bernard Berelson and Morris Janowitz, eds., *Reader in Public Opinion and Communication* (New York: Free Press, 1966), pp. 464-466.

11. See Jack M. McLeod, Lee B. Becker, and James E. Byrnes, "Another Look at the Agenda-Setting Function of the Press," *Communication Research* 1, 1974, pp. 131-166, where the authors claim that the press and the public exert a strong reciprocal relationship on one another. Which one was leading the agenda-setting dynamic changed as circumstances changed. This thesis muted the claims of Maxwell E. McCombs and Donald L. Shaw in "The Agenda-Setting Function of the Mass Media," *Public Opinion Quarterly* 36, 1972, which saw the media exerting a powerful effect on opinion formation.

12. For a discussion of how leaks to the press looked from inside the Truman White House see Oral History Interview: Eben A. Ayers, pp. 71-76. Harry S. Truman Library. Independence, Missouri. The impression Ayers gives is that there was suspicion between holdovers from the Roosevelt administration and the people Truman brought to his staff. International News Service correspondent Robert Nixon believed Truman was poorly served by many of the aides he brought to the White House with him. See Oral History Interview: Robert G. Nixon, pp. 170-175. Truman Library.

13. An insight into the Truman administration's nurturing of the press can be found in Walter Millis, ed., *The Forrestal Diaries* (New York: Viking Press, 1951), pp. 117, 124, 128, 169, 193, 243 and 399. See also, Papers of Eben A. Ayers. General File. Palestine. Papers of George M. Elsey. Foreign Relations. Palestine. Box 60. And

Oral History Interview: George M. Elsey, pp. 34, 77-78 and 249. The Ayers and Elsey collections and the Elsey oral history interview can be found at the Truman Library. For background, see Ronald T. Farrar, *Reluctant Servant: The Story of Charles G. Ross* (Columbia: University of Missouri, 1969) and Francis H. Heller, *The Truman White House: The Administration of the President*, 1945-1953 (Lawrence: Regents Press of Kansas, 1980), pp. 78-87, 106-121, 145-148 and 164.

14. *Foreign Relations of the United States 1948*, Volume 5 (Washington: Government Printing Office, 1976), pp. 538, 604, 609, 677, 764, 856, 876, 974 and 996.

15. *Ibid.*, pp. 963 and 993. Also, M. Truman, p. 387. And, Postal and Levy, pp. 329-330. The importance of favorable public opinion in helping a faction within government to win consensus for its policy is analyzed by S. Nelson Drew, "Expecting the Approach of Danger: The 'Missile Gap' as a Study of Executive-Congressional Competition in Building Consensus on National Security Issues," *Presidential Studies Quarterly* 19, 1989, pp. 317-335.

16. *FRUS 1948*, 5, pp. 634, 649, 757, 842, and 879. See also, Millis, pp. 118, 129, 181, 193, 441, and 515. And Barnet Litvinoff, ed., *The Letters and Papers of Chaim Weizmann*, volume 2 (New Brunswick: Transaction Books, 1984), his introduction and p. 486. See also, Richard S. Kirkendall, *The Truman Period as a Research Tool: A Reappraisal* (Columbia: University of Missouri, 1974), p. 20. H. Truman, *Memoirs*, volume 2, pp. 140 and 143-155. Elmer E. Cornwell, Jr., "The Presidential Press Conference: A Study in Institutionalization," *Midwest Journal of Political Science* 4, 1960, pp. 378-379.

For background on perceptions within the press of divisions within the Truman White House see Robert S. Allen and William V. Shannon, *The Truman Merry-Go-Round* (New York: Vanguard, 1950), pp. 15-43. Joseph and Stewart Alsop, *The Reporter's Trade* (New York: Reynal, 1958), pp. 84-98 and 120-121. Robert Donovan, "Harry S. Truman," in Kenneth W. Thompson, ed., *Ten Presidents and the Press* (Lanham, Md.: University Press of America, 1983), pp. 29-48. Douglass Cater, *The Fourth Branch of Government* (Boston: Houghton Mifflin, 1959), pp. 22-46.

17. For an analysis of the pressure the Zionist movement and the Jewish press were able to bring to bear on the Truman administration see Elsey Papers. Foreign Relations. Palestine. Box 60. Also, Papers of David K. Niles. Civil Rights and Minority Affairs. Jewish Affairs. 1933-1948. Box 27. Folders 5 and 6. Also, Niles Papers. Israel File. July 1946-December 1948. Box 30. Folders 2, 3, and 4. All files available in the Truman Library. Compare to File 4-11. The Harry Shapiro File. American Zionist Emergency Council Papers. The Temple. Cleveland, Ohio.

The commitment of AZEC President Abba Hillel Silver to building public pressure for a Jewish state in Palestine is described by his colleague Emanuel Neumann in the foreward to Abba Hillel Silver, *Vision and Victory: A Collection of Addresses by Dr. Abba Hillel Silver, 1942-1948* (New York: The Zionist Press of America, 1949). Also, Doreen Bierbrier, "The A.Z.E.C.: An Analysis of a Pressure Group," *American Jewish Historical Quarterly* 60, 1970, pp. 82-105. And, Marc Lee Raphael, *Abba Hillel Silver: A Profile in American Judaism* (New York: Holmes and Meier, 1989), chapter eight.

18. M. Truman at p. 384 states that during 1947, 1948 and 1949 the White

House received 86,500 letters, 841,903 postcards, and 51,400 telegrams on the Palestine issue. These numbers were compiled by Andie L. Knutson of the State Department staff in 1951 and do not reflect the messages received by the State Department itself. See also, Ian J. Bickerton, "President Truman's Recognition of Israel," *American Journalism Historical Quarterly* 58, 1968, p. 229. See also, *New York Times*, November 30, 1947, Section E, p. 10.

19. On Truman's perception that the *New York Times* represented informed public opinion and required particular cultivation see Oral History Interview: W. McNeil Lowry, p. 66. Oral History Interview: Jack Bell, p. 72. Oral History Interview: Walter Trohan, p. 70. And Heller, pp. 120 and 146. Oral history interviews available at Truman Library.

On the role of the *New York Times* in self-consciously participating in the policymaking process as an interpreter of news and by providing a "vital link" between policymakers and the public see remarks by Arthur Hays Sulzberger at meeting of the American Society of Newspaper Editors in April, 1947. *Problems of Journalism*, volume 25 (Washington: American Society of Newspaper Editors, 1947), pp. 67-74. In the same proceedings see comments by *Times* senior Washington correspondent Arthur Krock, pp. 171-174. A letter from E. Clifton Daniel, the Times Middle East correspondent in 1947 and 1948, to the author, dated April 15, 1988 also emphasizes the unique role the paper saw itself playing in the development of American foreign policy in the postwar period. See also, Lester Markel, ed., *Public Opinion and Foreign Policy* (New York: Harper, 1949), pp. 33-35. Also, Meyer Berger, *The Story of the New York Times*, 1851-1951 (New York: Simon and Schuster, 1951), pp. 473-475 and 529. James Reston, *The Artillery of the Press* (New York: Harper and Row, 1967), introduction. Arthur Krock, *Memoirs: Sixty Years on the Firing Line* (New York: Funk and Wagnalls, 1969), pp. 181-182. Cyrus L. Sulzberger, *A Long Row of Candles* (New York: Macmillan, 1969), pp. 362-363.

20. Bell Oral History Interview, p. 72.

21. Truman made the observation at his press conference on October 17, 1947. For transcript see Ayers Papers. Press Conference File. Box 62. Members of Truman's staff also provided the President with daily excerpts of press coverage. See Elsey Papers. Foreign Relations. Palestine. Box 60. For a sense of the importance Truman attached to such summaries see Elsey Oral History Interview, p. 77. Truman Library.

22. Margaret Truman, *Letters from Father* (New York: Arbor House, 1981), p. 98, which cites a Truman letter to his daughter on October 1, 1947, suggesting that editors and publishers of what Truman termed "sabotage sheets" were nothing more than "traitors." See also, Papers of Harry S. Truman. Memoirs. Press. Post-Presidential. Truman Library. and, Bell Oral History Interview, p. 47.

23. Oral History Interview: Richard L. Strout, pp. 1-2. Oral History Interview: Robert L. Riggs, p. 14. Oral History Interview: Raymond P. Brandt, p. 25. Bell Oral History Interview, p. 37. All interviews are in the Truman Library. Also, Alsops, pp. 84, 97-98 and 120. And, Allen, pp. 18-25.

24. Oral History Interview: Carleton Kent, pp. 10-13. Oral History Interview: Loy W. Henderson, pp. 34-35 and 104-105. Truman Library. Alonzo L. Hamby, "The Accidental Presidency: Truman Vs. Dewey, The 1948 Election," *Wilson Quarterly* 13,

1988, p. 49.

25. Merle Miller, *Plain Speaking: An Oral Biography of Harry S. Truman* (New York: G. P. Putnam's Sons, 1973), p. 217. Also, Transcript. Presidential Press Conference. Press Secretary Files. Papers of Harry S. Truman. Box 62. Truman Library. And, White House Official Reporter. Working Papers. Statement of President Truman's remarks before the Radio News Editors Group on November 13, 1947. Papers of Harry S. Truman. Box 30. That selection also contains a similar statement given on April 17, 1948 before the American Society of Newspaper Editors. Truman Library. The sense of the statement is clearly restated in Truman's Memoirs, volume 1, p. 47. And, *New York Times*, March 28, 1947, Section E, p. 3.

26. The need to appear "presidential" is an image that presidents need to cultivate if they intend to lead public opinion and obtain support for their policies. See Doris A. Graber, *The President and the Public* (Philadelphia: Institute for the Study of Human Issues, 1982), pp. 1-14. Edwards and Wayne, pp. 103-104. Michael Baruch Grossman and Martha Joynt Kumar, *Portraying the President: The White House and the News Media* (Baltimore: Johns Hopkins University, 1981), pp. 3-5. James A. Nathan and James C. Oliver, *Foreign Policy Making in the American Political System* (Boston: Little, Brown, 1987), p. 108. Alexander L. George writes that the criticism that Truman was not up to the job of being president made him "overly eager to appear decisive." See Alexander L. George, *Presidential Decisionmaking in Foreign Policy: The Effective Use of Information and Advice* (Boulder: Westview Press, 1980), p. 32. At least one reporter who covered the Truman White House agrees with this assessment. See Allen, pp. 22, 25 and 30.

27. Robert D. Schulzinger, *The Making of the Diplomatic Mind: The Training, Outlook, and Style of U.S. Foreign Service Officers, 1908-1931* (Middletown: Wesleyan Press, 1975), pp. 6-8, 81-93 and 98. See also A. Miller, pp. 167-168, 176-178 and 185. Martin Weil observes that in the early days of the Cold War the State Department was determined to "set the bounds for the debate" and Truman, because of his inexperience in foreign policy, was dependent and eager to follow their lead. See Martin Weil, *Pretty Good Club: The Founding Fathers of the U.S. Foreign Service* (New York: W. W. Norton, 1978), pp. 220-223. Hugh De Santis writes that intellectual independence among foreign service officers led to their isolation. This situation assured the State Department would speak in one voice to Truman. See Hugh De Santis, *The Diplomacy of Silence: The American Foreign Service, the Soviet Union and the Cold War, 1933-1947* (Chicago: University of Chicago, 1980), pp. 201-204.

For an analysis of Near East experts at the State Department and their determination to dominate public opinion see Phillip J. Baram, *The Department of State in the Middle East* (Philadelphia: University of Pennsylvania, 1978), pp. 78 and 328-329. Thomas J. Bryson, *American Diplomatic Relations with the Middle East, 1784-1975* (Metuchen, N.J.: Scarecrow Press, 1977), pp. 17-24, 59 and 135-148. John DeNovo, *American Interests and Policies in the Middle East, 1900-1939* (Minneapolis: University of Minnesota, 1963), pp. 6-9.

28. M. Truman, Harry S. Truman, p. 387. Also, James F. Byrnes, *Speaking Frankly* (New York: Harper, 1947), p. 247.

29. Byrnes, pp. 243-256. Byrnes' conviction that the press should cooperate with the government in winning public support for its foreign policy can be seen in his

remarks before the nation's newspaper editors in April, 1943. See *Problems of Journalism*, volume 21 (Washington: American Society of Newspaper Editors, 1943), pp. 36-43. Also, Leigh, pp. 99-102. For background, see Department of State, *Bulletin* 10, January 15, 1944. And, Lester Markel, ed., *Public Opinion and Foreign Policy* (New York: Harper, 1949), pp. 3-6.

    30. Markel, pp. 19-21 and 33-36. Also, Lester Markel, "The Real Sins of the Press," *Harper's*, December 1962, pp. 85-86. Berger, pp. 533-535. Arthur Hays Sulzberger, ASNE address, pp. 66-69.

    31. Letter from Doris A. Graber to author, dated 3 April 1991.

    32. See Doris A. Graber, *Processing the News: How People Tame the Information Tide* (New York: Longman, 1984), pp. 201-216. And, Kathleen Frankovic, "The 1984 Election: The Irrelevance of the Campaign," *PS* 18, 1985, pp. 39-47. And Page and Shapiro, pp. 175-189.

    33. Ralph B. Levering makes use of Gallup poll data results in describing those conditions in which the public is most alert to the foreign policy scene. See Ralph B. Levering, *The Public and American Foreign Policy, 1918-1978* (New York: William Morrow, 1978), pp. 28-31. Barry H. Hughes notes that the public exercises its greatest control over foreign policy issues it finds of greatest "salience." They would include economic and security issues that have developed over a long period of time, allowing public sentiment time to crystallize. See Barry H. Hughes, *The Domestic Context of American Foreign Policy* (San Francisco: W. H. Freeman, 1978), p. 224.

    A case study in the latent power of a mobilized press and public opinion used to constrain presidential policymaking can be seen in Montague Kern, Patricia W. Levering, and Ralph B. Levering, *The Kennedy Crises: The Press, the Presidency, and Foreign Policy* (Chapel Hill: University of North Carolina, 1984), pp. 175-176 and 195-204. A subsequent study saw Kennedy's successor as no more successful than he was in reversing negative trends in public and press opinion. See Kathleen J. Turner, *Lyndon Johnson's Dual War: Vietnam and the Press* (Chicago: University of Chicago, 1985), pp. 12-14. For an analysis of how several administrations tried to manage negative press coverage of failed foreign policies, see Nicholas O. Berry, *Foreign Policy and the Press: An Analysis of the New York Times Coverage of U.S. Foreign Policy* (Westport, Conn.: Greenwood Press, 1990.

    For background studies on the relationship of the press and the public in political communication, see Dennis McQuail, "The Influence and Effects of Mass Media," in Morris Janowitz and Paul Hirsch, eds., *Reader in Public Opinion and Mass Communication* (New York: Free Press, 1981), pp. 361-385. Joseph Wagner, "Media Do Make a Difference: The Differential Impact of Mass Media in the 1976 Presidential Race," *American Journal of Political Science* 27, 1983, pp. 407-428. F. Christopher Arterton, *Media Politics: The News Strategies of Presidential Campaigns* (Lexington, Mass.: Lexington Books, 1984), pp. 183-184.

One

Palestine and the Coming of the Cold War, January 1947–March 1947

During the winter of 1947, the future of Palestine became immersed in East-West policy considerations extending far beyond the Eastern Mediterranean. Britian's sudden retreat from empire enabled American Zionists and the U.S. State Department to exploit rising war jitters as they competed with one another in the mass media to create a new conventional wisdom on Palestine. The American Zionist Emergency Council (AZEC) insisted American involvement in Greece and Turkey should be followed by support for a Jewish state. The State Department's Near East desk argued that policy would only lead to Communist gains throughout the oil-rich region. Both sides attempted to use the American mass media, particularly the *New York Times*, to win converts to their cause. They competed in describing a vision of reality that would serve as the context for policymaking. The beginning of this struggle to shape conventional wisdom at the outset of the Cold War and the role the mass media played in that conflict is the subject of this chapter.

Americans reading the daily press and listening to the nation's network commentators in the opening days of 1947 had reason to believe that the world was entering an era of peace. Although a state of war still technically existed, President Harry S. Truman on December 31, 1946 declared the hostilities of World War II officially terminated. Emergency laws exercised by the Executive Branch since 1941 were ended. A presidential proclamation pledged the United States would work with other nations in building a world in which justice would replace force.[1]

The *New York Times* reported that American Secretary of State James F. Byrnes and Soviet Foreign Minister Vyacheslav M. Molotov had just completed negotiations in New York that amicably resolved differences on more than forty issues. United Nations Secretary General Trygve Lie indicated in his New Year's message that a "sound foundation" had been laid and he

looked to the future with "sober confidence." The chief United States delegate
to the United Nations, Warren R. Austin, told a radio audience that he was
convinced the United States and the Soviet Union "had come to a better
understanding of each other" and that he had "great faith" that a start had
been made on the "long road away from war." The nation's foremost radio
commentator, Hans V. Kaltenborn of the National Broadcasting Company
(NBC), caught this spirit of optimism when he told listeners, "the days ahead
will confirm mankind's steady march to better things." The United States,
Kaltenborn was convinced, had "seized the torch of freedom and held it aloft
for others to see and follow."[2]

The New Year's cheer proved short-lived. The British, bankrupted by
the war and wracked by labor problems, abruptly announced in February a
pullback from their commitments in the Eastern Mediterranean. The collapse
of the British economy and the Labour government's sudden fallback from
empire jolted *New York Times* publisher and board chairman Arthur Hays
Sulzberger, who remained convinced that the "common good" of the free
world required a strong Britain. The prospect of a disintegrating British empire
had *Times* editorial writers fearing the emergence of a world in which the
United States stood alone in defense of democratic freedoms everywhere under
attack. Kaltenborn shared this sense of sudden foreboding. Gone was the "new
age of peace" that seemed to have been dawning only weeks before. The
British cabinet's decision to reduce Britain's armed forces by 340,000 men,
plus the acute shortages of food, fuel and clothing throughout the United
Kingdom, created a "dangerous situation," Kaltenborn believed, in the postwar
world.[3]

Britain's pullback from the Eastern Mediterranean exposed misgivings
long held by members of the American media and the State Department over
the Soviet Union's postwar aims. In the fifteen months that followed, the
world was rhetorically split into two hostile camps, one Soviet, the other
American, separated by "deep distrust and mutual suspicion."[4] Palestine, a
country with a violent history of its own, became absorbed within the East-
West war of words when Britain, eager to trim a costly 100,000 man
peacekeeping force, announced in late February it was turning the Palestine
problem over to the United Nations. It was these events that set the stage for
a mass-mediated battle for public opinion at the beginning of the Cold War.

JOURNALISM'S FIRST DRAFT ON HISTORY

The early postwar rhetoric of Kaltenborn and Sulzberger reflects a
journalism of self-promotion and self-conscious public service, if not self-
abnegation. Each man intended to play a bigger part in policymaking than
either was permitted during the war years. Born in Milwaukee, Kaltenborn

joined the Fourth Wisconsin Voluntary Infantry to fight in the Spanish-American War. In the two decades that followed he hustled stories for the German language press in Wisconsin before joining the staff of the *Milwaukee Journal*, and later Herbert F. Gunnison's *Brooklyn Daily Eagle*. On April 4, 1922 Kaltenborn presented a radio address at the Army Signal Corps station in New York City, which years later he billed as "the first editorial opinion over the air." He made news when he climbed Mt. Fuji in 1927 and visited the Soviet Union two years later. In 1932 he covered the Democratic National Convention for the Columbia Broadcasting System (CBS), later interviewed Hitler and Mussolini, reported on the Spanish Civil War and the appeasement at Munich.[5]

Kaltenborn considered himself a "contemporary historian" and saw his fifteen-minute newscasts for NBC during the war as first drafts of history. NBC nourished this image and on October 16, 1941 organized a town meeting in which Kaltenborn answered questions about the war from two hundred of San Francisco's "outstanding citizens." NBC also arranged for a newsreel cameraman to be present. Subsequently, Kaltenborn appeared weekly in newsreels shown across the country. During the first six months of the war, more than one million theatre goers asked for Kaltenborn's views. While he admitted that he "didn't know all the answers," he believed it was his responsibility to "guide public opinion."[6]

Both Kaltenborn and Sulzberger saw the press as a major player in postwar policymaking. Kaltenborn observed that the responsibility to lead opinion belonged to the press as much as to those "who place their hands over the *Bible* and swear to do their duty in public office." Each made democracy possible by their public service. Sulzberger told the nation's leading editors that how the press handled its "sacred and special mission" might well "determine the destiny of the world." The war had shown too clearly, Sulzberger claimed, that only "an informed democracy" was strong enough to survive in a world where totalitarianism was on the march.[7]

During the war the press had been an agreeable, if at times, reluctant partner in reporting the Roosevelt administration's war news and views. Part of the reason was that the press generally supported the war effort. In April, 1942, Kaltenborn endorsed the idea that total war required a cooperative press in April 1942. "We want freedom of speech and press for patriotic Americans whose one concern is to win the war," he noted. "We want silence from all others." But as the war went on, many in the press wearied in the role of messenger service for the Roosevelt administration. Radio newsmen in May, 1943 went public with a complaint that government censors often left "the Japs better informed than Americans." Wire service reporters were convinced a false image of the war was being communicated through the government's determination to "hold back and play down American casualties." The

American Society of Newspaper Editors, representing the nation's largest dailies, resented the growth of "pernicious propaganda" disseminated by government bureaucrats. It charged in April, 1944 that news management had confused the American people.[8]

Arthur Krock, the *Times* veteran Washington correspondent, believed the war and the controversy growing out of government efforts to manage the news would alter the policymaking environment in the immediate postwar period. Krock thought the press would be less likely to accept the administration's call for a non-partisan foreign policy. He wrote that the State Department would be incapable of managing postwar foreign policy without significant participation by the Congress and the American people. *Times* management shared Krock's conviction. Sulzberger conceived of the *Times* as an "American institution" called upon to preserve the country's fragile freedoms through vigorous editorial crusading. Charles Merz, the paper's editorial page chief, determined to "stir the American people and the Congress to their responsibilities." Sunday editor Lester Markel saw that responsibility as "educating public opinion" to what diplomatic correspondent James Reston described as "the changes and convulsions in the world in which America must operate."[9]

The determination of *Times* management to participate in postwar policymaking was a significant departure from the days when Adolph S. Ochs seriously considered scrapping the paper's editorial page. The Ohio country boy turned grocer's clerk and druggist's apprentice told an interviewer that he could get a larger circulation by printing a newspaper with all advertisements and no news rather than a paper with all news and no advertisements. His work as an assistant in the composing room of the *Knoxville* (Tenn.) *Tribune* and as staff writer and editor of the *Chattanooga Times* convinced him that "news which told the exact truth so far as possible" also made good economic sense. In 1896 he became publisher and controlling owner of the *New York Times*, then a struggling enterprise in the era of the yellow press dominated by Joseph Pulitzer and William Randolph Hearst. Ochs' determination to cultivate an elite, monied readership resulted in a twenty fold increase in *Times* earnings during the first generation of his stewardship, and it led to the *Times'* dominance "within its own sphere of usefulness." Ochs reasoned that only one in 100 readers read all the news that *Times'* editors saw fit to print. But that one "would tell the other ninety-nine" and the *Times* would get the reputation of being the "complete newspaper."[10]

Sulzberger saw interpretation and leading elite opinion as central to the postwar role of the *Times*. Sulzberger had been a member of a noteworthy Jewish family that featured philanthropists, scholars and jurists, when he married Ochs' only daughter in 1917, positioning himself as the heir apparent within the *Times* hierarchy. On Ochs' death in 1935, Sulzberger became publisher, president, and chairman of the board at the *Times* and wielded his power to pick associates who shared his commitment to a journalism of "public service." Sulzberger saw protecting the nation's freedom from totalitarian intrusion at the center of that service. He warned fellow editors that the press was like the canary miners took down into the shafts with them. "It fell over at the least sign of poisonous gas," Sulzberger pointed out, and this warning gave others a chance to escape. While the *Times* primarily considered Soviet foreign policy before and during World War II in terms of that nation's security interests, by the winter of 1947 it was beginning to smell poison gas. "Communists and fellow travelers" represented a threat to the American way of life, Sulzberger told the nation's editors in April, 1947; the publisher who "knowingly employed a communist or any other type of totalitarian" or gave him "any place of influence" in news or editorial departments "threatened the United States itself." The defeat of Nazi Germany did not mean fascism was dead, *Times* diplomatic correspondent Herbert L. Matthews wrote, expressing this new orthodoxy. Communist authoritarianism was a "Red Fascism."[11]

Sulzberger and the *Times* were seen as an important target for those within the Truman administration who were pressing for a get tough policy toward the Soviet Union. In December, 1945 Navy Secretary James V. Forrestal told Sulzberger and Brooks Atkinson, the paper's Moscow correspondent, that "the only thing (the Russians) recognize is stark force." Forrestal's case to Sulzberger was that the Russians had "no respect for the normal human weaknesses, such as justice, kindliness and affection." At a cabinet meeting three weeks later Forrestal urged President Truman to call an emergency meeting of Sulzberger and other leading newspapermen, as well Kaltenborn and the nation's leading radio commentators, impressing on them "the seriousness of the present situation."[12]

Shortly before becoming the nation's first Secretary of Defence, Forrestal pressed his anti-Soviet campaign with Krock, asking him and the *Times* to join the administration in a partnership to combat Soviet propaganda. Forrestal urged the *Times* to get the facts of Soviet postwar imperialism "before the world, but most importantly, before our own people." Krock embraced Forrestal's argument, decried "the infiltration of Communists and crypto-Communists within the official structure" and castigated Truman for demobilizing too quickly after the war. "The demobilization was an act of deference to public opinion," Krock wrote, "that had been beguiled by Roosevelt's blunder of counting on a cooperative U.S.S.R. postwar foreign policy." The postwar *Times* was determined that error would not be repeated.[13]

As winter 1947 deepened, the *Times* pointed with approval to the nation's news media's growing awareness of postwar perils. A press institute at Columbia University attracting the nation's leading editorial writers had devoted three-quarters of its time to reviewing American foreign policy. The *Times* noted this reconsideration was necessary if the country's major dailies were to "inform and lead public opinion." Lester Markel observed that constructing an "enlightened citizenry" was the "number one problem in the world today" and required a joint undertaking by the nation's media and its government leaders. Sulzberger preached "faith in the intelligence of our constituents."[14]

Kaltenborn shared Sulzberger's sense that media should serve as an instrument of informed consent. He believed that the British retreat from empire created a postwar world that required an aggressive American response. In February he left his NBC show to embark on a widely publicized worldwide fact-finding tour. At the end of the war he had hoped that the Soviet Union "would devote itself to the establishment and maintenance of democracy in the world."[15] But Britain's crisis now forced a reassessment of Kaltenborn's first draft of history.

THE VIEW FROM FOGGY BOTTOM

On January 7, 1947 James F. Byrnes, who had begun his public career as an editor on the *Aiken* (South Carolina) *Journal and Review*, resigned his post as Secretary of State. Seven terms in the House of Representatives, two in the Senate, and a brief stint on the United States Supreme Court had convinced Byrnes that effective government required a press that cooperated with national leaders. While certain that reporters and editors were "patriotic," Byrnes charged that they did not take their responsibilities seriously enough. Criticism of the government during a national crisis, he warned, could destroy the consensus that sustained policy initiatives.[16]

Byrnes believed that the executive branch's dominance over postwar foreign policymaking required a favorable press and public. That the press could influence a public generally inattentive to the complexities of foreign policy was taken as an article of faith among those in the diplomatic community who worked to maintain good press relations. Noted poet, Librarian of Congress and war propagandist Archibald MacLeish, argued it was "not the government which shaped the public mind" but the press to whom "people in this country turn for counsel in the difficult and dangerous business of making up their minds." Therefore, it was not enough, MacLeish maintained, for journalists "to claim the right to influence opinion." It was necessary for them to "accept responsibility for the opinions which resulted."[17]

By war's end many in the media had grown impatient with senior diplomats who believed they could manage public affairs without significant participation by the public or the press. Krock charged that MacLeish had used the Office of Facts and Figures to "conduct psychological warfare with this data" designed to manipulate public opinion to serve administration purposes. Krock urged his colleagues to resist.[18]

Part of the *Times* problem with the foreign service during and immediately after the war was the secrecy of its operation. The *Times* Sunday editor, Lester Markel, observed that there were too many career diplomats "who looked upon themselves as Brahmins and upon fact-seekers as Untouchables." Markel wrote that too many of these officials felt public opinion had no place "in the frock-coated world in which both their bodies and their minds move." Far too many foreign service officials, Markel believed, failed to recognize that the public now demanded a full accounting of their country's foreign policy because they intended to participate in its formation.[19]

If senior officials within the State Department grudgingly accepted the necessity of public support for sustaining department initiatives, they openly resented making the public a partner in developing those initiatives. "We used to discuss how much time that mythical average American citizen put in each day listening, reading, and arguing about the world outside his own country," remarked former Secretary of State Dean Acheson in his memoirs. "It seemed to us that ten minutes a day would be a high average."[20]

Acheson's disdain for public opinion was not unique. The training of diplomats accentuated the sense that only professionals were equipped to manage foreign policy. Public opinion was to be molded to fit the world as seen by those men who were convinced they saw the world most clearly. Secretary of State Cordell Hull had been appalled by the public's apparent lack of knowledge concerning the nation's foreign policy. In January of 1944 he organized the Office of Public Information to collect and analyze data on public attitudes, and to carry the department's message to the public. Hull's successors, Edward Stettinius and James Byrnes, expanded the Office of Public Affairs, as it became known, to reach regularly opinion leaders in more than two hundred organizations across the country. The office sought the opinions of American voters through regular polling and subscribed to more than 100 newspapers and magazines to sample daily press opinion. But as Francis Russell, director of the office under President Truman saw it, the real purpose of the effort was not to follow American public opinion but to lead it.[21]

In public, the department suggested its public affairs operation had a different purpose. Byrnes heralded the bureau as an important instrument in assuring that a "people's foreign policy" would be carried out. It showed that the department was becoming "increasingly sensitive to public opinion," Byrnes suggested, and that it welcomed "criticism and suggestions on pending issues." The era of secret and private arrangements between rulers was over, Byrnes argued. The bureau represented a break "from the diplomatic habits of the past."[22]

Privately, however, few in the department took Byrnes' public proclamation seriously. The department's press officer, Charles Bohlen, saw the Office of Public Affairs as a strategy to fend off objectionable public opinion rather than adapt to it. This point was not lost on the *Times*. What the department's postwar planners did not properly appreciate, Markel warned, was that America's "new role in the world" required an end to the "white-shuttered era" in which the department's "High Priests" sat in "velvet prudishness and metallic sternness," while "hiding the most important secrets of the world." The man in the street would have his say in postwar foreign relations, Markel predicted, and never more so than when those relations seemed most critical.[23]

Markel's warning was well understood by department veteran Loy Henderson, who continuously urged the Truman administration to use the mass media to win public support for a get tough policy with the Soviets. Henderson's experience with the American Red Cross in the Baltic states during the Bolshevik period persuaded him that Communists were prepared "to destroy millions of human beings to see a Communist world." This conviction guided Henderson's surveillance in the 1920's of the international Communist movement; its relation to the American Communist Party and his attendance during the 1930's of Stalin's show trials."[24]

As head of the Near East desk at the State Department, Henderson had a deep distrust of Soviet postwar plans and was determined to prevent Soviet expansion in a region whose oil wealth the department considered crucial to Western security interests. Henderson's division had long opposed Zionist ambitions in Palestine and argued that creation of a Jewish state in Palestine contradicted traditional American policy of following the "wishes of a large majority of the local inhabitants with respect to their form of government."[25]

To Henderson's mind, the possibility of Soviet penetration into Palestine made it even more urgent the United States do nothing to alienate the region's Arabs. Critics, including President Truman, claimed anti-Semitism undergirded the division's attitude on Palestine. They saw the department as hostile to all "hyphenated Americans" who "meddled" in the department's "private reserve"---foreign policymaking. Henderson died in 1986 still denying these charges and insisting that his only purpose was to make Truman see the grave dangers in the postwar world before it was too late.[26]

Truman's eventual conversion to the department's anti-Soviet stand was facilitated by the "Long Memorandum" written by American minister-counselor and charge d'affaires in Moscow, George F. Kennan. Kennan's thesis, which soon became gospel for many within the Truman White House, saw Soviet postwar expansionism springing from the authoritarian character of its leadership as much as from ideological necessity. The Kremlin's view of world affairs was essentially "neurotic," driven by "the instinctive Russian sense of insecurity."[27]

Kennan's contentions won consensus within America's diplomatic community not only because they appeared to fit the reality of the postwar world but because the interpreters of that reality shared a common background, training and outlook. Educated at Groton and the "better schools," department careerists were inculcated with the values of professional solidarity and conformist patriotism, as well as a sense of public service. Advancement within the ranks came from seeing the world as your superiors did. These circumstances encouraged junior foreign service officers to accept conventional wisdom about the Soviet menace and to form a united front in the face of criticism.[28]

In September of 1946, the patience and persistence of Henderson, Forrestal, Kennan, Acheson and other senior diplomats paid off. President Truman's Special Counsel Clark Clifford and the nation's Joint Chiefs of Staff, accepted their warnings concerning the Soviet postwar threat. In a six chapter, 100,000 word study that Krock called the blueprint of Truman's postwar strategic planning, Clifford suggested the United States "should be prepared to use force to protect its vital security interests" in the Middle East. The Joint Chiefs echoed this sentiment less than a month later. Implicit in long range military planning, they argued, was the necessity of keeping Western Europe, China, Japan and the oil rich Middle East out of the Soviet grip.[29]

THE VIEW FROM MADISON AVENUE

When the executive committee of the American Zionist Emergency Council (AZEC) met at 342 Madison Avenue in New York City on the afternoon of January 29, 1947, its members hardly suspected that a major policy review then underway in Washington would have a profound effect on their eight-year-old organization. In the opinion of its presiding officer, Cleveland Rabbi Abba Hillel Silver, Zionism had come to a dangerous crossroad. Silver feared the public airing of divisions within world Jewry had crippled chances of establishing a Jewish state in Palestine anytime soon. A December meeting of the World Zionist Congress in Basel, Switzerland had ended acrimoniously. A faction headed by Silver and David Ben-Gurion of the Jewish Agency in Palestine was charged with the responsibility of intensifying the movement's political and propaganda activities in support of Jewish statehood. It was a blow to the movement's old guard, which had shepherded the Zionist movement for half a century and strongly believed that quiet diplomacy yielded the best results. Rabbi Stephen S. Wise, an intimate of Theodore Herzl, the founder of the modern Jewish state movement, severed his ties with American Zionism in protest and granted an interview with the

New York Times to state the reasons why.[30]

    Times foreign correspondent, C. L. Sulzberger, the nephew of the paper's publisher, had sought out Wise's long-time colleague Chaim Weizmann in London. Weizmann had been largely responsible for getting the British government to issue the Balfour Declaration in November, 1917, committing its leaders to work for the creation in Palestine of a homeland for the Jewish people. But following the Basel convention, he too no longer had any formal ties to the movement he had long led. Sulzberger found the usually upbeat Weizmann "depressed and gloomy." Zionism in Palestine, he told Sulzberger, had been taken over by "misguided idealists and ordinary racketeers" led by "that damned fascist Ben-Gurion." Weizmann worried that the position of the Jews in Palestine "was worse than it had been at any time since World War I." He feared that the eagerness of Zionist leaders to push the British out of Palestine would "force an eventual conflict between the British and the Jews of Palestine" that would resemble the destruction that came to the Jewish people when two millennia before they had fought Rome.[31]

    Differences of opinion were nothing new to the Zionist movement. Silver himself had been at the center of many such storms. What made the current controversy so destructive from his point of view was that it prevented Zionists from speaking "in one voice" at a time when the future of the Jewish state's future "hung in the balance." To understand Silver's apprehensions in late January, 1947, and in the sixteen months which followed, one must recognize that the whole of his activities were directed at "the winning of public opinion" that he felt certain would prove decisive for the Zionist movement.[32]

    Silver had been forced to give up his post as head of the American Zionist movement in 1944 after failing to win White House endorsement for a Congressional resolution increasing Jewish immigration to Palestine. The defeat underscored what had long been the pattern. American Zionists could agitate for a Jewish state in Palestine, and at times even carry a majority of the House and Senate with them. But Zionists could not break the State Department's hold on America's Middle East policy nor the White House's willingness to go along with that policy.[33]

    Silver was not contrite for long. In his years out of power, he travelled throughout the country building support for his initiatives. By the end of 1946, his efforts were rewarded. The twenty-second World Zionist Congress recognized his hold over the American Zionist movement and the more than four hundred local emergency councils he had helped establish. It gave Silver leadership over the effort to mobilize American public opinion to make real Herzl's dream of a Jewish state by the middle of the Twentieth Century.[34]

    The executive committee of AZEC had worked feverishly throughout

1946. Its meetings with the nation's editors and newspaper publishers resulted in 1,500 column inches of Zionist views finding their way into the country's press. Along with the Zionist Organization of America, AZEC had weekly co-sponsored "Palestine Speaks," a radio program that had aired on 207 American stations throughout the year. This supplemented eighty-eight nationwide demonstrations that had been launched during the year demanding unrestricted Jewish immigration there and its immediate representation before the United Nations.[35] The committee was convinced that eventually this propaganda campaign would push the American government to support Zionist objectives in Palestine. For more than a year, polls had been indicating that eight in ten American Jews favored the creation of a Jewish state in Palestine, and of the three in four Americans who followed the debate over Palestine, more than half favored partition.[36]

The reporting of this public sentiment was not lost on Truman. On the eve of Congressional elections he had announced his support for the "creation of a viable Jewish state in control of its own immigration and economic policies in an adequate area of Palestine instead of the whole of Palestine." The statement, prepared by Zionists, at the last minute had been altered by the State Department to indicate the United States was proposing no new initiative on Palestine but was seeking only to "bridge the gap" between British proposals for a federated, unitary state, and Zionist demands for their own state. But to the delight of Zionists, the American press emphasized the part about partition. Eliahu Epstein, representative of the Jewish Agency in Washington, privately reported that newspaper readers were getting the right message: "Truman supports a Jewish state."[37]

THE VIEW FROM TIMES SQUARE

The continuing opposition of the *New York Times* to any talk of a Jewish state in Palestine tempered Zionist euphoria. *Times* publisher Arthur Sulzberger and Arthur Krock, the paper's chief Washington correspondent since 1933, were seen by AZEC as mortal enemies of the Zionist movement. AZEC considered Krock the "most informed and influential" of the nation's Washington columnists and a man whose intimacy with official Washington allowed him to serve as a "mouthpiece of high officials in the State Department." A fourth generation son to German immigrant parents, Krock admitted to "what is called Jewish descent." But his father was a "free thinker" whose first wife had been a "Kentucky Anglo-Saxon." It left Krock free to choose a life "without a creed of any kind." He acknowledged being an "early agnostic, who remained through life that way." His attitude to a Jewish state in Palestine was influenced not by his Jewishness but by State Department logic. Like Henderson, he believed both political parties exploited the issue with little regard to the consequences the policy would have in American relations to the Arab states or their British ally.[38]

Sulzberger's opposition to the Jewish state was more personal and followed in the tradition of his father-in-law Adolph S. Ochs. Ochs may have usually eschewed editorial crusading as a way of distinguishing his own commercial venture from his competitors in the yellow press, but when it came to the Jewish state movement, Ochs was prepared to make an exception. The rift between the *Times* and the American Zionist community began in earnest in 1922 when the *Times* editorially attacked Massachusetts Senator Henry Cabot Lodge for his introduction of a resolution favoring a Jewish homeland in Palestine. The *Times* charged that Lodge's action was a blatant effort to attract Jewish votes in his upcoming Senate race.[39]

Sulzberger went beyond editorial opposition to the Jewish state movement when he announced the creation of the American Council for Judaism. The purpose of the council, the *Times* observed, was to oppose Zionism and its "philosophy of defeatism which does not offer a practical solution to the Jewish problem. Such radical ideas," the paper observed, "were inimical to the welfare of Jews living in Palestine as well as America." In June, 1946, Sulzberger took the unprecedented step of banning from the pages of the *Times* all advertisements from the American League for a Free Palestine. While the *Times* prided itself on running advertisements from certain Zionist groups with which it "violently disagreed," Sulzberger drew the line at advertisements that threatened the "common good." Advertisements implying the British were "not acting in good faith" in Palestine "overstepped certain bounds" and were "calculated to do harm in the world situation." Sulzberger claimed the *Times* commitment to preserving peace in the postwar world required the ad to be pulled.[40]

In explaining the *Times'* position, E. Clifton Daniel, the paper's chief Middle East correspondent beginning in 1945 and Truman's future son-in-law, believes that Sulzberger was "very definitely an assimilationist Jew." Daniel suggests this meant Sulzberger stood ideologically opposed to the Zionist insistence that only the creation of a Jewish state would assure Jewish existence. Instead, Sulzberger's self-image was that of "an American of Jewish faith" who believed Jews could make it in America. Sulzberger considered himself a perfect example of that success story. Daniel writes that it was not until after the Israeli War of Independence that a new generation of *Times* ownership, flushed with Israel's military successes, changed its editorial position in support of a Jewish homeland. In this regard, Sulzberger and Krock were characteristic of German Jews whose immigrant parents had come to America during the Nineteenth Century. They felt secure in their assimilation and steadfastly opposed the Zionist movement, which they saw as a reactionary crusade of Eastern European "paupers" to the persecution of living within the pale. The families of Krock and Sulzberger hardly shared the nostalgia of recent immigrants to one day return to the Promised Land. For Krock and

Sulzberger, America was the promised land; they resented any movement they feared might threaten the status they had struggled for so many years to obtain.[41]

Daniel argues that Sulzberger's editorial position in no way influenced the *Times* coverage of events in the Middle East during his tour there, which lasted into 1947. Before taking the assignment, Daniel asked Sulzberger if there were any "special considerations" that he should observe in his coverage of the Palestine story. Sulzberger told him "there were none, and that I should cover the story as I would any other story---that is, accurately, fairly and without bias toward any point of view."[42]

AZEC was not so persuaded. It took the organization six months to arrange a forty-five minute meeting with *Times* editor Anne O'Hare McCormick, only to find that the paper was simultaneously interviewing warring Zionist factions.[43] AZEC organizers were convinced that they would have to fight both the *Times* and the State Department to establish a Jewish homeland in Palestine. More than once Abba Hillel Silver was convinced the *Times* reporting was "pure invention." His daily reading of the paper often led to his call to friends in the Congress or sources within the White House, checking on the veracity of *Times* reporting. Throughout the partition controversy, AZEC saw the *Times* as a "special case" needing special cultivation.[44]

THE VIEW FROM TEN DOWNING STREET

The failure of January's London conference to settle the conflict that had plagued Palestine stimulated new calls in the House of Commons and in the British press for the end of Britain's generation long mandate over Palestine. Former British Prime Minister Winston Churchill charged Britain's continued presence in Palestine "is covering us with blood and shame." He urged that either the United States be brought in to serve as an equal partner in administering the mandate or the future status of Palestine be handed over to the United Nations "in all its bloodshed, opium, trouble, and expense."[45]

The nation's press reflected similar misgivings. The *New Statesman and Nation*, with close ties to the British cabinet, asked readers if the country could afford a 1,385,000 member armed force when it needed 600,000 of them to work in key domestic industries and half a million more to run the country's export trade. The *Sunday Tribune*, after surveying the nation's defense chiefs, predicted that the Labour government would have difficulty in bringing home half the men it needed to rebuild the country's struggling economy.[46]

From the beginning of the Palestine crisis, Labour leaders had handled the public relations of the problem poorly. Foreign Secretary Ernest Bevin, a labor organizer with limited foreign policy experience, and Prime Minister Clement Attlee, were convinced that President Truman's announcement in October, 1946, declaring his support for increased Jewish immigration to

Palestine had destroyed any chance of reaching a settlement there. Attlee was outraged at Truman's action and privately told the *New York Times*' C. L. Sulzberger as much. Bevin went public with his bitterness; pounding a table at the House of Commons, he blasted the Truman administration for "wrecking the Palestine talks" by its pandering for a few Jewish votes in a key election state. Bevin's outburst prompted a four-column front-page article in the *New York Times* and provoked angry replies the following day from both the White House and Capital Hill. When Bevin arrived in America to meet with administration and Zionist leaders, the drumbeat of negative publicity continued. New York dock workers were so incensed over Bevin's charges they refused to move his luggage.[47]

Bevin's swipe at Truman and the negative publicity following it, indicated the profound pressure the British government was feeling to find a solution to the problems of Palestine. It also reflected Whitehall's irritation at what Joseph Alsop correctly observed in his syndicated column to be the "self-righteous criticism being directed at them from the sidelines." What particularly infuriated British leaders was America's handling of the Jewish refugee problem. The United Nations Relief and Rehabilitation Administration was reporting a million displaced persons living in camps throughout Western Europe in January, 1947, one third of them Jews.[48] The United Jewish Appeal, under the general chairmanship of former Treasury Secretary Henry Morgenthau, collected $102 million for these war victims in 1946 and was seeking $170 million for 1947. American Zionists, however, were not anxious to see Jewish refugees brought to America, nor did they want the administration to expand the nation's annual immigration rate, which processed only 7,000 European refugees in a single year. A presidential commission found that the majority of Europe's displaced Jews, two-thirds of them survivors of the Polish death camps, wanted to go to Palestine. Silver's conviction was that the longer they held that resolve, but were forced to remain in camps, the stronger would be the pressure on the British to ease barriers on their coming to Palestine.[49]

The British problems on the ground in Palestine were going from bad to worse. The kidnapping of a British official prompted an order that British women and children be evacuated from Palestine immediately. This move provoked speculation in the press that the next step of the British government would be to impose martial law and turn the problem of Palestine over to the United Nations. Bevin's hope was that the United Nations would give international legitimacy to his call for a bi-national state in Palestine under Arab majority rule. The Jewish Agency of Palestine was given seven days to cooperate with British authorities in the rounding up of "Jewish terrorists" or "face the consequences" of its refusal. Not unexpectedly, Jewish leaders rejected the ultimatum, charging it would turn Jew against Jew. The Associated Press reported Palestine's Arab representatives were making plans for a "holy war." By February 10, British authorities had issued death sentences for three

Jewish underground members, and Gene Currivan of the *New York Times*, predicted it would only be a matter of days before the problem was turned over to the United Nations. Two days later, Bevin confirmed to Charles Egan of the *Times* that that was the proposal he was bringing to the British cabinet. At week's end Egan could report that the cabinet had overwhelmingly approved Bevin's proposal.[50]

Delegate counting at the United Nations had persuaded British leaders that they could win a final vote on the future disposition of Palestine while gaining international legitimation for British policies in the region. But British leaders failed to anticipate how world opinion would overwhelm their careful calculations. The British decision would be seen in the context of Krock's warning in mid-February that the world was entering "a very critical situation." Krock told Sunday readers of the *New York Times* that he could not remember a time since the Second World War when the international situation had been more dangerous and that the future status of Palestine must be seen in that uncertain context. Soviet foreign policy, the *Times* argued editorially, was "aggressive and expansionist." In a public forum on March 5, the *Times* James Reston shared the concern of a growing number of American officials that the Soviet Union had not given up world communist domination. Reston argued that sentiment was growing in official Washington that if the British could not hold the Soviets off in the Eastern Mediterranean, the United States would. The *Times* United Nations correspondent Thomas Hamilton sounded a note of warning, however. Neither Britain nor the United States could expect the United Nations to provide a police force to blunt Soviet expansion into the Eastern Mediterranean. The Soviets could block any U.N. initiative with which they disagreed. Hamilton cautioned that this situation would leave the United States and the Soviet Union staring across a barrel at one another in Greece, Turkey, or perhaps Palestine.[51]

The view from London was that the problems of Palestine could be contained and that the United Nations was the best place to contain them. But events would show how feeble the British were in fighting either of the battles that lay before them. British bungling in Palestine and within the halls of the U.N. General Assembly was exceeded by their complete failure to win the public relations war on Palestine. The power to define the "realities" of Palestine and what was ultimately at stake took on special importance once the matter was turned over to the "court of world opinion." And it was here that proponents and opponents of a Jewish state would wage their fiercest battle.

THE BATTLE FOR PUBLIC OPINION

The decision announced in mid-February by the British to leave Greece by the end of March and their declaration that they were turning the problem of Palestine over to the United Nations, created a dilemma for the U.S. State Department. Acheson wrote Secretary of State Marshall on

February 21 that the administration would have a difficult time convincing Congress in such a short time that America's vital interests required it to take over British burdens in Greece. Acheson's fears sprang from the department's own polling of the public, which showed only a small fraction of Americans favoring a get tough policy toward the Soviets. This result was consistent with department polling throughout 1946, which had shown that fewer than half of all Americans were attentive to the nation's foreign policy.[52]

President Truman recognized this problem as he prepared a major address before a Joint Session of the Congress. C. L. Sulzberger, writing from Europe, was convinced that Washington finally understood how "urgently important" to American interests was the Eastern Mediterranean. Truman's major concern in March, 1947, was delivering a speech that would make the public see it as well. He rejected initial language sent to him by the State Department. He did not want the speech to sound "like an investment prospectus." Instead, it needed to be "clear and free of hesitation or double talk." The final draft argued that United States "support(s) free people who are resisting subjugation by armed minorities or by outside pressures." Failure to commit to these objectives would bring "confusion and disorder throughout the Middle East."[53]

The Truman Doctrine of March 12 not only linked the fate of the Middle East to East-West relations but also reflected the conviction of the President, members of his State Department and the AZEC executive that mobilizing American public opinion through the mass media constituted an important link in America's postwar foreign policy. It was not that Truman looked to that fraction of the American public attentive to foreign policy issues for advice but rather he understood that initiatives he had taken could not be long sustained in the absence of public support.[54]

Truman and his aides appear to have seen the media as a key to getting their message to the American public. They also used the media to gauge public attitudes toward that policy. Truman believed the press could exert a powerful influence over public opinion, particularly in foreign policy matters where public attention was limited and its convictions sometimes ephemeral. George Elsey, an assistant to the President and one of his speech writers, believed that Truman understood his job was "to lead public opinion rather than waiting for public opinion to tell him what to do." The White House view, according to Elsey, was that the mass media should perform an educational role in mobilizing support for policy initiatives. It ought to tell the public, in Truman's words, why the President had done what he had done in the hope that they would understand and support his action.[55]

Truman often saw himself as a "glorified public relations man" whose principal power rested in his ability to persuade others to follow him. First among those who needed persuading were members of the media. And Truman saw media support for the broad outlines of American foreign policy as a kind of patriotic duty. Truman reportedly told reporters that he considered them a fundamental part of the bi-partisan foreign policy that represented the national interest. While there was much talk about men in "striped trousers" who made foreign policy, Truman was convinced "far more influence is exerted by the baggy pants of managing editors." Truman believed that for better or worse "no private group was given as all-important a role as the press in determining what the nation as a whole will do."[56]

In the case of his call to contain Communism through Greek aid, Truman was not disappointed. The *New York Times* considered it a speech of the "first magnitude." It agreed with the President's logic that "if Greece should fall under Communist domination, the effect upon the whole Middle East, and upon all European countries now struggling to maintain their freedom, would be disastrous, not only for them but for us." The *New York Herald-Tribune* thought Truman's speech gave hope to the "shattered peoples of the world that the American system offers a working alternative to the totalitarian order." The *Washington Post* considered it a necessary "tocsin aimed at countering Soviet aggression." The *Philadelphia Inquirer* saw it as a recognition that "many harassed nations will have their liberty disappear if we fail them." The *Memphis Commercial-Appeal* said it was "fully aware that the President is right when he says the course he proposes is serious," and warned, "we think he is also right when he says the alternative is more serious."[57]

Even some of the papers that had been Truman's bitterest enemies did not fault the President's logic as much as they worried where his policy would lead the nation. The *Chicago Tribune* feared "the outcome inevitably will be war. It probably will not come this year or next year, but the issue is already drawn and cannot be tempered or withdrawn." The *St. Louis Post-Dispatch* felt "the President's address has committed the nation to an all out diplomatic action just as a declaration of a shooting war must necessarily follow when the President asks for it." There can scarcely be an American, the *San Francisco Chronicle* suggested, "who doesn't have that pit-of-the-stomach awareness of impending danger."[58]

Many of the nation's leading radio commentators thought the United States had no alternative but to take that risk. Joseph Harsch, who had covered the Nazi blitzkrieg from Berlin to London told his Columbia Broadcasting System (CBS) listeners that the United States would either "inherit the British empire or let nature take its incalculable cost." Communism was a "heavy liquid which flows down into the swamps of poverty," Harsch warned, and America must be sure it spread no further. Clifton Utley, who for eleven years had been the director of the Chicago Council on Foreign Relations, told his listeners at NBC that the United States would either shape the future "to our liking or permit the Russians to shape the world to theirs." Even the self-proclaimed liberal Cecil Brown of Mutual Broadcasting, who decried "hysterical radio commentators" who thought the United States and Russia were about to go to war, had to admit that the stakes were too high for

America "to desert its friends in their hour of great need." His experience in
the Middle East and Far East during World War II had persuaded him that the
free world could not submit itself to "total enslavement" at the hands of
"barbarian forces." He hoped that men learned by their mistakes, "but if they
do not learn, then the mistake is doubly, horribly tragic."[59]

When AZEC's Abba Hillel Silver arrived in Jerusalem the day after
President Truman's speech, he told the *Times*' Clifton Daniel that he was
cautiously optimistic the United States government was now "prepared to go
a little farther" in its policy on Palestine. Silver offered Daniel what was to
become over the next eight months the Zionist's clarion call to American
public opinion. The American people must be made to realize, he told Daniel,
"that the Middle East is a part of the world that you cannot treat piecemeal."
A commitment to embark on a new policy in Greece necessarily required a
new policy in Palestine.[60]

In the next few weeks, as the United Nations prepared to consider the
case of Palestine, the Zionists continued to make Silver's argument. President
Truman, AZEC pointed out, had publicly linked Palestine to East-West
relations. American support to Greece and Turkey would be "the camel's nose
in the proverbial tent." This was the message that AZEC's Eliahu Ben-Horin
took to the American editors. In meetings with publishers and chief editorial
writers in Detroit, Pittsburgh and Kansas City, he hammered away at what
Zionists saw as the logic of their position. The American stand on Greece, he
argued, required its linkage to a just settlement in Palestine. The sooner the
United States recognized that fact, the better.[61]

The struggle to shape reporting on the future of Palestine quickly
became absorbed in international tensions extending far beyond the borders of
Palestine. Bright prospects of postwar peace had receded as rapidly as the
British retreat from Greece. Now, according to some commentators, it was a
short step from the fall of Greece to World War III. The emerging image of
Palestine was a backward place in a strategic region. It would either remain
in the Western camp or fall to the Soviets.

The media did not come to portray the issues of Palestine in this
fashion by inadvertence or accident. The British and American governments,
as well as Zionists and Arabs, and the divisions within these camps, each had
messages to get out on Palestine. In the months that followed, each would be
forced to define and redefine for the press what was at stake. What had been
determined during the first months of 1947 was that each of the major parties
to the dispute would be compelled to speak the language of the Cold War. This
development gave the U.S. State Department an enormous early advantage
because that was a language in which they had been proficient for more than
a year.[62]

The other major fact to emerge in the days preceding and the weeks
following the announcement of the Truman Doctrine was that the United
Nations would be the site of the future struggle over Palestine. As events

turned out, it was the future of the United Nations itself that became implicated in those deliberations. This linkage was in part the consequence of the way in which the media played the story of Palestine in the spring and summer of 1947, a period during which Palestine would be projected onto the world stage, across its front pages and along its many airwaves.

NOTES

1. *New York Times*, January 1, 1947, p. 1.

2. *New York Times*, December 29, 1946, Section E, p. 1; January 1, 1947, p. 28; and January 5, 1947, p. 1. Also, H. V. Kaltenborn Radio Script. December 24, 1946. H. V. Kaltenborn Papers. Box 181. Folder 1. State Historical Society of Wisconsin. Madison, Wisconsin.

3. *Problems of Journalism*, Volume 25 (Washington: American Society of Newspaper Editors, 1947), p. 71. *New York Times*, February 14, 1947, p. 22. Kaltenborn Radio Script. February 21, 1947. Box 181. Folder 1. Kaltenborn Papers.

4. *New York Times*, December 29, 1946, Section E, p. 1.

5. Biographical notes on Kaltenborn can be found in H. V. Kaltenborn Papers. Box 1. Folder 1. S.H.S.W.

6. H. V. Kaltenborn, *Europe Now: A First Hand Report* (New York: Didier, 1945), xi. Kaltenborn appeared in Embassy newsreel theatres in New York City and Telenews theatres outside of New York City. See H. V. Kaltenborn, *Kaltenborn Edits the News* (New York: E. P. Dutton, 1942), p. 2. Kaltenborn Radio Script. December 4, 1946. Kaltenborn Papers. Box 181. Folder 1.

7. Kaltenborn Radio Script. December 4, 1946. Kaltenborn Papers. Box 181. Folder 1. *Problems of Journalism*, Volume 25 (Washington: American Society of Newspaper Editors, 1947), pp. 67, 70 and 74.

8. See Richard W. Steele, "News of the Good War: World War II News Management," *Journalism Quarterly* 62, 1985, pp. 707-717 and 783. Also, Patrick S. Washburn, "The Office of Censorship's Attempt to Control Press Coverage of the Atomic Bomb during World War II, *Journalism Monographs*, Number 120, 1990, pp. 11-26 and 33-35. Jean Folkerts and Dwight L. Teeter, Jr., *Voices of a Nation: A History of Media in the United States* (New York: Macmillan, 1989), pp. 351-355. John Morton Blum, *V Was for Victory: Politics and American Culture during World War II* (New York: Harcourt, Brace, Jovanovich, 1976), pp. 5-14. Edward S. Corwin, *Total War and the Constitution* (Freeport, N.Y.: Books for Libraries Press, 1970), pp. 106-108. For background see, Richard W. Steele, *Propaganda in an Open Society: The Roosevelt Administration and the Media, 1933-1941* (Westport, Conn.: Greenwood, 1985), pp. 106-111.

See also, Kaltenborn, *War News, pp. 83-84. Variety, May 5, 1943*, p. 32. Remarks by Erwin D. Canham, managing editor of the *Christian Science Monitor* to Associated Press managing editors meeting in September, 1943, published in "The Newspaper's Obligation in War Time," *Journalism Quarterly* 20, 1943, pp. 315-317. *Problems of Journalism*, Volume 22 (Washington: American Society of Newspaper Editors, 1944), p. 154.

9. *New York Times*, December 6, 1944, pp. 15 and 22; December 10, 1944, Section E, pp. 2 and 3. Meyer Berger, *The Story of the New York Times, 1851-1951* (New York: Simon and Schuster, 1951), p. 529. Lester Markel, *Public Opinion and Foreign Policy* (New York: Harper, 1949), pp. 33-35. Bruce J. Evensen, "Surrogate State Department? *Times* Coverage of Palestine, 1948," *Journalism Quarterly 67*, 1990, pp. 391-400. James Reston, *The Artillery of the Press* (New York: Harper and Row, 1967), introduction.

10. Berger, p. 527. *Editor and Publisher*, February 16, 1924, pp. 3-4. See also, Michael Schudson, *Discovering the News: A Social History of American Newspapers* (New York: Basic Books, 1978), pp. 106-120. Berger, pp. 109-125. Elmer Davis, *History of the New York Times, 1851-1921* (New York: The New York Times, 1921), pp. 193-208. Benjamin Stolberg, "The Man Behind the New York Times," *Atlantic Monthly* 138, 1926, pp. 721-731. For background, see Gerald W. Johnson, *An Honorable Titan* (New York: Harper, 1946).

11. *Problems*, Volume 25, pp. 67-70. For an assessment of the pro-Soviet line taken by the *Times* during Sulzberger's first decade as publisher, see Thomas R. Maddux, "American News Media and Soviet Diplomacy, 1934-1941," *Journalism Quarterly* 58, 1981, pp. 29-37. Also, Marco Carynnyk, "The Famine the *Times* Couldn't Find," *Commentary* 76, 1983, pp. 32-40. Herbert L. Matthews, "Fascism Is Not Dead," *Nation's Business* 34, 1946, p. 40. Les K. Adler and Thomas G. Paterson, "Red Fascism: The Merger of Nazi Germany and Soviet Russia in the American Image of Totalitarianism," *American Historical Review* 75, 1970, p. 1046. Howard K. Smith, *The State of Europe* (New York: Knopf, 1949), p. 67.

12. Walter Millis, ed., *The Forrestal Diaries* (New York: Viking, 1951), pp. 118 and 128, which include Forrestal's diary entries of December 14, 1945 and January 11, 1946.

13. *Ibid.*, pp. 243-244, which includes diary entry of February 7, 1947. Also, Arthur Krock, *Memoirs: Sixty Years on the Firing Line* (New York: Funk and Wagnalls, 1968), p. 234.

14. *New York Times*, January 16, 1947, p. 22. Lester Markel, "The Real Sins of the Press," *Harper's*, December 1962, pp. 85-86. Also, *Problems*, Volume 25, p. 69.

15. Kaltenborn, *Europe Now*, p. 180.

16. *Problems of Journalism*, Volume 21 (Washington: American Society of Newspaper Editors, 1943), pp. 36-38.

17. *Problems of Journalism*, Volume 20 (Washington: American Society of Newspaper Editors, 1942), p. 119.

18. *New York Times*, December 6, 1944, p. 15.

19. Markel, *Public Opinion*, pp. 6-7.

20. Dean Acheson, *Present at the Creation: My Years in the State Department* (New York: W. W. Norton, 1969), p. 375.

21. Robert D. Schulzinger, *The Making of the Diplomatic Mind: The Training, Outlook and Style of U.S. Foreign Service Officers, 1908-1931* (Middletown: Wesleyan University, 1975), pp. 6-8, 81-93 and 98. Also, Aaron D. Miller, *Search for Security: Saudi Arabian Oil and American Foreign Policy, 1939-1949* (Chapel Hill: University of North Carolina, 1980), pp. 167-168, 176-178 and 185. Phillip J. Baram, *The Department of State in the Middle East* (Philadelphia: University of Pennsylvania, 1978), pp. 78 and 328-329. Thomas A. Bryson, *American Diplomatic Relations with*

the Middle East, 1784-1975 (Metuchen, N.J.: Scarecrow Press, 1977), pp. 17-24, 59 and 135-148. John De Novo, *American Interests and Policies in the Middle East, 1900-1939* (Minneapolis: University of Minnesota, 1963), pp. 6-9.

 See also, Bernard C. Cohen, *The Public's Impact on Foreign Policy* (Boston: Little, Brown, 1973), pp. 58-63 and 103-113. Bernard C. Cohen, *The Press and Foreign Policy* (Princeton: Princeton University, 1963), pp. 222-245. Gabriel A. Almond, *The American People and Foreign Policy* (New York: Praeger, 1961), pp. 136-143. Cordell Hull, *The Memoirs of Cordell Hull*, two volumes (New York: Macmillan, 1948), pp. 1529-1536. James F. Byrnes, *Speaking Frankly* (New York: Harper, 1947), pp. 233-256 and 277-297. Acheson, pp. 169-171 and 734-737. George F. Kennan, *Memoirs: 1925-1950* (Boston: Little, Brown, 1967), pp. 109 and 134-139. Evan M. Wilson, *Decision on Palestine—How the U.S. Came to Recognize Israel* (Stanford: Hoover Institution Press, 1979), pp. 41-42 and 51-52.

 22. Department of State, *Bulletin* 10, January 15, 1944. For background see Michael Leigh, *Mobilizing Consent: Public Opinion and American Foreign Policy, 1937-1947* (Westport, Conn.: Greenwood Press, 1976), pp. 104-105. Oral History Interview: Francis Russell, pp. 18-25 and 35-45. Harry S. Truman Library. Independence, Missouri. Also, Cohen, *The Public's Impact*, pp. 44-46 and 69-72. Acheson, pp. 101-102. Thomas G. Paterson, "Presidential Foreign Policy, Public Opinion, and Congress: The Truman Years," *Diplomatic History* 2, 1979, pp. 7-8.

 23. Byrnes, pp. 243, 247 and 256.

 24. Charles E. Bohlen, *The Transformation of American Foreign Policy* (New York: W. W. Norton, 1969), pp. 89-90. Markel, *Public Opinion*, pp. 3 and 6.

 25. Oral History Interview: Loy W. Henderson, pp. 20-21 and 34-35. Harry S. Truman Library. Independence, Missouri. Also, Martin Weil, *A Pretty Good Club: The Founding Fathers of the U.S. Foreign Service* (New York: W. W. Norton, 1978), pp. 52-53. George W. Baer, ed., *A Question of Trust: The Origins of U.S.-Soviet Diplomatic Relations, The Memoirs of Loy W. Henderson* (Stanford: Hoover Instituion Press, 1986), introduction, particularly, xxiv.

 26. *Foreign Relations of the United States 1945*, Volume 8 (Washington: Government Printing Office, 1973), pp. 727-730. Between 1933 and 1938, the Jewish population of Palestine more than doubled to 450,000, or 28 percent of all the inhabitants of Palestine. By 1946, the number had risen to 600,000, or 32 percent of the total. Whereas there were seven Arabs for every Jew in Palestine in 1921, the ratio was only two to one in 1946. See Joseph Heller, "The Anglo-American Commission of Inquiry on Palestine: The Zionist Reaction Reconsidered," in Elie Kedourie and Sylvia G. Haim, eds., *Zionism and Arabism in Palestine and Israel* (New York: Frank Cass, 1982), pp. 137-146. Amritzur Ilan, "Withdrawal Without Recommendations: Britain's Decision to Relinquish the Palestine Mandate," in Kedourie and Haim, pp. 183-209.

 See also, Acheson, p. 169. Hull, pp. 1532-1533. Millis, p. 323. *Foreign Relations of the United States 1943*, Volume 4 (Washington: Government Printing Office, 1971), pp. 795 and 807-810. *Foreign Relations of the United States 1944*, Volume 5 (Washington: Government Printing Office, 1972), pp. 563-564.

 27. On anti-Semitic attitudes within the State Department and Henderson's defense against those charges, see Baram, pp. 83-86 and 262-263. Weil, pp. 46-48. Hugh De Santis, *The Diplomacy of Silence: The American Foreign Service, the Soviet Union, and the Cold War, 1933-1947* (Chicago: University of Chicago, 1980), pp. 12-

14. Miller, pp. 185-187. Henderson Oral History Interview, pp. 161-162. See also, Abba Eban, *An Autobiography* (New York: Random House, 1977), p. 71. For Truman's assessment see Truman Memoirs. Foreign Palestine. Palestine. Post Presidential. Truman Library. A passionate critic of the Truman administration, Walter Trohan, the Washington correspondent for the *Chicago Tribune*, for once agreed with Truman. See Oral History Interview: Walter Trohan, p. 52. Truman Library. Truman's press office came to the same conclusion. See Diary entry. March 25, 1948. Papers of Eben A. Ayers. Box 16. Folder 5. Truman Library. For a recent discussion of this issue plus State Department plans to settle Jews in Alaska or Uganda, see *Jerusalem Post*, International Edition, January 19, 1991, p. 8.

28. *Foreign Relations of the United States 1946*, Volume 6 (Washington: Government Printing Office, 1974), pp. 696-709. Harry S. Truman, *Memoirs: Year of Decision* (New York: Doubleday, 1955), pp. 551-442. Kennan, pp. 292-295. For background, see Robert Messer, *The End of an Alliance: James F. Byrnes, Roosevelt, Truman and the Origins of the Cold War* (Chapel Hill: University of North Carolina, 1982), pp. 152-180. Donald Yergin, *Shattered Peace: The Origins of the Cold War and the National Security State* (Boston: Houghton Mifflin, 1977), pp. 138-178.

29. Baram, pp. 5-6 and 327-328. Weil, pp. 46-63. De Santis, pp. 199-204. For background, see Howard Jablon, *Crossroads of Decision: The State Department and Foreign Policy, 1933-1937* (Lexington: University of Kentucky, 1983), pp. 135-138.

30. Krock, pp. 224-231 and 419. For a complete text of Clifford's memorandum, see Krock, pp. 421-482. *Foreign Relations of the United States 1946*, Volume 1 (Washington: Government Printing Office, 1974), pp. 523-532.

31. See File 4-2. Correspondence. Minutes: American Zionist Emergency Council. January 29, 1947. The Temple. Cleveland, Ohio. A particularly bitter outcome of the Zionist Congress was the ouster of Chaim Weizmann from any formal connection to the organization. Dr. Israel Goldstein, chairman of the steering committee of the Zionist Organization of America, charged Weizmann with spreading "slurs" against the American Zionist Emergency Council and the American Zionist movement. See "Bulletin of the Twenty-second World Zionist Congress." Box 1219. American Jewish Archives. Cincinnati, Ohio.

See also, Philip Ernest Schoenberg, "The Wise-Silver Controversy: An Analysis of Zionist Policy Aims in the United States, 1939-1945," pp. 2-9. Box 1039. American Jewish Archives. Cincinnati, Ohio. Also, Marshall Blatt, "The Attempt of the American Jewish Committee to Unite the Force of Political Jewry and to Influence U.S. Foreign Policy on the Palestine Question: 1942-1948," pp. 4-16. Box 1293. American Jewish Archives. Cincinnati, Ohio. Also, *New York Times*, January 6, 1947, p. 4.

32. *The Times* (of London), November 9, 1917, p. 1. See also, Carl J. Friedrich, *American Policy Toward Palestine* (Washington: American Council on Public Affairs, 1944), pp. 3-8 and 57. Reuben Frank, ed., *America and Palestine* (New York: Arno Press, 1977), pp. 33 and 438-460. For background on the Balfour Declaration and its troublesome aftermath consider J. C. Hurewitz, *Middle East Dilemmas: The Background of United States Policy* (New York: Harper, 1953), pp. 116-124. William Roger Louis, *The British Empire in the Middle East, 1945-1951: Arab Nationalism, the United States, and Postwar Imperialism* (Oxford: Clarendon Press, 1984), pp. 382-396. Walter Laqueur and Barry Rubin, eds., *The Arab-Israeli*

Reader: A Documentary History of the Middle East Conflict (New York: Facts on File, 1985), pp. 85-104.

See also, C. L. Sulzberger, *A Long Row of Candles: Memoirs and Diaries, 1934-1954* (New York: Macmillan, 1969), p. 339. Weizmann's letters of early January, 1947, make it apparent he considered establishing a rival Zionist group to counter the policies of Ben-Gurion and Silver. See Barnet Litvinoff, ed., *The Letters and Papers of Chaim Weizmann*, Volume 12, May 1945-July 1947 (Jerusalem: Israel Universities Press, 1979), particularly Weizmann's letter to Leonard Stein, dated January 5, 1947, p. 212; Weizmann to Stephen S. Wise, January 6, 1947, p. 213; and Weizmann to Felix Frankfurter, January 7, 1947, pp. 213-214.

33. File 4-2. Correspondence. Minutes: American Zionist Emergency Council. January 29, 1947. See also, Abba Hillel Silver, "A Year's Advance: A Political Report Submitted to the Convention of the Zionist Organization of America," October 15, 1944, p. 13. Published by the American Zionist Emergency Council. The Temple. Cleveland, Ohio.

34. Baram, pp. 4-18, 67-69, 85-88 and 288-313. Bryson, pp. 90-96 and 124-134. DeNovo, pp. 167-209. Frank E. Manuel, *The Realities of American-Palestinian Relations* (Washington: Public Affairs Press, 1949), pp. 271-307. Hull, pp. 1528-1536. Acheson, p. 169.

35. Abba Hillel Silver, *Vision and Victory: A Collection of Addresses by Dr. Abba Hillel Silver, 1942-1948* (New York: The Zionist Organization of America, 1949), see especially the foreward by Emanuel Neumann. See also, "Bulletin of the Twenty-second World Zionist Congress." Box 1219. American Jewish Archives. Cincinnati, Ohio.

36. Marshall Blatt, "The Attempt of the American Jewish Committee to Unite the Force of Political Jewry and to Influence U.S. Foreign Policy on the Palestine Question: 1942-1948," pp. 16-17. Each column inch contained approximately 500 words of copy. See also, *The American Israelite* (Cincinnati), April 19, 1945, p. 1.

37. Barry Schwardon, "Zionism and Pro-Palestinian Activities," *American Jewish Yearbook, 1946-1947* (Philadelphia: American Jewish Committee, 1947), pp. 243-244. The author cites a Roper Poll. *Foreign Relations of the United States, 1946*, Volume 7 (Washington: Government Printing Office, 1974), p. 682. See also, Harry S. Truman, *Memoirs: Years of Trial and Hope* (Garden City: Doubleday, 1956), p. 134. For State Department anger at Truman, see Wilson, pp. 51-52. *New York Times*, October 5, 1946, p. 1. *New York Herald-Tribune*, October 5, 1946, p. 1. *Washington Post*, October 5, 1946, pp. 1 and 3. Letter from Eliahu Epstein to Nahum Goldmann, October 9, 1946. The Weizmann Archives. Rehovoth, Israel.

38. File 4-2. Correspondence. Minutes: AZEC. January 29, 1947 and February 24, 1947. Also, Krock, pp. xii, 8 and 214.

39. For background on the *Times*-Lodge dispute see Melvin Urofsky, *American Zionism from Herzl to the Holocaust* (Garden City: Doubleday, 1975), pp. 307-308. See also, Berger, pp. 527-528.

40. *New York Times*, August 31, 1943, p. 22. For background on the animosity between Sulzberger and American Zionists see Samuel Halperin, *The Political World of American Zionism* (Detroit: Wayne State University, 1961), pp. 255-256. Sulzberger's letter to the American League for a Free Palestine is dated June 10, 1946 and appears in *Problems of Journalism*, Volume 25 (Washington: American Society of Newspaper Editors, 1947), pp. 70-71.

41. Letter from E. Clifton Daniel to author, dated April 15, 1988. Daniel may be about a year off in his dates, however, since *Times* editorial support for the Jewish state remained consistent from November 29, 1947, the date of the United Nations' decision to partition Palestine into separate Jewish and Arab states. Also, Krock, pp. 1-8, 13, 19 and 23. For background on the clash of Reform Jews and Conservative/Orthodox Jews over Zionism, see Marshall Sklare, ed., *The Jews: Social Patterns of an American Group* (Glencoe: Free Press, 1958), pp. 16-18. Halperin, pp. 66-102. Bernard A. Rosenblatt *Two Generations of Zionism: Historical Recollections of an American Zionist* (New York: Shengold Publishers, 1967). Louis Lipsky, *Thirty Years of American Zionism* (New York: Nesher Publishing, 1927), pp. 22, 46-54 and 61. Isidore S. Meyer, ed., *Early Years of Zionism in America* (New York: Arno Press, 1977), pp. 63-68. Rufus Learsi, *The Jews in America: A History* (New York: KTAV Publishing House, 1972), pp. 43-45. Alpheus T. Mason, *Brandeis: A Free Man's Life* (New York: Viking, 1946), pp. 451-453.

For studies of Jewish immigration patterns to America and its impact on Jewish social patterns and political beliefs see Moses Rishchin, *The Promised Land: New York Jews, 1870-1914* (Cambridge: Harvard University, 1962), pp. 78, 126-127, 158 and 167. Ronald Sanders, *Shores of Refuge: A Hundred Years of Jewish Immigration* (New York: Henry Holt, 1988), pp. 165-166. Ronald Sanders, *The Downtown Jews: Portrait of an American Generation* (New York: Harper and Row, 1969), pp. 6, 108, 217, 257 and 434-436. Oscar Handlin, *The Uprooted* (New York: Grosset and Dunlap, 1951), pp. 61-62. Irving Howe, *World of Our Fathers* (New York: Harcourt, Brace, Jovanovich, 1976), pp. 11-12. Samuel Joseph, *Jewish Immigration to the United States from 1881-1910* (New York: Columbia University, 1914), introduction.

42. Letter from Daniel to author, April 15, 1988.

43. Silver saw publicly holding out for all of Palestine as a Jewish state, rather than partititioning it between separate Jewish and Arab states, as a necessary starting point in subsequent negotiations. See his comments at the AZEC executive meeting of January 29, 1947. Compare to File 4-2. Correspondence. Minutes: AZEC December 11, 1947. In this meeting, held right after the United Nations vote for partition, Silver claims the historical rightness of his position. For difficulties getting a meeting scheduled with the *Times*, see File 4-11. Letter from Anne O'Hare McCormick to Eliahu Ben-Horin, February 12, 1947. Letter from Ben-Horin to Arthur Lourie, February 19, 1947. For background see Ben-Horin to Harry Shapiro, January 19, 1947. AZEC Files.

44. Letter from Abba Hillel Silver to Abe Tuvim, dated June 13, 1947. File 1-4-42. AZEC Files. Also, Correspondence. Minutes: AZEC. January 21, 1948. File 4-2. AZEC Files. The special problem of the *New York Times* is mentioned most decisively at this meeting, but concerns over the *Times* coverage can be found in nearly every AZEC executive meeting between January 29, 1947 and April 27, 1948.

45. *New York Times*, February 1, 1947, p. 22.

46. *The New Statesman and Nation*, January 18, 1947, p. 1. *Sunday Tribune*, January 18, 1947, p. 1.

47. Cabinet Meeting. 47/6. Minute 4. Confidential Annex. January 15, 1947. The Public Record Office. Kew Gardens, England. *FRUS 1946*, Volume 7, pp. 704-705. Sulzberger, p. 369. *New York Times*, February 26, 1947, p. 1 and February 27, 1947, p. 1.

48. Letter from Joseph Alsop to Frances Gunther, dated February 17, 1948. Box 3. Papers of Joseph Alsop. Library of Congress. Washington, D.C. Alsop's note speaks of British attitudes in the wake of President Truman's Yom Kippur address. Also, *New York Times*, January 5, 1947, Section E, p. 5.

49. *New York Times*, January 11, 1947, p. 18 and January 24, 1947, p. 20. Correspondence. Minutes: AZEC. January 29, 1947. File 4-2. AZEC Files.

On June 22, 1945 President Truman instructed Earl G. Harrison, the dean of the University of Pennsylvania law school, to investigate the conditions under which Europe's displaced persons were living, their needs and their desired destination. Harrison's report, given to the President sixty days later, described the appalling conditions of those detention centers and the overwhelming desire of its Jewish internees to be permitted to emigrate to Palestine. For the impact the Harrison Report had on Truman, see *Memoirs: Years of Trial and Hope*, chapter ten.

Also, Clark M. Clifford, "Factors Influencing President Truman's Decision to Support Partition and Recognize Israel," a speech delivered to the American Historical Association, on December 28, 1976, in Washington, D.C., pp. 2-3. A text of the Harrison Report can be found in Department of State, *Bulletin* 13, September 30, 1945. For background, see J. C. Hurewitz, *Diplomacy in the Near and Middle East, A Documentary Record: 1914-1956* (Princeton: D. Van Norstrand, 1956), pp. 249-257.

50. *New York Times*, January 29, 1947, p. 1; February 1, 1947, p. 1; February 2, 1947, Section E, pp. 1 and 5; February 4, 1947, p. 1; February 6, 1947, p. 1; February 13, 1947, p. 18 and February 15, 1947, p. 1. *Washington Post*, February 7, 1947, p. 5.

51. David Horowitz, *State in the Making* (Westport: Greenwood Press, 1981), pp. 139-143. Also, *New York Times*, February 15, 1947, Section E, p. 3. Jon Kimche, *Seven Fallen Pillars: The Middle East, 1945-1952* (London: Secker and Warburg, 1953), pp. 65-77. *New York Times*, February 15, 1947, Section E, p. 3; February 19, 1947, p. 24 and March 5, 1947, p. 16.

52. *FRUS 1947*, Volume 5, p. 31. Also, "American Attitudes on U.S. Policy Toward Russia," February 19, 1947, a nationwide survey conducted by the Survey Research Center of the University of Michigan and available at the National Archives. Modern Military Branch. Record Group 165. Section 1-D. Washington, D.C. And, George H. Gallup, *The Gallup Poll: Public Opinion, 1935-1971* (New York: Random House, 1972), Volume 1, pp. 561 and 604, and Volume 2, p. 852.

53. *New York Times*, March 5, 1947, p. 18. Truman, *Memoirs: Years of Trial and Hope*, pp. 100-131. Lloyd C. Gardner, *Imperial America: American Foreign Policy Since 1898* (New York: Harcourt, Brace, 1976), pp. 182-185. And, *Congressional Record*, Volume 93, p. 1999. Daily edition. March 12, 1947.

54. Even those scholars who charge that President Truman paid little attention to public opinion in devising his postwar foreign policy, acknowledge that Truman was aware he could not hope to sustain that policy without public endorsement. See Manfred Landecker, *The President and Public Opinion* (Washington: Public Affairs Press, 1968), pp. 64-65. Thomas G. Paterson, "Presidential Foreign Policy, Public Opinion, and Congress: The Truman Years," *Diplomatic History* 3, 1979, pp. 2-3.

55. Truman, *Memoirs: Year of Decision*, p. 47. Truman saw his relations with the press as being of the "utmost importance." By way of the press he saw himself maintaining "a direct contact with the people." See also a statement by Truman before

the American Society of Newspaper Editors on April 17, 1948. Papers of Harry S. Truman. White House Official Reporter. Working Papers. Public Statements of the President. Box 30. Truman Library. Also, Oral History Interview: George M. Elsey, Volume 1, pp. 32-35 and 74-79. See also, Volume 2, pp. 243-251. Truman Library.

56. Margaret Truman, *Harry S. Truman* (New York: William Morrow, 1973), p. 356. Clinton Rossiter, *The American Presidency* (New York: Harcourt, Brace, 1956), p. 122. Landecker, pp. 64-65. Several reporters who covered the Truman White House felt that the President's insistence that partisanship stopped at the water's edge made him especially thin-skinned when his foreign policy initiatives came under attack. See Oral History Interview: Robert G. Nixon, pp. 445-446 and 673-696. Also, Oral History Interview: Robert K. Walsh, pp. 60-62. Both interviews are in the Truman Library. See also, Truman's remarks before the American Society of Newspaper Editors in *Problems of Journalism*, Volume 28 (Washington: American Society of Newspaper Editors, 1950), p. 49.

57. *New York Times*, March 13, 1947, p. 26. *New York Herald-Tribune*, March 13, 1947, p. 14. *Washington Post*, March 13, 1947, p. 22. *Philadelphia Inquirer*, March 13, 1947, p. 23. *Memphis Commercial Appeal*, March 13, 1947, p. 11.

58. *Chicago Tribune*, March 13, 1947, p. 8. *St. Louis Post-Dispatch*, March 13, 1947, p. 15. *San Francisco Chronicle*, March 13, 1947, p. 8.

59. Joseph Harsch Radio Script. March 12, 1947. Box 11. Folder 3. Joseph Harsch Papers. Clifton Utley Radio Script. March 12, 1947. Box 47. Folder 3. Clifton Utley Papers. Cecil Brown Radio Script. March 5, 1947. Box 12. Folder 1. All scripts are at the State Historical Society of Wisconsin. Madison, Wisconsin. Also, Cecil Brown, *Suez to Singapore* (New York: Random House, 1943), pp. ix, x, 17 and 530-531.

60. *New York Times*, March 14, 1947, p. 4.

61. Letter from Eliahu Ben-Horin to Harry Shapiro, dated February 4, 1947. File 4-11. AZEC Files. Also, letter from Ben-Horin to Arthur Lourie, dated February 19, 1947, File 4-11. AZEC Files. Efforts to translate the American interest in Greece to support for the Zionist cause in Palestine are described in AZEC's March 10, 1947 executive meeting. See Correspondence. Minutes: AZEC March 10, 1947. File 4-2. AZEC Files.

62. Correspondence. Minutes: AZEC April 7, 1947. File 4-2. AZEC Files.

Two

The Debate to Create a Committee of Inquiry: Zionists Divide and Fail to Conquer, April 1947–June 1947

Divisions within Zionism were never more apparent nor self-defeating than during the spring of 1947. The British decision to turn the problems of Palestine over to the United Nations gave Zionists the opportunity they had long sought to win international support for their cause. But instead of speaking in one voice, Zionists argued with one another publicly and privately over personalities and tactics. The squabbling destroyed the movement's efforts to determine the shape of the political debate on the future status of Palestine and allowed the U.S. State Department to argue only the Soviet Union would win if a Jewish state was created in Palestine.

Zionism's spring-long struggle brought to a head lingering disagreements within the American Zionist Emergency Council (AZEC) on how to achieve its stated objective of creating a Jewish homeland in Palestine. Zionism's old-line leadership, headed by Russian-born chemist Chaim Weizmann, was convinced that behind the scenes bargaining with world leaders, particularly the British and American governments, was the best course. Weizmann pointed with pride to long-standing ties to political leaders across much of Europe and was supported in his gradualist approach by American Reform Rabbi Stephen Wise, who could claim access to Franklin Roosevelt's Oval Office.

The Weizmann-Wise faction, however, was thrust aside by world Zionists in December 1946. The collision in Basel between forces loyal to Cleveland Rabbi Abba Hillel Silver and those supporting Weizmann led to rupture and recrimination that deepened by the following spring. In essence, the dispute centered on the merits of mass mobilization versus quiet diplomacy in achieving Zionist goals. Silver was certain that only overwhelming political pressure generated by an effective use of the mass media could assure Zionist success. Silver argued that unless Zionists mobilized "a mighty chorus of voices" to support immediate Jewish statehood, the opportunity would be lost, perhaps for a generation.

Silver's elevation to the executive of the Jewish Agency, the group responsible for the coordination of worldwide Zionist activities, and the ending of any formal connection between Weizmann and world Zionism in December 1946, showed the ground gained by those demanding a more militant Zionism. But by the following spring, the real winner of this conflict was still unclear. Weizmann, in London, brooded and planned revenge. Silver, in New York, labored to lead Zionist forces in the days leading to U.N. consideration of Palestine, but he encountered powerful opposition. Silver's public plea for a Jewish state in Palestine to serve as sanctuary for Holocaust survivors was undermined by Weizmann gradualists, who privately suggested Zionists might be satisfied with something less than a state. The double-minded message was no match for State Department insistence that a Jewish state only facilitated Soviet expansion, a warning made all the more credible by Moscow's abrupt advocacy of Jewish statehood.

As a U.N. committee of inquiry bound for Palestine prepared to leave New York, Silver, seeing Zionism at a "crossroads," feared the future. The press was reporting Weizmann would be in Palestine to testify when the committee reached Jerusalem. Silver's concern was that the Jewish Agency, torn by divisions, would do little to "control" Weizmann. A breakdown in communication with the executive left Silver "reading the papers" to find out "what's going on." Silver's strategy of creating the conventional wisdom by which the fate of Palestine would be sealed was in retreat by June. It was for American Zionism's chief agitator and publicist an unwelcome lesson in the limits of mass mobilization. As long as Zionists remained divided, Silver predicted, what was possible in Palestine would be defined by others.

ZIONISM'S DIVIDED HOUSE

Born in Lithuania, raised in New York City, converted to Zionism at an early age, Abba Hillel Silver was a fifth generation rabbi of unquestioned oratorical and organizational skill. Many of his contemporaries thought Silver had the self-conscious bearing of an Old Testament prophet and that he led his movement like a Moses, or in the manner of a dictator, depending on one's point of view. Silver galvanized a deeply-divided Zionist movement at the close of World War II with his single-minded certainty that the survival of the Jewish people required a state where they could be masters of their fate and his conviction that the mass media were an indispensable tool in winning that state.[1]

When Zionists met in London in August, 1945, Silver urged delegates to learn the lessons of the Holocaust. "We are living in a hard and brutal world," he told them. "The gentle, patient and personal diplomatic approach of yesterday is not entirely adequate for our days." He warned that, "if we speak too softly our voices are likely to be drowned in the cacophony of the world today. Sometimes it is the height of statesmanship to be unstatesmanlike."[2]

The London Conference was not the first time Silver had rebuked the "statesmanlike gradualism" of Chaim Weizmann, Zionism's elder statesman. A 1921 showdown of world Zionists in Cleveland splintered the movement for two decades. Silver was among American Zionists who supported Supreme Court Justice Louis Brandeis' break with Weizmann. The Brandeis group wanted to accelerate the pace of Jewish immigration to Palestine and to mobilize non-Jewish Americans in support of Zionist objectives. The Weizmann faction insisted on exerting central authority over all Zionist chapters and warned that public pressure would only alienate the world leaders whose good will Zionists should carefully cultivate.[3]

The feuding among Zionists stifled the Jewish state movement for a generation. When the Great Depression began there were only 18,000 active Zionists in the United States, and that was lower than 1922 levels. The Zionist Organization of America, which served as an umbrella for a host of Zionist activities, was unable to meet expenses. As economic times worsened, Zionists were resented by many in the Jewish community for their endless quarreling and fundraising projects that seemed to produce little in the way of results. It was during these lean years that Silver solidified his position with the Zionist rank and file. His active speaking schedule took him to churches, temples and community centers nationwide, where he argued for the building of a Jewish homeland in Palestine.[4]

In May of 1942 at the Biltmore Conference Silver further alienated the Weizmann faction when he proposed that the Jewish homeland in Palestine be a state and nothing less. Weizmann had won British backing in 1917 for a Jewish homeland in Palestine and thirty years later still considered that the preferred solution for the region. Silver's demand for an independent, self-governing authority greatly irritated Weizmann ally, Rabbi Stephen Wise, who had studiously avoided making any such demand in his semi-annual visits with Franklin Roosevelt. When Silver's supporters displaced Wise in August, 1943, as head of the AZEC, the political action arm of American Zionism, Wise was convinced Silver was attempting to destroy him.[5]

The council, under Silver's aggressive leadership, established 400 local chapters through 1945 and 1946, linking them to editors, columnists and commentators across the country, as well as town councilmen, mayors, governors and state assemblymen. Business and labor leaders were also approached by AZEC operatives, as well as movie stars and writers, who pressed for increased Jewish immigration to Palestine in nationwide radio spots and highly publicized mass demonstrations.[6]

Loy W. Henderson, the director of Near East Affairs at the State

Department, could see trouble coming and warned his colleagues the department's long opposition to Jewish statehood would be threatened by the "more militant" Silver. Henderson's hope was that President Truman would be "turned off" by Silver's tenacity. There is evidence that he was. Silver's primary contact in the White House, Minority Affairs assistant David K. Niles, told Jewish Agency representative Eliahu Epstein that Truman had developed an allergy to "that rabbi from Cleveland" and his intense advocacy of special interests. The suspicion was reciprocated. Silver, a registered Republican, had supported Roosevelt in his first two terms, before getting both political parties to adopt Zionist planks at their national conventions in 1944. But Roosevelt walked away from his commitment a month after the election was won. And although Truman endorsed the immediate immigration of 100,000 Jews to Palestine in October, 1946, Silver was convinced it was nothing more than "a smart election move" that would be forgotten when the election was over.[7]

Silver's capacity to make powerful enemies extended to Weizmann, who by the spring of 1947 was old, ill and bitterly angry over the "humiliation" of being ousted by an upstart like Silver from a movement he helped found. Initially, Weizmann told supporters within the Zionist movement he would wash his hands of the "slime" of the Basel Congress and allow the Zionist movement under "that demagogue Silver" to fend for itself. However, the more Weizmann pondered his "political assassination" the angrier he became. He began comparing Silver to Hitler in his determination to eliminate all political opposition. Weizmann warned Meyer Weisgal and other American Zionists to defeat "a Fascist streak in the Movement" which had led Zionism to a "grave crisis."[8]

Weizmann would not go quietly. He wrote former Treasury Secretary Henry Morgenthau that although "it had been my intention to retire," he could not abandon the movement "in its present decisive stage." By January of 1947 Weizmann began to build "a moderate group of thinking Zionists" who might yet "save our movement from a collapse" brought on by "the evil machinations of a man like Silver." Although Weizmann insisted he "did not wish to undermine in any way the authority of the Jewish Agency," it was necessary to point out that the organization was now being run by individuals "who have been enemies of mine from time immemorial" and whose actions would inexorably lead "to the destruction of all that we have built up."[9]

Weizmann resented Silver's use of the media in pursuing "his own agenda," and he believed members of the press, Jewish and secular, had joined in a Silver-led conspiracy to oust Weizmann from leadership in the Zionist movement. Weizmann urged his followers to ignore "any false interviews of mine forged by some of the correspondents of American newspapers." Without naming them, Weizmann charged such reporters with exploiting him for a few sensational headlines. But he was refusing all interviews and photographs. "So whenever you read something of an alarming nature," he warned, "you can take it for granted that in 99 cases out of 100 it is false."[10]

Weizmann was, however, not keeping his "reserve," as he claimed. On April 19, 1947 he wrote a long letter to the editor of *The Times* of London in which he broke with Jewish Agency policy and urged perpetuation of the British mandate over Palestine. The agency, through Silver and its chairman David Ben-Gurion, was preparing to argue in Flushing Meadow for the creation of a Jewish state in Palestine. But Weizmann wrote that he could not remain "silent" or "aloof" while the future of Jewish national hopes in Palestine were further "imperilled." Silver and the AZEC executive believed Weizmann's "appeasement" of the British had confounded the press over Zionism's commitment to a Jewish state. The press appeared to be "buying" a story concocted by Weizmann supporters that their man had been selected by the Jewish Agency to speak in behalf of world Zionism.[11]

Weizmann, however, was less expert at managing the media than Silver's faction feared. Although he maintained close ties with Jacob Landau, the director of the Jewish Telegraph Agency, which acted as a wire service for most of America's 175 Jewish periodicals, Weizmann saw much of the Zionist press as Silver's ally and his mortal enemy. He warned that American Zionism was taking on "the characteristics of a totalitarian regime" supported by a "servile press, whose object is to glorify the leader and vilify any opposition." Weizmann asked Joseph Heftman, the chairman of the Palestine Journalists' Association and in charge of credentials for reporters assigned to the region, to censure reporters who "spread vain rumours" in an "organized campaign to discredit me." Particularly galling to Weizmann was the appearance in mid-March of a largely factual story by Shlomo Yitzhaki, Palestine correspondent of the New York Yiddish daily *Jewish Morning Journal*, which reported Weizmann's effort to establish a group to challenge the Jewish Agency leadership of Silver and Ben-Gurion. Weizmann reiterated his public posture that he "would do nothing that might disturb the work of the Jewish Agency, or that might appear to be a breach of national discipline."[12]

The battle by Zionists to create the conventional wisdom by which the United Nations would consider the final status of Palestine was also a battle within the movement to determine which faction would speak in behalf of Zionism. As the United Nations prepared to debate the matter, the Silver faction had an enormous advantage over the Weizmann stalwarts. Flushing Meadow was in their backyard and Weizmann was half a world away. Just as important, a significant majority of American Jews and their press had been won to Silver's cause and were urging immediate Jewish statehood. In the spring of 1947, eight in ten of America's 5.6 million Jews favored the creation of a Jewish homeland in Palestine, with one of the remaining two "undecided." The Jewish press reflected this sentiment. Even if *The Yiddisher Kemfer* and other leaders in the Yiddish press continued to take verbal "potshots" at Silver and the stridency of AZEC, the Holocaust had made them supporters of the Zionist cause. The oldest and most prestigious of the Yiddish dailies, *The Forward*, founded in 1897 in New York and managed by Abraham Cahan, had by the spring of 1947 abandoned its anti-Zionist stand. Some Yiddish dailies such as *The Day* continued to resist formal alliance with Zionist organizations while supporting Zionist objectives in their columns.[13]

ON THE OFFENSIVE

As delegates from fifty-five nations gathered at Flushing Meadow on the morning of April 28, 1947 to prepare for the opening of the United Nations special session on Palestine, the *New York Times* published maps for those readers who wanted to attend the meeting and see history made. That evening from a booth overlooking the convention floor, NBC's H. V. Kaltenborn reported live on a debate he was convinced would mean much to global security. Network commentators made much of the East-West conflict that overshadowed consideration of Palestine's future. Clifton Utley observed that the "most important" aspect of the problem was "the rivalry between Russia and the West." Western leaders must make certain, he argued, that vital oil reserves were kept out of Soviet hands. Mutual Radio's Cecil Brown agreed with the logic of that argument if not its morality. "If the conscience of the world were the issue," he told his listeners, "then the murder of five million Jews in Europe and the fate of the ragged, miserable surviving one and a half million" would mean more than oil. The current consideration of Palestine, he claimed, was "a vivid example of what has happened to the world's sense of justice and fairness and decency."[14]

The Truman administration did not welcome the General Assembly session but was careful to avoid giving that impression in the media. The State Department feared giving the Soviets a forum to rail against American aid to Greece and Turkey. But the British were not cooperating. Eager for the United Nations to begin its work, the British embassy circulated a story that Washington was blunting a hearing on Palestine. Robert McClintock of the Office of Political Affairs at the State Department grew nervous. Washington could not appear to be impeding discussions on Palestine even though that is what it was doing. McClintock had the department's press office bring in reporters and deny the story.[15]

The difficulty of the administration's position was reflected in public opinion polls. In the days following the Truman Doctrine speech leading up to the U.N. special session on Palestine, the public was apprehensive about America's commitment to Greece and fearful that commitment would be broadened to Palestine. A majority of taxpayers opposed any unilateral American initiative in the Eastern Mediterranean and favored turning the problem of aid to Greece and Turkey over to the United Nations. Four in five surveyed said they were aware of the problems of Palestine, but two in three wanted the United States to avoid keeping the peace there. Three-quarters of those polled specifically disapproved of sending American troops to the region.[16]

Public reticence tended to magnify the administration's ambivalence on Palestine in the days leading up to the opening of the U.N. special session. Truman sent a message to Zionists saying he had no intention of assuming British responsibilities in Palestine. He said he hoped to find "some proper way" to take care of the displaced persons in Europe who wanted to go to Palestine because these individuals were "in a pitiful plight" and because American taxpayers "were paying to feed most of them."[17]

Silver was hardly satisfied with the President's position and began preparations for a major publicity campaign designed to capture American public opinion and through it to create the best possible climate for the talks about to begin at the United Nations. AZEC's strategy from its April 7 executive meeting onward was to make the Truman administration publicly link its aid plan to Greece and Turkey with finding a solution to the problems of Palestine. The State Department told Silver that the Greek aid was "very urgent" but that Palestine required "a long-range solution and further study." Silver asked long-time allies, Republican senators Robert Taft of Ohio and Owen Brewster of Maine to make Foreign Relations Committee Chairman Arthur Vandenberg, a Republican, see that connection but made little progress.[18]

More irritating to Silver than Congressional and State Department "foot shuffling" was the failure of the Jewish Agency in Jerusalem to authorize immediate action to gain the propaganda offensive at the United Nations. Silver complained that precious time had been wasted while workers in AZEC's nationwide network sat idly waiting word from headquarters. At the root of the impasse were Silver's growing differences with Ben-Gurion. Silver threatened to resign from the Jewish Agency executive because of "the inept and willful" interference by Ben-Gurion's representatives in AZEC propaganda efforts. Silver charged the creation of a separate agency office in Washington undermined AZEC activities with the press and political leaders, leaving both "completely in the dark" over who spoke for Zionism.[19]

The differences between Silver and Ben-Gurion were not only personal but substantive. Ben-Gurion had indicated to the press his support for a partitioned Palestine; Silver opposed partition. Ben-Gurion was prepared to accept a portion of a divided Palestine as a home for a Jewish state; Silver and his supporters were demanding the whole of Palestine as a Jewish state. In light of these differences and "the urgency of the moment," Silver decided to act independently of the Jewish Agency in advance of the General Assembly debate. His organization, Silver was convinced, knew what needed to be done and alone realized that conditions required immediate and dramatic action.[20]

AZEC's first initiative was to bombard President Truman and Secretary of State George C. Marshall with telegrams registering "emphatic protest" over the exclusion of the Jewish Agency and its American section from participating in the U.N. debate on Palestine. AZEC argued the effect would be "catastrophic on world opinion" since the Arab states had five voting members in the General Assembly and only their side of the argument would be heard. A week before the General Assembly was to convene, the *New York Times* chief diplomatic correspondent James Reston noted the publicity campaign was having its effect. The administration, he wrote, would have to reluctantly support Zionist participation in the Flushing Meadow debate despite State Department fears that debate could not be contained. Reston observed that the administration had formulated no specific solution to the Palestine problem and seemed to favor a short session in which the General Assembly appointed a neutral fact-finding commission to study the case.[21]

AZEC was hoping for a great deal more, especially an immediate easing of British immigration restrictions, and was assisted in making this case by an old ally, the American Christian Palestine Committee (ACPC). The organization was born in 1942, through the efforts of Reinhold Niebuhr, professor of applied Christianity at Union Theological Seminary in New York. Its purpose was to end the persecution of Jews in Europe through the creation of a Jewish homeland in Palestine. The organization's effort sought to shape American public opinion in the interests of "simple humanity." By the spring of 1947, ACPC had grown to include more than 3,000 clergymen, mainly Protestant and all sympathetic to the Zionist cause. The organization was not only aggressive in its support of AZEC policy objectives, but received financing through AZEC.[22]

There was close cooperation between Daniel Poling, ACPC co-chairman, and Silver. In a bulletin to Christian committee members, Poling urged his fellow clerics to make their words multiply. The restoration of the Jewish state would signify not only the fulfilling of "civilization's broken vow to the Jewish people," but it would also lead "to the world's moral and spiritual recovery" following the war. Poling was convinced there could be no physical recovery of war-stricken states until their spiritual dilemma was first resolved. Recovery would begin "with the reopening of Palestine to the Jew." The coming months would prove "decisive to our cause" and hopes for a Jewish state.[23]

Poling's work for ACPC supplemented his column for the *New York Post* and his editing of the *Christian Herald*, a newspaper read by church leaders and laymen. These responsibilities left the day to day activities of ACPC in the hands of Howard M. LeSourd. LeSourd had been for ten years the dean of the Graduate School of Boston University when he took a leave in

1944 to direct ACPC propaganda activities. When he returned to the university in the fall of 1947 it was to direct its newly organized School of Public Relations.[24]

LeSourd relied on two arguments in urging ACPC's nationwide network to act. The local press, religious periodicals and radio stations needed to be convinced that developments in Palestine were directly connected to postwar recovery in Europe. Committee members were urged to make the point that the opening of Palestine to Jewish immigration would greatly ease the economic strain on fragile European economies while making a moral statement "of tremendous importance and far-reaching consequence." While LeSourd took the high road, ACPC chairman Carl Hermann Voss took the low. Voss, a leader in the ecumenical Church Peace Union, founded by Andrew Carnegie on New York City's Fifth Avenue, openly charged that anti-Semitism was behind British policymaking in Palestine. Voss deplored British police for "clubbing and gassing Jewish refugees who tried to enter their national home" as a "unilateral breech of international covenants." Voss was certain the Christian world "would not turn its head away" as individuals were sacrificed to imperial interests.[25]

ACPC's appeal was bolstered by growing restlessness in Europe's displaced persons camps. In a mass meeting held on March 14 at detention centers in Frankfurt, which housed more than 100,000 Jews, a direct appeal was made to the governments of the United States, Great Britain, France and the Soviet Union, urging an end to a situation which had plunged Holocaust survivors into "bitterness, hopelessness, and spiritual depression." An appeal sent directly to a foreign ministers meeting in Moscow charged: "Our homes are destroyed. The places where we lived are cemeteries. We cannot revive the dead. The only solution for those who survived is to escape to Palestine."[26]

By the end of March Jewish desperation led to the well-publicized spectacle of Jewish immigration boats captured by British naval patrols before arriving in Palestine. Failure to make progress in resolving the immigrants' final status led to what the *New York Times* characterized as "a revolt" of several thousand displaced persons who had marched on the British consulate in Munich. Their protest was reinforced just before the General Assembly was to take up the Palestine struggle when two members of the Jewish underground cheated the British hangman by "blowing their hearts out" with explosives smuggled to their Jerusalem jail cell.[27]

As the United Nations began three weeks of debate on the Palestine problem, Sumner Welles, former undersecretary of state, along with *New York Herald-Tribune* columnist Walter Lippmann embraced AZEC's argument that the Truman administration would be unable to stabilize the situation in Greece or Turkey without taking a "decisive hand in Palestine." Welles told Benjamin Akzin, his contact within AZEC, that Welles' syndicated column in the

Washington Post would contend that "a just and permanent settlement of the problems of Palestine" were of "primary importance if greater tragedies were not to befall the Jewish people." These friendly columns were supplemented by AZEC's call for America's 2,000 rabbis and five million Jews to pray and fast for "Jewish justice."[28] The effort was a prelude to "Action for Palestine" week, the most ambitious use of the media in American Zionist history.

ACTION FOR PALESTINE

The "Action for Palestine" week had the dual purpose of discrediting the British handling of the problems of Palestine while increasing the pressure on the Truman administration to take the lead in supporting Zionist objectives in the U.N. debate. AZEC's Harry Shapiro, working through the organization's 400 local chapters, urged local radio stations to run public service spots suggesting the U.N. debate over Palestine would decide "the fate of the Jewish people." Every American "with a sense of fair play" was told to "side with justice" and to write President Truman insisting the United States "stand by its pledges to the Jewish people." Support for the concept of a Jewish homeland was portrayed as every American's patriotic duty. Certain radio spots emphasized the continuity of American foreign policy with every president since Woodrow Wilson endorsing the idea of a Jewish homeland. Other spots were a direct appeal to emotion arguing that only a national home for the Jews in Palestine could put an end to the suffering of homeless Jews while "removing a blot from the conscience of the civilized world." By urging the President to "take the initiative," the ads argued, Americans would make good "on a sacred pledge they had made to the Jewish people."[29]

During the week of May 4, radio stations in forty-four American cities ran the spots, as well as newspapers in thirty-one more. In addition, fifty-seven cities held mass meetings of concerned citizens at which similar points were made. The campaign provoked a massive letter writing response. Everyone from community leaders to school children participated. Letters to President Truman were sent by eighteen state governors, and AZEC was told that more were on the way. Silver was convinced the pressure finally persuaded Washington to permit Zionists to participate in the U.N. debate while making it more difficulty for the administration to "hide behind a cloak of neutrality." That opinion was also held by the *New York Times*.[30]

"Action for Palestine" week was planned as a way of bringing the weight of mass sentiment to bear on political decision-makers. But an important part of Silver's campaign was also to fire up Zionist troops and to keep them fired up. This goal was accomplished in large measure by the more than 100 Jewish periodicals that, by the spring of 1947, had aligned themselves with the Jewish state movement. These papers relied on a series of news syndicates that fed the Jewish press daily reports and weekly features. The oldest and most prestigious of these services was the Jewish Telegraph Agency, which published news and special features on Jewish topics in both English and Yiddish. Launched in 1917 out of offices in New York City, its owner, Boris Smolar, was never formally identified with any Zionist group but was sympathetic in his syndicated column to AZEC initiatives under Silver.[31]

In addition to Smolar's operation was the venerable Nathan Ziprin and his Seven Arts Feature Syndicate. Begun in 1922 as a supplement to Smolar's work, by 1947 it commanded a broad audience interested in reading background pieces on the major figures shaping Zionism. A third major source for the Jewish press was provided by J. L. Teller and his Palcor News Service. With a stridently Zionist message, Teller's agency began to target the Jewish community in 1932 from offices in New York City's Union Square. Palcor received wide play in the Jewish English language press during the spring of 1947. Its message was unrelentingly clear. American Jews needed to apply maximum pressure to get their government to act in support of Zionist goals in the crucial debate that was about to open at the United Nations.[32]

Behind the Jewish press lay the country's 4,500 Jewish congregations, 1,500 of which issued weekly or fortnightly synagogue bulletins and some of their own press releases. AZEC worked through its local chapters to enlist the support of congregations and succeeded by early 1947 in creating an anti-British atmosphere within the Jewish community, as reflected in propaganda efforts by some of its largest congregations.[33]

An anti-British bias and a growing dismay over American failure to take the lead at Flushing Meadow filled the pages of the Jewish press in the first days of the debate on the future status of Palestine. Reports in *The Times* of London that the British government felt no responsibility in carrying out any decision of the General Assembly with which it disagreed drew the wrath of the Jewish press. "If the United States says the word firmly enough," the *Jewish Advocate* of Boston charged, "it can tell Mr. Bevin what to do, and he'll do it." Yet the fact remained that "while the United States has the power to command, she hesitates to do so." The silence of the American delegation, the *Kansas City Jewish Chronicle* reported, allowed Britain, "a once great country, now exhausted by war, to imitate Hitler in a policy of depravity that has no parallel in modern English history."[34]

The only way to awaken the Truman administration to its responsibilities, *The American Hebrew* told its readers, was for an aroused American public opinion to insist on it. Local emergency councils under Shapiro were generating letters and wires by the tens of thousands, and chapter representatives were told how to employ different kinds of stationery to disguise the organized nature of the campaign. The blitz was aided by a grouping of liberal organizations whose publicity campaign included Freda

Kirchwey, owner of *The Nation* magazine, former editor Herbert Bayard
Swope, who served as the director of the National Conference of Christians
and Jews and network radio commentator Raymond Gram Swing. The *New
York Times* took note of the unprecedented display of Zionist energy while
noticing it had failed to move the administration to embrace the Zionist
agenda.[35]

     "The American attitude has been deplorably unclear," charged the
English-language *Palestine Post* on the day that Jewish Agency chairman
David Ben-Gurion boarded a plane for America. A week into the U.N. debate
no one knew where the United States or the Soviet Union stood, Palestine's
right-wing Hebrew newspaper *Haboker* protested. Each appeared to be waiting
on the other while watching developments in world public opinion.[36]

     Silver's speech to the General Assembly on May 8 and Ben-Gurion's
address to the same delegates four days later represented the culmination of
weeks of Zionist agitation. Silver's remarks were free of the rhetoric that
sustained much of his printed statements in the days leading up to his
appearance. The headline to emerge from his thirty minute talk was his
insistence that the development of a Jewish national home in Palestine be
considered the "basic and irreducible minimum" for a future settlement in the
region. At the same time, Silver urged the United Nations to investigate the
status of Jews held in detention centers throughout Europe. "See with your
own eyes," he urged, "the appalling human tragedy which mankind is
permitting to continue unabated two years after the end of the war."[37]

     The thrust of Ben-Gurion's remarks of May 12 before the United
Nations downplayed his differences with Silver and AZEC on whether a
Jewish state should occupy all or part of Palestine. Instead, Ben-Gurion
reiterated the themes AZEC advocated in the days leading up to his testimony.
The return of the Jews to their ancestral homeland, Ben-Gurion observed on
front pages across many of America's most prestigious dailies, was a "work
of self-liberation and self-reconstruction" contributing to the development of
Palestine as a whole. There was every reason to see the interests and
aspirations of Jewish and Arab peoples to be "compatible and complementary."
But there was no possibility the Jews were contented with being "a dependent,
subordinate minority" in a land to which they had already given so much. "The
Jewish nation in its own country," Ben-Gurion told the delegates, "must
become a free and independent state with a membership in the United
Nations."[38]

     The special session of the U.N. General Assembly ended three days
after Ben-Gurion's presentation in a spirit that satisfied AZEC strategists. An
eleven member U.N. investigating team was given the responsibility of
reporting back to the General Assembly in September recommendations on the
future status of Palestine. Over bitter Arab protests, the committee of inquiry

would probe the broader problems of Palestine in an investigation not necessarily bound by Palestine. As Thomas J. Hamilton of the *New York Times* noted, that meant the committee would invariably link the status of Europe's refugee population to any future settlement in Palestine.[39] This position had been held by AZEC all along. Though AZEC's efforts failed to persuade the President to take the lead in supporting a Jewish state, another delegation, quite surprisingly, was persuaded. And it was the announcement by that delegation that threw Palestine into the center of the East-West maelstrom.

BACK TO THE COLD WAR

When Andrei Gromyko, the deputy foreign minister of the Soviet Union, announced on May 14, 1947 that his government now supported the partitioning of Palestine into separate Arab and Jewish states, a betrayed Arab delegate told the *Times'* Thomas Hamilton that the Soviets "were following a policy laid down in Nietzsche's 'Beyond Good and Evil.'" Not only the Arabs and the Jews, but the delegates from each of the Great Powers were astonished at the Soviet decision. The announcement seemed abrupt because the committee of inquiry had yet to begin its work, and it seemed self-contradictory since the Soviets had throughout the General Assembly debate seemed to side with the Arabs.[40]

The Jewish Agency for Palestine could not believe the news. "What's the catch?" they asked *New York Times* Middle East correspondent Clifton Daniel, when he sought their reaction. "This is pure Zionism," they told him. The Jerusalem press was overjoyed. "The Soviets have given us their own Balfour Declaration," cheered *Ha'aretz*. "An event of extraordinary importance!" celebrated another. A decision "standing in sharp contrast to the coolness of the Anglo-Saxon states," said a third.[41]

The Soviet declaration sent a shudder through the Anglo-American alliance and left Harry Truman brooding over the mess he had on his hands. On the morning after the Soviet announcement Truman called to the office his special advisor on minority affairs, David K. Niles. The President was angry that the Zionist propaganda campaign had gotten out of hand. "We could have settled this Palestine thing," the President told Niles, "if U.S. politics had been kept out of it." Silver had particularly gotten under the President's skin. "Terror and Silver are the contributing causes of some if not all of our troubles," the President argued. According to Niles, what infuriated Truman most was Silver's suggestion at a U.N. press conference that the United States was prepared to sacrifice homeless refugees for Arab interests.[42]

Part of Truman's irritation also stemmed from the political payoff Silver's speech at the United Nations had made among Republican Presidential hopefuls. Silver and Taft had long been political allies. Now Arthur

Vandenberg and Thomas Dewey were joining the club. Vandenberg wrote Silver, "If we could now have aggressive American leadership, it seems to me that---at long last---there ought to be an answer to our dreams." The Senator then assured Silver that he would "continue to be at your service in any way I can be helpful." That was also Dewey's sentiment. "Unrestricted Jewish immigration and colonization," he announced, was a necessary pre-condition of building a Jewish state in Palestine. The Jewish refugees of Europe, Dewey argued, "should be permitted to go to Palestine in large numbers."[43]

The idea horrified the British, who were still reeling from their miscalculation on the Soviet stand. The Soviets seemed to be throwing away good relations with the Arab states, and the British foreign office could not understand what they were getting out of it. The State Department's Director of Special Political Affairs Dean Rusk could only guess. In a letter to outgoing undersecretary Dean Acheson, Rusk reviewed Moscow's long-standing opposition to partition and suggested that perhaps the Soviets were now playing "both ends against the middle" in hopes of assuring an early British departure from the region.[44]

The Soviet announcement on Palestine came at a time of rapidly deteriorating relations with the West and at precisely the moment in which the U.S. State Department was attempting to lay the groundwork for a new foreign policy initiative. That initiative was embodied in a State Department Policy Planning Staff report of mid-May 1947, which concluded that massive American relief aid, in part fueled by Middle Eastern oil, was urgently needed for the reconstruction of postwar Europe. Policy planners were persuaded that psychological malaise had gripped the continent and was a greater threat to its nations than the possibility of Soviet attack. The policy document urged the United States to provide the means and for Europeans to administer a program designed to lead economic recovery. In the meantime, the report urged the American press be courted so that they might give the best possible play to the department's plan.[45]

James Reston and the editorial board of the *New York Times* got the message. Ten days before Secretary of State George Marshall publicly outlined the program that would become the Marshall Plan for the reconstruction of Europe, the *Times* was advocating a "Continental Plan" for the economic development of all European nations devastated by war and now threatened by Communism. Reston pointed out that such a scheme would allay the fears in Congress that in supporting aid to Greece and Turkey it was setting a dangerous precedent America's limited resources could not hope to fulfill. Reston reported that official Washington was coming to recognize "that the old policy of shoring up the shattered economies of individual European nations and feeding their hungry is insufficient to bring about real recovery."[46]

The *Times* editorial quickly endorsed the signing of the Greek and

Turkish aid bills by the President, seeing the policy as an effort designed to prevent further Communist conquest of the free world. This attitude by the *Times* brought a quick rebuke from J. M. Lomakin, a Soviet representative at the United Nations. He charged the *Times* was a leader of the "war-mongering press," which had "promoted distrust and provoked trouble" between wartime allies. Holding up a *Times* editorial at a meeting with reporters, Lomakin charged that "if a man from Mars visited earth and read certain American newspapers, he would think enemies, not allies, were conferring" on the future of the war-torn world.[47]

The collapse of the Moscow summit to decide the future status of Germany accelerated media criticism of the Soviet Union and was followed by a rare nationwide radio address in which Marshall warned that if the Soviets were not prepared to cooperate with the West in bringing peace to Europe, Western nations would proceed without them. Marshall's grim warning was echoed in the news and editorial pages of the *Times*. The paper reported that after a brief period where peace seemed possible, even imminent, "the Soviet Government has again rung down the Iron Curtain" and shown itself to be "a danger to the rest of the world." The Soviet attitude, the *Times* was certain, "lent new urgency" to considerations then underway at the highest levels of the Truman administration on what to do about it.[48]

On June 5, 1947, at a commencement address at Harvard University, Marshall suggested the mass of facts presented by the press and daily on the radio should not confuse "the man on the street" to the current crisis his nation faced. What he needed to understand was that there could be "no assured peace" without "economic health in the world." Marshall pledged the full cooperation of the U. S. government to facilitate economic recovery of Europe in a program the Europeans themselves would administer. The purpose of such a plan, he charged, would not be directed against any country or doctrine, but against "hunger, poverty, desperation and chaos."[49]

The nation's press and radio commentators saw the Marshall Plan as a deliberate attempt by the Truman administration to blunt Soviet gains in Europe and along the shores of the Mediterranean. "Russia and her satellites could participate in the program," the *Times* reported, but it was the Soviets' failure to cooperate in postwar recovery that had necessitated the program in the first place. According to NBC commentator Clifton Utley, the Marshall Plan would inevitably provoke "the greatest debate and decision this country has been called upon to undertake since the Civil War." Utley reasoned that while entrance into the two world wars had been thrust upon the United States, the decision over the Marshall Plan would be one that was freely taken. At stake was the salvation of Europe and the "free institutions upon which America stood." The alternative was a "completely totalitarian Europe, run from Moscow." America, Utley argued, had fought two wars to prevent one country from dominating Europe, and if necessary, would fight another.[50]

PALESTINE AND THE COLD WAR

The collapse of the Moscow summit followed by the public articulation of the Marshall Plan came at a bad time for Zionists. Instead of capitalizing on the momentum of the U.N.'s decision to investigate broadly the problems of Palestine and of the Soviet endorsement of partition, Zionists found themselves unable to move the Truman administration to action. On the day the Marshall Plan was announced, the President issued a public statement urging all Americans not to prejudice the outcome of the U.N. inquiry by promoting violence in Palestine. The presidential action followed a demand by the British government that it rein in the activities of American Zionists who urged attacks against British authority in Palestine. The flap was stirred when American writer Ben Hecht, representing the American League for a Free Palestine, told Evelyn Webster, a reporter on the *London Evening Standard*, that he had urged members of the Jewish underground "to kill British troops." Though later denied by Hecht, the charge was repeated in the *New York Times* two days later.[51]

The controversy over Hecht's statements reflect the divisions in the Zionist movement as the U.N. committee planned to launch its inquiry. Hecht's organization had run full page advertisements in New York newspapers that purported to speak for the American Jewish community. One series of ads likened British conduct to that of the Nazis. The Jewish resistance was told that "every time you blow up a British arsenal, or wreck a British jail, or send a British railroad train sky high, or rob a British bank, or let go with your guns and bombs at the British betrayers and invaders of your homeland, the Jews of America make a little holiday in their hearts." The American Jewish Committee, which opposed partition but favored a U.N. trusteeship over Palestine, told the press Hecht's group did not speak for American Jews and added that "terrorism is hostile to the spirit of the Jewish religion and Jewish tradition." Jewish Agency spokesman Nahum Goldmann found the media campaign of Hecht and his allies "disgusting, because it confused the American public, which does not realize the group does not represent American Jewry."[52]

It was not simply Hecht's activities, however, that added to the public impression Zionism did not speak in a single voice. Divisions between Silver and Weizmann on a Jewish state and between Silver and Ben-Gurion on partition appeared in a May 15 article by Homer Bigart in the *New York Herald-Tribune*. Hasty efforts by AZEC to publicly paper over those differences only made matters worse. A Jewish Agency representative on the AZEC executive charged the denial "irresponsibly" implied AZEC's opposition to partition was the official Zionist position. This claim only "served to confuse" American public opinion since Ben-Gurion had already gone on record endorsing partition. AZEC media consultant Harold Manson snapped back that it was Ben-Gurion's unauthorized statements about partition that had "confused" AZEC's own members. He wondered how it would be possible for Zionists to rally public opinion behind their cause when they could not agree among themselves what that cause was.[53]

AZEC's euphoria following Silver's appearance before the United Nations proved to be short-lived. Zionism's historic divisions and personality clashes, which long crippled the movement, had resurfaced in print. Added to this controversy was the diplomatic and media fallout following Soviet endorsement of a Jewish state. Silver knew that as long as Zionist media messages remained double-minded, those messages would be unable to overcome Cold War jitters and rally American opinion to AZEC's cause. Clifton Daniel's report from Jerusalem that Chaim Weizmann "may well resume the role of world Zionism's chief spokesman" when the committee of inquiry arrived in Palestine, only deepened Silver's dismay. When published reports in June indicated Weizmann would be meeting with U. N. investigators when they arrived in Jerusalem, the AZEC executive considered ways of preventing that meeting. Silver conceded his organization's problem was one of information. The Jewish Agency had been silent on any meeting. All Silver knew was "what appears in the press."[54]

AZEC's decision to separate itself from the world Zionist hierarchy and to launch a propaganda campaign under its own authority in advance of the U.N. debate on Palestine now isolated it. Gene Currivan, writing from Jerusalem for the *Times*, thought he detected "a new line" among Zionists. They had abandoned, Currivan thought, "an all or nothing attitude and indicated a willingness to compromise." Currivan came to this conclusion following the release of a statement by Jewish Agency chairman David Ben-Gurion indicating "there was little chance for a Jewish state in all of Palestine at this time" and suggesting that the "Zionist plan might be to accept a form of partition." AZEC considered issuing a statement to the press denouncing the stand taken by Ben-Gurion, but Silver worried such a move would only deepen the public impression that Zionism was a house divided against itself. Once the committee of inquiry arrived in Palestine, it would be impossible for American Zionists to control either developments there or how the press was likely to report them.[55]

While the nation's press prepared for what it billed as the "debate of the century" on the Marshall Plan and America's position in the postwar world, the United Nations quietly went about its work in Palestine. Silver and the AZEC executive became concerned that in the sixty days it would take the committee to complete its probe and issue its report, their cause would be lost.

So they desperately sought an issue that would put Palestine back on the front pages of the nation's press in a context furthering their cause. With the *Exodus* incident, Zionists both contrived and were given such an issue. Favorable publicity growing out of the controversy was as much a product of Zionist ingenuity and the timing of their efforts, as the heavy-handedness of the British particularly Foreign Secretary Ernest Bevin, in the handling of the affair. And when it was over, Zionist leaders, despite their many differences, succeeded in transforming the chronic problem of Europe's displaced persons into an international debate on the efficacy of a Jewish state in Palestine. Most importantly, it was a debate that progressed and was covered by the world's media on their terms.

NOTES

1. Marc Lee Raphael, *Abba Hillel Silver: A Profile in American Judaism* (New York: Holmer and Meier, 1989), introduction and pp. 181 and 214. See also, Abba Hillel Silver, *The World Crisis and Jewish Survival: A Group of Essays* (New York: Richard R. Smith Publishers, 1941), preface and p. 49. Abba Hillel Silver, *The Democratic Impulse in Jewish History* (New York: Block Publishing, 1928), pp. 38-43. Alon Gal, "The Mission Motif in American Zionism," *American Jewish History* 75, 1986, pp. 363-385. For background, see Harold Manson File. File 1-4-1. American Zionist Emergency Council Files. The Temple. Cleveland, Ohio.

2. Remarks by Abba Hillel Silver at the Zionist London Conference of August 3 through August 7, 1945. Silver spoke on August 3. His comments can be found in the conference protocol. Folder S/25. Central Zionist Archives. Jerusalem, Israel.

3. Louis Lipsky, *Thirty Years of American Zionism* (New York: Nesher Publishing, 1927), pp. 62 and 71-72. Edward Victor, ed., *Meyer Weisgal at Seventy: An Anthology* (London: Weidenfeld and Nicolson, 1966), pp. 11-16. Bernard A. Rosenblatt, *Two Generations of Zionism: Historical Recollections of an American Zionist* (New York: Shengold Publishers, 1967), pp. 89-93. Melvin I. Urofsky, *American Zionism from Herzl to the Holocaust* (Garden City: Doubleday, 1975), pp. 243-293.

4. Urofsky, pp. 305-311. Lipsky, pp. 29-30, 100 and 231-248. Raphael, p. 69.

5. Raphael, p. 84.

6. Marshall Blatt, "The Attempt of the American Jewish Committee to Unite the Political Force of American Jewry and to Influence U.S. Foreign Policy on the Palestine Question, 1942-1948," p. 16. Box 1039. American Jewish Archives. Cincinnati, Ohio. Also, *The American Israelite* (Cincinnati), April 19, 1945, p. 1. For background on President Truman's growing concern over the refugee problem, see Harry S. Truman, *Memoirs: Years of Trial and Hope* (Garden City: Doubleday, 1956), chapter 10. Clark M. Clifford, "Factors Influencing President Truman's Decision to

Support Partition and Recognize Israel," a speech to the American Historical Association on December 28, 1976 in Washington, pp. 2-3. Department of State, *Bulletin* 13, September 30, 1945. Jacob C. Hurewitz, *Diplomacy in the Near and Middle East, A Documentary Record: 1914-1956* (Princeton: D. Van Nostrand, 1956), pp. 249-257. Despite repeated assurances concerning the importance of resolving the refugee problem, the *New York Times* of January 24, 1947 pointed out that the United States had processed only 7,000 European refugees in 1946.

7. Note from Loy Henderson to Joseph Grew, undersecretary of state, dated July 22, 1945. U.S. State Department File 867.01/6-2245. National Archives. Washington, D.C. Also, Eliahu Elath, *The Struggle for Statehood: Washington, 1945-1948* (Tel Aviv: Am Oved, 1982), pp. 80-81. Carl J. Friedrich, *American Policy Toward Palestine* (Washington: American Council on Public Affairs, 1944), pp. 101-103. Reuben Fink, ed., *America and Palestine* (New York: Arno Press, 1977), pp. 32, 78-84 and 153. Letter from David Ben-Gurion to Abba Hillel Silver, dated October 9, 1946. Weizmann Archives. Rehovoth, Israel.

8. Letters from Chaim Weizmann to Stephen Wise, dated January 6, 1947; Weizmann to Felix Frankfurter, January 7, 1947; Weizmann to Meyer Weisgal, March 20, 1947; and Weizmann to Eliezar Kaplan, March 27, 1947. Each letter appears in Barnet Litvinoff, ed., *The Letters and Papers of Chaim Weizmann*, Volume 22 (Jerusalem: Israel Universities Press, 1979), pp. 213, 283-286 and 291-292.

9. Letters from Chaim Weizmann to Marc Jarblum, dated January 13, 1947; Weizmann to Harold Laski, January 13, 1947; Weizmann to Henry Morgenthau, Jr., January 13, 1947; and Weizmann to Richard H. S. Crossman, March 12, 1947, in Litvinoff, pp. 218, 219, 221-222 and 264-266.

10. Letter from Chaim Weizmann to Meyer Weisgal, dated March 20, 1947, in Litvinoff, pp. 283-286.

11. Letter from Chaim Weizmann to the Editor of *The Times* (London), dated April 19, 1947, in Litvinoff, pp. 312-314. Also, Minutes: American Zionist Emergency Council. May 19, 1947 meeting. File 4-2. American Zionist Emergency Council Files. The Temple. Cleveland, Ohio.

12. Letter from Chaim Weizmann to Jacob Landau, dated October 19, 1947, in Barnet Litvinoff, ed., *The Letters and Papers of Chaim Weizmann*, Volume 23 (Jerusalem: Israel Universities, 1980), p. 15. Also, letter from Chaim Weizmann to Joseph Keftman, dated March 14, 1947, and letter from Weizmann to Eliezar Kaplan, March 27, 1947, in Litvinoff, ed., pp. 273-274 and 291-294.

13. *American Jewish Yearbook, 1947-1948* (Philadelphia: American Jewish Committee, 1948), pp. 713-721. *The New Palestine News Reporter Issue*, January 24, 1947, p. 8 and April 25, 1947, p. 5. Martin Mart, *The Religious Press in America* (New York: Holt, Rinehart and Winston, 1963), pp. 142-145.

14. *New York Times*, April 28, 1947, pp. 1 and 2. Also, H. V. Kaltenborn Radio Scripts. April 28, 1947. H. V. Kaltenborn Papers. Box 182. Folder 3. Clifton Utley Radio Scripts. April 27, 1947. Clifton Utley Papers. Box 48. Folder 2. Cecil Brown Radio Scripts. April 14, April 22 and April 25, 1947. Cecil Brown Papers. Box 12. Folders 1 and 2. All scripts are in the State Historical Society of Wisconsin. Madison, Wisconsin.

15. Letter from Robert McClintock, Office of Special Political Affairs, to

Dorothy Fosdick, U.S. delegate to the United Nations, March 28, 1947. Letter titled, "Confidential: British Press Tactics on Palestine." Robert McClintock Refernce File. M1175. Roll 8. National Archives. Washington, D.C.

16. George H. Gallup, *The Gallup Poll*, Volume 1 (New York: Random House, 1972), pp. 530, 535 and 639. Charles H. Stember, *Jews in the Mind of America* (New York: Basic Books, 1966), pp. 174 and 177.

17. Official File. 204 Misc. Papers of Harry S. Truman. Box 773. Folder 5. Harry S. Truman Library. Independence, Missouri.

18. Correspondence. Minutes: American Zionist Emergency Council. April 20, 1947. File 4-2. AZEC Files.

19. Letter from Abba Hillel Silver to David Ben-Gurion, dated October 9, 1946, in Michael J. Cohen, ed., *The Rise of Israel: The Holocaust and Illegal Immigration, 1939-1947*, Volume 31 (New York: Garland Publishing, 1987), pp. 265-271.

20. This break between Silver and Ben-Gurion became particularly clear during and after the United Nations debate. See *New York Times*, May 10, 1947, p. 4; May 13, 1947, p. 12; May 24, 1947, p. 5; and May 27, 1947, p. 11. Also, Correspondence. Minutes: AZEC. April 20, 1947. File 4-2. AZEC Files.

21. Press release from AZEC. April 20, 1947. File 1-4-6. AZEC Files. Also, *New York Times*, April 15, 1947, p. 16.

22. News releases from the American Christian Palestine Committee bear a striking resemblance to AZEC press releases in form and content. See Hertzel Fishman, *American Protestants and a Jewish State* (Detroit: Wayne State University, 1973), pp. 73-74. The historical relationship between Zionism and its Christian supporters within the United States is described in Robert T. Handy, "Zionism in American Christian Movements," in Moshe Davis, ed., *Israel: Its Role in Civilization* (New York: Harper, 1956), pp. 280-285. Also, Shirley J. Case, *The Millennial Hope* (Chicago: University of Chicago, 1918), chapters. 4 and 5. Wilmer T. Clark, *The Small Sects in America* (New York: Abingdon-Cokesbury, 1949), chapter 4. Alan Heimert, *Religion and the American Mind* (Cambridge: Harvard University, 1968), pp. 368-373.

For background, see also David A. Rausch, *Zionism Within Early American Fundamentalism, 1878-1918* (New York: Edwin Mellen Press, 1979), chapters 3, 5 and 8. Michael J. Pragai, *Faith and Fulfillment: Christians and the Return to the Promised Land* (London: Vallentine, Mitchell, 1985), pp. 25-40. Yonathan Shapiro, *Leadership of the American Zionist Organization, 1897-1930* (Urbana: University of Illinois, 1971), chapters 7 and 8.

23. American Christian Palestine Committee Bulletin, "Our Works Must Multiply." January 1947. Manson File. 4-1-2. AZEC Files.

24. Harold Manson File. 4-1-2. AZEC Files.

25. ACPC Memorandum from LeSourd to ACPC Liasons and Co-Workers. January 13, 1947. Manson File 4-1-2. Also, copy of "From One Parson to Another: An American Clergyman Writes to a British Clergyman," written by Carl Hermann Voss, and appearing in *The Churchman* on February 1, 1947. Manson File. 1-4-42. AZEC Files.

26. *New York Times*, March 25, 1947, p. 5.

27. *New York Times*, March 31, 1947, p. 1; April 18, 1947, p. 15 and April 22, 1947, p. 1. *New York Herald-Tribune*. April 1, 1947, p. 1 and April 5, 1947, p. 1. *Boston Globe*, April 8, 1947, p. 6.

28. ACPC Bulletin to members. March 1947. File 4-1-2. AZEC Files. The Lippmann critique of American policy is the centerpiece of the ACPC logic. Also, letter from Sumner Welles to Benjamin Akzin, copied to Abba Hillel Silver. April 25, 1947. File 1-4-42. AZEC Files. *New York Times*, April 25, 1947.

29. Memo from Shapiro to chairmen of local emergency committees. April 22, 1947. File 1-4-17. AZEC Files. For background, see Stember, pp. 8-13, 50-55, 60-61, 77-92 and 101-128. Stember offers poll data results showing Americans were slow to identify with the Zionist cause. In a 1944 poll, Jews were found to be the least desirable of all immigrant groups with the exception of citizens from Germany and Japan. When asked directly if Jews had "too much power and influence in the United States," two-thirds of all respondents said yes. One possible interpretation of Stember's findings is that Americans, in part, supported Jewish settlements in Palestine as an alternative to settlement in the United States. In 1948, 60 percent of all respondents agreed a specific limitation should be placed on the number of Jewish refugees to be admitted to the United States---a percentage only slightly greater than the number who wished a limit applied to German immigrants.

30. Correspondence. Minutes: AZEC. May 19, 1947. File 4-2. AZEC Files. *New York Times*, May 11, 1947, Section E, pp. 1 and 5.

31. *American Jewish Yearbook, 1947-1948*, pp. 720-721. Also, memo from Harry Shapiro to chairmen of local emergency committees, dated April 22, 1947. File 1-4-17. AZEC Files.

32. *American Jewish Yearbook, 1947-1948*, pp. 713-716. Palcor's clients included leading Jewish weeklies in Kansas City, Detroit, St. Louis, Los Angeles, Cleveland, Cincinnati, Philadelphia, Boston, New York and Chicago.

33. A majority of the nation's synagogues printed weekly, bi-monthly or monthly bulletins as well as press releases, which frequently contained AZEC propaganda in behalf of Jewish statehood. A good example is the January 12, 1947 press release issued by Congregation B'nai Jeshuvim of New York City. It attacked British efforts to "create dissension along racial and religious lines" in the United States and challenged British allegations that Jewish Americans were guilty of dual loyalties.

34. *The Times* (of London), April 28, 1947, p. 11. *The Jewish Advocate* (Boston). "Let the U.S. Speak Out!" May 1, 1947, p. 2. *Kansas City Jewish Chronicle*. "The Palestine Executions." April 25, 1947, p. 2.

35. *The American Hebrew* (New York). May 2, 1947, p. 4. *New York Times*, May 5, 1947, p. 2.

36. *Palestine Post*, May 4, 1947, p. 1. *Haboker*, May 4, 1947, pp. 1 and 2.

37. *New York Times*, May 9, 1947, p. 1. See also, *Vision and Victory: A Collection of Essays by Dr. Abba Hillel Silver, 1942-1948* (New York: The Zionist Organization of America, 1949), pp. 124-133.

38. *New York Times*, May 13, 1947, pp. 2 and 3. *New York Herald-Tribune*, May 13, 1947, pp. 1 and 2. *Philadelphia Inquirer*, May 13, 1947, p. 2. *Baltimore Sun*, May 13, 1947, p. 1.

39. *New York Times*, May 13, 1947, p. 1 and May 14, 1947, p. 1.

40. *New York Times*, May 15, 1947, p. 1.

41. *New York Times*, May 16, 1947, p. 3. *Ha'aretz*, May 15, 1947, p. 1.
Palestine Post, May 15, 1947, p. 1.

42. See David Niles' notes of conversation, dated May 13, 1947. PSF Subject
File. Folder: Foreign-Palestine. Box 184. Papers of Harry S. Truman. Truman
Library. Niles quotes Truman as saying, "I sure wish God almighty would give the
children of Israel an Isaiah, the Christians a St. Paul, and the sons of Ishmael a peep
at the Golden Rule. Maybe he will decide to do that." Also, Elath, p. 81.

43. Letter from Vandenberg to Silver, dated May 19, 1947. File 4-4-42.
Letter from Dewey to Silver. May 15, 1947. File 4-4-26. AZEC Files. Also, *New York
Times*, May 20, 1947, p. 6.

44. Foreign Office. 371/61875. E3245 and E4898. May 15, 1947. The Public
Record Office. Kew Gardens, England. Also, note from Rusk to Acheson. May 27,
1947. *Foreign Relations of the United States 1947*, Volume 3 (Washington:
Government Printing Office, 1975). pp. 1088-1089.

45. *FRUS 1947*, 3, pp. 224-230.

46. *New York Times*, May 26, 1947, p. 22.

47. *New York Times*, May 24, 1947, Section E, p. 3 and May 27, 1947, p.
10.

48. *New York Times*, April 28, 1947, pp. 1 and 4; April 29, 1947, p. 1; May
3, 1947, p. 16; and June 3, 1947, p. 24.

49. Department of State, *Bulletin* 16, June 5, 1947.

50. *New York Times*, June 8, 1947, Section E, p. 12. And, Clifton Utley
Radio Scripts. June 15, 1947. Clifton Utley Papers. Box 48. Folder 4.

51. *New York Times*, May 28, 1947, p. 12 and June 6, 1947, pp. 1 and 5.
London Evening Standard, May 27, 1947, pp. 1 and 8.

52. Ben Hecht, *A Child of the Century* (New York: Simon and Schuster,
1954), p. 615. Also, Memo from British Foreign Office. May 20, 1947. Foreign
Office. 371/61754. The Public Record Office. *New York Times*, June 5, 1947, p. 17.

53. Correspondence. Minutes: AZEC. May 19, 1947. File 4-2. AZEC Files.
Also, *New York Herald-Tribune*, May 15, 1947, p. 1.

54. *New York Times*, May 10, 1947, p. 4. Also, Correspondence. Minutes:
AZEC. June 4, 1947. File 4-2. AZEC Files.

55. *New York Times*, May 24, 1947, p. 5. Also, Correspondence. Minutes:
AZEC. June 4, 1947. File 4-2. AZEC Files.

Three

Reporting the Second Exodus: Zionist Propaganda, British Bungling and a High Seas Melodrama, July 1947– September 1947

To a journalism historian, the most interesting aspect of the *Exodus 1947* incident, a case involving the capture of a boatload of 4,500 Jewish refugees bound for Palestine and their reshipment to Germany, is that Zionists from the outset subordinated the goal of actually landing those refugees in Palestine to the public relations benefits of attempting to do so. The episode was contrived by the Jewish underground to cast international media attention on the refusal of British authorities to admit more than a handful of the half million displaced Jews of Europe to Palestine. Zionist leaders on both sides of the Atlantic were convinced that publicizing the wretched plight of Holocaust survivors struggling to return to the "Promised Land" was the strongest case they could make for Jewish statehood. The bold plan to sail the *Exodus* was conceived months before a U.N. Committee of Inquiry was given international authority to travel to Palestine and make a final recommendation on the future status of the region. As historical coincidence and British bungling would have it, the story of the ship's bloody confrontation with the His Majesty's Navy became a made to order media event that greatly aided the Zionist cause.

As U.N. committee members left New York for Palestine, Zionists appeared poised to fumble a promising moment. Divisions between Silver-led zealots and Weizmann stalwarts, compounded by Silver's break with Ben-Gurion over partition, created a mixed message in the American media and led to Silver's admission that neither Zionists nor their opponents understood where the Zionist movement stood on the size or necessity of a Jewish state. That the *Exodus* incident retrieved the situation for Zionists owed much to their early recognition that the simple story of a ship trying to run a British blockade could be transformed into a morality tale of good and evil, of homeless women and children and their stubborn resistance to British brutalization.[1]

The British were an unwilling, and for the most part, unwitting accomplice in undermining their own Palestine policy in the *Exodus* affair. British Foreign Secretary Ernest Bevin was determined to prevent illegal Jewish immigration to Palestine and to teach the *Exodus* passengers a lesson that would deter others in the future. He rejected the persistent recommendation of middle level advisors who accurately predicted how the international news media would play the story. They repeatedly urged Bevin to avoid actions which could be interpreted as instances of British imperialism and callous insensitivity. But Bevin did not grasp the power of the press to transform the events it covered nor the Zionist success in creating images that seemed to affront the collective dignity of readers and listeners. Among those most affronted by the spectacle of the battered *Exodus* and its beleaguered passengers, were members of the U.N. committee sent to Palestine to recommend its future status. It was these men, with backgrounds opposing colonialism and Great Power geopolitics, whose votes gave international legitimacy to a separate Jewish state in Palestine. It was a legitimacy Zionists would exploit all the way to their declaration of Israeli independence in May, 1948.

THE DISPLACED OF EUROPE

To understand the impact of the *Exodus* incident on U.N. committee members as well as the public imagination and why it was treated in the world press the way that it was one must consider conditions in Europe in the summer of 1947. Two years after World War II ended still found a continent struggling from the catastrophic consequences of that war. Seventeen and a half billion dollars of American aid failed to revitalize the continent's productive capacity nor to relieve the "growing crisis" of many of its major cities. It was not simply that European democracies lacked the physical means to restore some semblance of the prewar world, but that, beaten down by years of war, they lacked the will to do so. Army Chief of Staff Gen. Dwight D. Eisenhower, just back from a tour of Europe, found it gripped by "chaos, disorder and hysterical fear." He urged that an organized effort rebuild the continent and rehabilitate its peoples "if a way of life to which we are devoted was to survive."[2]

As the *New York Times* saw it, the Marshall Plan was a recognition that the war's physical destruction of Europe included the "dislocation of the entire fabric of the European economy." Confidence in local currencies was severely shaken; raw materials and fuel were in short supply; machinery was lacking or worn out. The continent's division of labor was "threatened with breakdown." Recovery would require concentrated, international cooperation, and guidance by a commitment to end human misery and the conditions perpetuating that hardship.[3]

Central to this suffering was the plight of 850,000 displaced persons who remained in detention camps throughout Europe. John H. Hilldring, assistant secretary of state, told a Congressional committee that three-fourths of Europe's non-repatriables were stationed in more than 300 camps staffed by U.S. personnel. The majority, he testified, could not be re-settled for religious or racial reasons. Nearly one-half of them were Jews.[4]

America's conservative and liberal press agreed the displaced persons of Europe represented a major postwar problem but disagreed on whose responsibility they were. The *Chicago Tribune*, a leader in what President Truman called "the sabotage press," charged the decision by Presidents Roosevelt and Truman to "give away half of Europe" inevitably produced "mass migration of hundreds of thousands left homeless and rootless." The *Tribune* and *U.S. News and World Report* thought the international community was responsible "for making sure these refugees do not remain on U.S. relief roles indefinitely." The *New York Times* and *The Nation* argued "the world's wealthiest nation" should lead the effort to resettle refugees by opening its borders to them.[5]

On June 4, 1947, Congressional hearings began on a bill introduced by Rep. William G. Stratton, an Illinois Republican, to permit 100,000 displaced persons to enter the United States for four consecutive years. The measure received the enthusiastic support of the Truman administration and several major East Coast dailies, but by mid-July, with Congress set to adjourn, the measure remained in committee. Opposition was led by veterans organizations charging that the refugees would complicate America's own employment and housing problems. They were joined by Representatives John M. Robison of Kentucky and Ed Gossett of Texas, who claimed that Jewish displaced persons were sent into American camps by Russia "for eventual fifth-column work in the United States." These warnings played well to postwar fears of Communist encirclement and forced an international relief agency to admit there seemed "no deepened sense of urgency or concern" in resolving the displaced persons problem.[6]

While the Stratton bill languished in committee, the four year life of the U.N. agency aiding the rehabilitation of Europe came to an end. It had spent $3 billion to assist seventeen countries in recovering from the war, three-quarters of that money contributed by the United States. Editors on the *New York Times* thought the passing of the U.N. Relief and Rehabilitation Agency made it all the more urgent that the Stratton Bill be passed. President Truman charged that passage of the measure was the least the United States could do to end "a human problem, a world tragedy." *Time* painted a sympathetic picture of one Jewish refugee, who survived the Warsaw ghetto, sustained only by "the will to live." Secretary of State George C. Marshall told House

Judiciary Committee members that rescuing pitiable refugees "is what the Statue of Liberty is all about." But by July 14, Senate Foreign Relations Committee Chairman Arthur Vandenberg reported Congress would adjourn before acting on the bill. A *Times*' editorial retorted, "Congress is in a hurry to get home. The refugees, who have spent two or more years in camps, without homes, are probably in a hurry to get somewhere, too."[7]

With the U.S. Congress deadlocked, many of Europe's displaced persons led by Jewish non-repatriables, were taking matters into their own hands. In March, 1947, Jews held a mass meeting within a detention center near Frankfurt, demanding that "the gates of Palestine be opened immediately so that Jews can begin a normal, productive life." One month later, 2,000 people angrily marched on the British consulate in Munich, shouting death to British authorities and demanding that British Foreign Secretary Ernest Bevin immediately lift immigration restrictions to Palestine. Jewish refugees also took to the high seas hoping to get to Palestine. The former American coastal steamer, *Hatikva*, carrying 1,200 unauthorized Jewish immigrants, was captured by British destroyers after a mid-sea collision. The conflict was given front page attention in the United States, along with the British decision to transport the passengers to detention facilities in Cyprus. Mid-June British appeals to the French, Italian and Greek governments temporarily dried up the supply of ships the Zionist underground planned to use on similar missions.[8]

Critics of the British action saw it only as a stop-gap measure. General Joseph T. McNarney, former commander of the American Occupation Forces in Europe, warned that life within the refugee camps of Germany was unbearable and that Jews were desperate to get out. He noted that the lapsing of U.N. assistance to European refugees would cut their daily ration from 2,200 to 2,000 calories, barely a subsistence level. The United Jewish Appeal, headed by former Treasury Secretary Henry Morgenthau, took out full page advertisements in the nation's press and urged private citizens to contribute up to $170 million for the one and a half million European Jews the organization hoped to reach. "Fear has gripped the Jewish community of Europe," the ads stated. "In this hour of crisis, it is now a matter of life and death." Published reports confirmed the urgency. Surveys found "four of ten Germans actively anti-Semitic and the other six passively so." Knowing anti-Semitism was "mounting steadily" made displaced persons "panic stricken" and created a climate of "explosive discontent."[9]

In early June, British intelligence began to suspect that the Jewish underground was in the process of organizing another illegal boatload of refugees bound for Palestine. There had been a similar suspicion at the time of the *Hatikva* in May. Published reports then suggested a second Jewish ship, with as many as 4,000 people aboard, was at sea, in the most ambitious effort yet to defeat the British blockade. The report was both erroneous and prophetic. As members of the U.N. Special Committee on Palestine arrived in Jerusalem in mid-June to conduct hearings on the future of the region, a 5,000 ton, American-built, former ferry boat, was being outfitted for a perilous journey through the Eastern Mediterranean that neither committee members nor the world media could easily ignore.[10]

THE PRESIDENT WARFIELD

Before the fateful voyage of the *Exodus*, news coverage of developments in Palestine had been going very badly for the Zionists. Testimony taking by the U.N. committee was submerged by reports of disunity and violence within Zionist circles. The Jewish Agency's efforts to preserve peace within Zionist ranks was shattered when the British sentenced three members of the Jewish underground to death and then refused to reverse that decision despite pleas from the committee of inquiry. Three days later an effort by the Jewish underground group, the Irgun, to kidnap a British officer failed. Attacks on British soldiers and police escalated during late June and early July, bringing a condemnation that made front page news from the committee of inquiry. Press attention to Jewish violence peaked on July 13, when the *New York Times*, the *New York Herald-Tribune*, and other major dailies ran double column front page stories reporting the kidnapping of two British army intelligence officers in the coastal town of Netanya. In a written communique, given to the press, Irgun chief Menachem Begin warned that the British soldiers would be executed if military authorities went ahead with their threat to hang three Irgun fighters. As British troops fanned out over seven villages, conducting a house to house search for their comrades, the drama was played out on the front pages of America's press, with reports on the committee of inquiry's work almost disappearing from view. The British refused to give in to what they saw as terrorist threats and demanded the immediate return of their men.[11]

A greater threat, however, to British control of events was off the southern coast of France. The British had been keeping a wary eye on a ship, the *President Warfield*, for quite some time. As early as May 1, 1947 the British cabinet had discussed the possibility of boarding the ship, then taking on stores at Genoa once the ship left port. But the interception was postponed because of the "embarrassing precedent" it might set for a nation publicly pledged to "the inviolability of the high seas." The Admiralty warned Whitehall to avoid the "special difficulty" that would follow the inevitable sabotaging of the ship's engines on interception and the "spectacle" of the ship being towed into harbor.[12]

Built in 1927 at a cost of $850,000 as the flagship of the Old Bay Line, the *President Warfield* plied the waters of Chesapeake Bay from

Baltimore to Norfolk at a cruising speed of 17 statute miles per hour. In the spring of 1942 she found herself moored at a pier in Baltimore harbor, "boarded up and freakish looking." Pressed into transport duty along the Seine during World War II, the steamship returned to a slip in Baltimore harbor in the summer of 1946, a "bedraggled, graying hulk" destined for the scrapheap. The rusty tub was, in the words of one *Exodus* crewman, "infested with rot and rats and thousands of leaks."[13]

The ship's reprieve came later that year when the Sonneborn Institute, an American-based Zionist group, purchased the ship and began outfitting the vessel for its mission in the Eastern Mediterranean. The institute, which enlisted Hank Greenberg, a New York born Nevada newspaper publisher, to smuggle guns to the Jewish underground army of Palestine, now found a "righteous Gentile" to play a unique role in publicizing the mission of the *President Warfield* to the displaced Jews of Europe. John Grauel was a lanky, 30-year-old Methodist minister from Worcester, Massachusetts. His shoulder length blonde hair, blue eyes and the gold cross that he wore on a chain around his neck created quite an impression on his fellow smugglers. He joined the American Christian Palestine Committee (ACPC) because of his concern for the future of the Jewish people, and he volunteered to join the crew of the *President Warfield* because he was "greatly disturbed" by the plight of the displaced Jews of Europe and "convinced that the death of Israel would be the death knell of Western civilization." In January of 1947 he made his way to the Haganah recruiting office in New York and later that month joined the ship's crew of forty-three, as cook and able-bodied seaman and as its only Gentile.[14]

Grauel's mission was also to serve as the ship's public relations officer and chief publicist. He had received credentials as foreign correspondent from *The Churchman*, the venerable publication of the Protestant Episcopal Press, which served as a sounding board for Carl Hermann Voss and other Zionists within the ACPC. Its editor, Guy Emory Shipler, was an ACPC executive board member. Grauel would later give a personal account to UNSCOP members and the world press of how "the British had dogged our steps" ever since the *President Warfield* put in at the Azores in early summer for refueling. British insistence forced Italian authorities to hold the ship for seven weeks until a bribe allowed port authorities to claim the darkened ship had escaped an Italian gunboat in the dead of night.[15]

On July 9 the *President Warfield* eased its way out of Port de Bouc and entered the harbor of Sete, sixty-five miles to the west. The ship's bulkheads were ripped out and replaced by bunkbeds, four and five high, with eighteen inches of space per person, the identical measurement so efficiently used in Hitler's death camps. Grauel remembers "gulping scalding coffee" just before dawn on that day when he heard the low rumble of the first of seventy-two trucks bringing 4,500 men, women and children out of their internment camps in Poland and Germany and down the cobblestone streets of the Mole St. Louis where the *President Warfield* waited. Grauel helped the first refugee aboard. She was a blonde-haired, brown-eyed, girl of fourteen "who looked like any other girl her age in America." As she lifted her pack from her shoulders, Grauel felt "a shiver pass over me" as he saw "a purple number branded into her flesh by the Nazis," an image that would repeat itself innumerable times in the five hours that followed.[16]

When British Foreign Secretary Ernest Bevin heard that the *President Warfield* escaped its French guard and set out to sea on the morning of July 12 he was outraged. He demanded Foreign Minister Georges Bidault tell him why the French government refused a British demand to detain the ship. Bevin vowed to "make an example" of the refugee ship and expected French support in capturing the vessel and disembarking her passengers.[17]

The intention of Ike Aranne, the captain of the ship, was simple enough. As a member of the Palmach, an elite corps within the Haganah, he had been planning since November of 1946 to land as many as 5,000 Jews in Palestine. Aranne's mission was to demonstrate the moral bankruptcy of British restrictions on immigration, which limited refugees to a maximum of 1,500 a month. Months of preparation and outfitting the *President Warfield* had gone into the effort. Finding 4,500 passengers prepared to pay between $100 and $300 to risk an open sea voyage to Palestine was not difficult. Aranne was taking his orders from Yosi Har-El, a senior officer with the Haganah, who accompanied the ship's crew out of Port de Bouc. As the Haganah saw it, the landing of the immigrants in Palestine was of secondary importance. The primary objective of the operation was its impact on world public opinion. Its purpose was to show "how weak and poor and helpless" the Jews were "and how cruel the British were."[18]

A British flotilla of five destroyers and a cruiser began tracking the *President Warfield* soon after it left Sete. The incident, however, was attracting less attention in the world's media than violent developments inside Palestine. Front page treatment was given to the refusal of Irgun leaders to release Clifford Martin and Mervyn Paice, the two men it kidnapped from a Netanya cafe. Clifton Daniel reported in the *New York Times* that Paice had many Jewish friends and spent his holidays in a Jewish settlement helping in irrigation projects. The Jewish Agency issued a highly publicized demand that the Irgun release its captives. The agency's call was joined by Jewish municipal leaders, including Netanya Mayor Oved Benami, who told the *New York Times'* Gene Currivan that he had done "everything I could think of to bring about the return of the kidnapped men."[19]

The American Zionist Emergency Council (AZEC), watching

developments from New York, feared the trend in reporting. Zionist infighting, Abba Hillel Silver told the AZEC executive, had sunk AZEC's spring-long offensive and allowed opponents within the State Department "to play for time" by claiming Jewish statehood welcomed Soviet penetration of the region. The testimony of the Jewish Communist party to the U.N. committee of inquiry on July 13 contributed to this impression. The *New York Times* reported that although the party's spokesman had not "slavishly followed the full outline of the Soviet position on Palestine," he had stuck very closely to it. The paper gave particular attention to the spokesman's claim that Palestine under the British "was being prepared for a new World War that would be carried out by Anglo-American imperialists." This outlook only deepened the *Times'* conviction that certain Zionist groups might want the British out of Palestine so they could welcome in the Soviets.[20]

A certain depression descended on the *Warfield* crew by the morning of July 16. A woman had died in childbirth. The child, a boy, would soon die in a Haifa hospital. During the woman's burial at sea, Grauel was reminded of the death in childbirth of his own wife and son. Bill Bernstein, an American crewman Grauel befriended, told Grauel the death of either of them would be a propaganda victory for the cause. The British flotilla was close enough now so that a voice over the loudspeaker could be heard shouting in German, "This is the Cruiser *Ajax*." It demanded the ship's surrender. Grauel and the crew remembered *Ajax*'s successful hunt of the *Graf Spee* but were not impressed. "You'll have to speak in English," Aranne shouted through a megaphone. "We are not the *Graf Spee*!" By evening the ship's radio room established contact with Haganah headquarters in Tel Aviv and with its illegal Jewish station, Kol Israel---the Voice of Israel. The Jewish underground gave the ship a new name "Yetziat Eiropah Tashaz" or *Exodus 1947*.[21]

By the afternoon of July 17, it was clear the voyage had failed to generate the hoped for headlines. A gloomy *Exodus* crew gathered in the ship's wardroom to open sealed orders on the final disposition of the ship. A macabre humor settled over the discussion. Aranne would make a run for the Palestine coast and prepare the ship for the violent British boarding expected once the *Exodus* arrived in Palestine's territorial waters. The clash, it was thought, would inevitably produce casualties. If they were Americans, it was reasoned, they would greatly assist the cause. "Particularly if the victim," someone remarked to Grauel, "was a Gentile."[22]

REPORTING THE ATTACK AND ITS AFTERMATH

A little past three in the morning, a dispatcher aboard the *Exodus 1947* reported to Palestine via radio the ebb and flow of a battle that began a half hour before. He reported seven separate rammings by British ships and waves of assaults led by British boarding parties, which left several passengers and crewmen seriously injured. The British hurled tear gas in boarding the *Exodus*, and refugees responded, according to Grauel, "with potatoes, canned goods, and whatever else came into our hands."[23]

The fierce defense of the ship filled Grauel with patriotic pride. He saw the struggle as a latter day Lexington and Concord. As he watched the fighting he saw "the rebirth of a nation." By four-thirty the result of the battle remained very much in doubt. Aranne controlled the ship from an emergency steering room below decks, although he was unable to navigate. Two persons were dead, Bernstein was dying and 200 refugees were in urgent need of medical attention. Aranne was prepared to beach the vessel somewhere along the Palestinian coast, but the Haganah's Har-El overruled him. At five, Har-El ordered that the surrender of the ship. He refused to risk the loss of passenger life in a desperate gamble to make the beach. In his mind, the immigrants and the Jews of Palestine had won "a stupendous victory in terms of world public opinion" because of the British attack on the ship. By five-fifteen the fighting stopped.[24]

The British attack on the ship, in what *Exodus* crew and passengers insisted was international waters, along with the violence of the ship's takeover proved a boon to Zionist propagandists. Those in Palestine who missed the radio play by play of the fight read about it in special editions of their daily press and in handbills updated hourly and distributed throughout the Jewish community in Palestine. At ten in the evening on July 17, with the *Exodus* approaching the Palestinian shoreline under British escort, Kol Israel broadcast a twenty-five minute program from the ship in Hebrew, English and French, complete with youth choir and an impassioned plea by Grauel directed toward members of the U.N. committee. Grauel's message implored committee members to investigate the "utter brutality" inflicted on ship's passengers by the British "who acted as the Nazis acted in clubbing and beating and shooting down in cold blood our women and children."[25]

At four o'clock on the afternoon of July 18, at the onset of the Jewish sabbath, radio sets in Palestine captured the *Exodus* drama unfolding in Haifa harbor. With the world's press suddenly interested and taking note, a choir of immigrant children aboard the vessel sang the "Hatikva" as their ship turned suddenly starboard and the hills of Haifa came into view. At quayside were Emil Sandstrom, Valado Simic, and Karel Lisicky, the committee of inquiry's chairman and its Yugoslavian and Czechoslovakian delegates. Also present were Gene Currivan and Clifton Daniel of the *New York Times*, Kenneth Bilby and Homer Bigart of the *New York Herald-Tribune*, Carter Davidson of the Associated Press, Vic Bernstein of *P.M.* (a liberal newspaper from New York City), Nat Barrow of the *Chicago Tribune*, Simon Eliav of United Press, as well as Moses Esolsky of the *Palestine Post* and Arieh Dissentchik representing the Hebrew daily *Ma'ariv*. Capturing the scene on film was British Paramount news producer Ben Oyserman. British authorities attempted to restrict press coverage by keeping reporters in an area far down the pier from the *Exodus* and behind a fence, which discouraged their view and prevented access to passengers or crew. But even at a distance the visuals were arresting. The ship was a sight. She was severely gashed in on both sides. Her decks were blackened with fuel oil. Her railings were ripped off. Her life rafts lay strewn across the bridge. Women and children "looking tired, very tired," Sandstrom remarked, disembarked first. Then stretcher cases were taken to waiting ambulances. By nine that evening the refugees were boarded into cages on three ships, *Ocean Vigour*, *Empire Rival* and *Runnymeade Park*, and in the early morning hours of July 19 appeared to set sail for detention facilities in Cyprus.[26]

Currivan reported Grauel's testimony that Americans had fought and died in the clash. One was the assistant cook, Arthur Ritzer of Brooklyn, and another was Cyril Weinstein, a former Guadalcanal marine, from New York. Currivan and other papers reported Grauel's observation that the passengers included many infants and young mothers. Reporters saw enough themselves to know that survivors appeared exhausted from the ordeal. One expectant mother had died in childbirth, they were reporting, and been buried at sea. Bernstein would be buried, as he had wished, in Palestine.[27]

British officials confiscated Grauel's passport and visa and sequestered him in Haifa's Savoy Hotel, pending deportation to the United States. Inside the bar at the Savoy, Grauel was able to tell his story to more than a dozen reporters. Then, at the instigation of Vic Bernstein and Gerold Frank of the Overseas News Bureau, Grauel was able to slip out of the Savoy through a back entrance to a bathroom. Frank and Bernstein then drove for four hours through British roadblocks with Grauel bundled in the backseat, before arriving at the Jerusalem apartment of Jorge Garcia-Granados, the Guatemalan representative on the U.N. committee. There Grauel told his story again. Granados had already been briefed by Sandstrom on the "pitiable" events in Haifa harbor and knew that the British attack had left two dead and nearly 200 wounded. Grauel's account so stirred Granados that he arranged for the American to have a private interview with Sandstrom in Sandstrom's apartment the following morning. At the end of the emotional presentation, Granados and Sandstrom became convinced that the British mandate over Palestine should not be considered an option for the future status of the country. They further decided to extend their inquiry to the displaced persons camps of Europe before going to Geneva to write the committee's final report. Simic summarized their feelings when he told reporters that the brutalization of *Exodus* refugees "is the best possible evidence that we can have" that the British mandate over Palestine should end.[28]

Currivan reported that the *Exodus* passengers, as they were now being called in print, were on their way to Cyprus where they would be held in detention centers. Their status was quickly becoming the number one international story in the American media. Gertrude Samuels in the *New York Times* saw a connection between the *Exodus* incident and the failure of the international community to adequately deal with the continuing tragedy of Europe's displaced persons. The *Nation* charged that by doing nothing, other nations contributed to the "tragic fate" of the *Exodus*. Cecil Brown at Mutual Radio argued Britain's "stupid" policy on immigration was now covered in "shame." *Time* sided with "embittered refugees" whose "hope was not lost." Even the *Chicago Tribune*, whose Middle East correspondent disparaged Grauel for wearing an armband displaying the American flag, gave front page play to the violence that erupted in Palestine's Jewish community following the deportation of the *Exodus* passengers. The *Chicago Times* captured press treatment of the *Exodus* affair in an editorial cartoon of a haggard looking man on a raft holding a tattered flag reading "Europe's War Homeless."[29]

The positive press emboldened AZEC to demand that the United States do something to end the tragedy. Silver was quoted as saying the incident "filled every right-thinking man and woman everywhere with indignation and horror." His organization embraced Bernstein as "the first American casualty in the Jewish struggle for Palestine." The Jewish press concurred. "This exodus, like the previous one," they proclaimed, was "dictated by a desire for survival." That is why *Exodus* passengers were "willing to risk all to reach the shores of haven and safety."[30]

On the morning of July 20, committee of inquiry members, having completed their work in Palestine, prepared to leave the country. The press reported the committee's decision to visit displaced persons camps in Europe as a major achievement by Zionists. Foreign Minister Bevin further complicated the British cause by deciding to return the *Exodus* passengers to France. Word of that decision led to a hunger strike by Jewish detainees aboard British transports. The British Ambassador to France, Alfred Duff Cooper, implored Bevin to rescind his order and to return the flotilla to Cyprus. The forcible removal of refugees from British ships at a French port, Cooper warned, "would provide lurid anti-British propaganda which French public opinion would associate with the Nazis." Cooper added that "the man on the street is totally ignorant of Palestine problems and will see the immigrants as a persecuted race seeking refuge in their national home."[31]

Bevin, however, had been antagonized by the violence of the Jewish underground and was determined to make an example of the *Exodus* refugees. His stubborn insistence that the detainees not be disembarked in Cyprus, where their ordeal would have been quickly lost on the back pages of the world press, kept the controversy alive. When his government attempted to cover up the fact that it illegally boarded the ship on the high seas, it was condemned by the press and excoriated at a mass meeting in New York's Madison Square Park, where Silver charged the British had committed "a piratical act." The *Washington Post* was outraged by the British action, charging it was "as senseless as it was cruel." The *Post* noted that the decision had already been "calamitous in the overcharged atmosphere of the Holy Land" and that the situation demanded "a sober and merciful second thought." The *Post* editorial was quickly reprinted as a full page advertisement in major papers across America.[32]

On the afternoon of July 23, the British government was informed by the French Council of Ministers that it would not help in forcibly removing Jewish refugees from their ships. The French indicated that they might not permit British officials to do so either. This statement again led Ambassador Cooper to urge Bevin to back down and "avoid a most unedifying spectacle," which, Cooper reported, "was sure to be captured by the journalists and photographers" now gathering at Port de Bouc. Bevin wired back that he understood Cooper's anxiety, but that there was no where else to send the refugees "without exposing us to ridicule" that would amount to "acknowledging defeat."[33]

The *New York Times* and the wire services emphasized divisions within the British government over the handling of the *Exodus* affair. Currivan in the *Times* was reporting that the British High Commissioner of Palestine, Sir Alan Cunningham, had vigorously opposed returning the refugees to France "for fear of repercussions in a country already at the boiling point." Associated Press was reporting the decision to re-ship the refugees to Europe had united Jews across Palestine and would likely lead to another wave of violence directed at British targets. United Press was reporting new pressures on the Truman administration to force the British into reversing their stand. And Reuters was reporting that the Colombian consul general in Marseilles had expressed his government's willingness to grant visas to every Jew being forced to return to France.[34]

The refusal of the French government to forcibly evict *Exodus* detainees at Port de Bouc led to a fateful decision by Bevin. The announcement Britain was returning the refugees to Germany drew heavy press criticism on both sides of the Atlantic and created a month's worth of headlines and pictures that well served Zionist propaganda. Zionists had long supposed that Bevin was a virulent anti-Semite.[35] Now, his policy in Palestine sparked a wave of anti-Semitism unprecedented in the postwar world, which was eagerly and aggressively detailed in the Anglo-American press.

REFUELING THE FIRE

The story of the *Exodus* had disappeared from the front pages of the American press by the end of July when the British government, quite unexpectedly, triggered its return. On July 28, the day the immigrants arrived in Port de Bouc, British police hanged three Irgun men in an Acre jail. An hour later, alarm sirens sounded over Jerusalem. Associated Press reported increased British patrols in Tel Aviv and Haifa anticipating violence. The *New York Times* reported the bodies of the Irgun men were taken for private burial to the Jewish holy city of Safad and that British military authorities had rejected last minute pleas for clemency by the chief rabbi of Palestine, Dr. Isaac Herzog.[36]

The *Palestine Post* published the final message of the Irgun fighters before their executions. It urged their family members not to grieve. "What we have done we did out of conviction," the *Post* reported them as saying. The paper also printed a pledge from Irgun leader Menachem Begin "to carry out the promise we have made." The *Post* warned that killing the two British sergeants would be seen as a deed "contrary to all human standards." Even a last minute appeal by Mervyn Paice's father to Begin was ignored. Irgun had made up its mind.[37]

On the morning of July 31, the bodies of two British sergeants were discovered by Jewish police, south of the seacoast town of Netanya. British officials, accompanied by a horde of journalists, were summoned. Photographers took pictures of the two hanging hooded men. That created a sensation in the British press. "A picture that will shock the world!" screamed the *London Daily Express* the next day. "They were kidnapped unarmed and defenceless," wrote *The Times* of London. "They were murdered for no offence. They had been denied a Christian burial. The bestialities practiced by the Nazis could go no further."[38]

Anti-Semitic riots broke out in London, Manchester, Cardiff, Devonport and Glasgow. A synagogue was put to the torch in Derby. Jewish businesses in a score of cities were attacked and looted. A Jewish cemetery in Birmingham was vandalized. In Liverpool, shop windows of 100 Jewish merchants were smashed, while crowds of 2,000, chanting anti-Semitic slogans, looked on. The weekly *Morecambe Visitor* in Lancashire urged its 17,500 readers to "rejoice greatly over the pleasant fact that only a handful of Jews despoil the population of our borough!" The paper warned, "Violence may be the only way to bring (Jews) to a sense of their responsibility to the country in which they live." Public indifference and isolated instances of official sanctioning of racial violence, *The Manchester Guardian* found, "was the ugliest aspect" of the administration's no-win Palestine policy.[39]

Gangs of British soldiers in Palestine were also on the rampage. Bus and shop windows in Tel Aviv were smashed and Jews randomly beaten. On the evening of July 31, one Jew was killed and three others wounded when a bus was fired on near the British compound in Tel Aviv. Fifteen minutes later, another bus was fired on in the Hatikva quarter of the city, and three more Jews were killed. Nearby, a grenade hurled by British police into a crowded cafe, killed one Jew and injured several others.[40]

British violence increased over the next several days. Currivan reported thirty-three Jews were wounded in clashes with British police on August 1. Anti-Semitic slogans appeared in a number of British cities, accompanied by random violence and muggings. A fire was begun in the Jewish section of a Liverpool cemetery and Jewish factories throughout the city were put to the torch. Clifton Daniel reported from Jerusalem that the Haganah promised to find and punish the Britons responsible for killings in Palestine. The Irgun told Reuters seven more British soldiers "are scheduled for the gallows."[41]

The American media was appalled by the violence in Britain and Palestine and blamed it on Bevin. "Terror feeds on terror," the *Nation* warned, in noting that Bevin had struck the first blow. British policy had produced "an eye for an eye" mentality, reported *Time*, in condemning "mob arithmetic." Brown lamented that Bevin's obduracy was "pushing Palestine to the brink of open warfare." Homer Bigart of the *New York Herald-Tribune* concluded that Britain was acting "as if it were dealing with gangsters only." The Jewish press was also incensed. It pictured Bevin in a royal commander's cap, under the caption, "finishing Hitler's work." Its editorial cartoons showed Bevin standing in a sea of Jewish blood.[42]

The *Exodus* detainees greatly complicated Britain's public relations problem when they refused to disembark when their ships arrived at Port de Bouc. This stand enabled pictures of the prison ships to cover the front pages of major American dailies along with closeups of some of the 650 children aboard the vessels. In the meantime, the resourceful Grauel had managed to communicate with members of the press gathering at Port de Bouc. He reported conditions aboard the vessels were unbearable, with temperatures on the decks of 90 degrees and heat in the holds making them life-threatening. Passengers already weakened by their ordeal at sea, he warned, were asked to live on a ration of two cups of water a day, and that supply was dwindling. Grauel's claims were amplified by interviews with French doctors who warned that 1,000 of the 4,500 refugees were seriously ill and needed immediate medical attention.[43]

The French press reported conditions aboard the ships could "only be likened to a floating Auschwitz." French nationalism now came into play. The *Figaro* reported the ships were an attack on French sovereignty and a "demonstration of British arrogance." Cooper wired Bevin on July 30 begging that the ships be withdrawn and pointing to press assertions that the incident had brought Anglo-French relations to a postwar low. But Bevin cabled back that local police should be given instructions to cooperate in emptying the ships by whatever force was necessary.[44]

The French refused Bevin's demand. They offered safe haven to any of the refugees who wanted to make their home on French soil, but that is as far as they went in trying to get the immigrants off the British ships. Reuters correspondent Boyd France was even given permission to take a launch up beside the *Ocean Vigour* to ask how many of the refugees were going to take the French up on their offer. "Nein, nein," he reported the crowd as shouting, as they raised the Star of David and broke into a chorus of the "Hatikva." The Haganah men aboard the ship continued to maintain discipline. Their warnings were used, when necessary, to prevent passengers from going ashore. The goal was to make the incident a public relations nightmare for the British.[45]

Initially Bevin's strategy was to wait the refugees out. But after three days, only eighty-two of the passengers had come ashore, and nearly all of these for medical reasons. The delay played into the hands of the Haganah publicity campaign while further inflaming French public opinion. Old criticisms of British imperialism began to appear in the French press. The *Franc-Tireur* captured French sensibilities when it published an editorial cartoon titled, "Alert in the Mediterranean," which portrayed eight Royal Navy warships and a squadron of British aircraft converging on a small sailing dinghy flying the flag of the Star of David.[46]

The American Zionist Emergency Council through its ally, the American Christian Palestine Committee, pushed the contrast between British and French handling of the affair. They received wide play in the media for a letter signed by forty prominent Americans who expressed their "deep sense of gratitude" for the "honorable and benevolent manner" in which France had attempted to intercede in behalf of the refugees. The statement, by noted physicist Albert Einstein, former New York City mayor Fiorello La Guardia, former undersecretary of state Sumner Welles and others, praised the French exercise of "democratic ideals for dispirited wanderers" compared to the "duplicity of the British."[47]

Welles argued in his syndicated column that the British administration in Palestine was "shot through from top to bottom with anti-Semitism," and the "pogrom" in the streets of Tel Aviv was the latest example of that hatred. In a broadcast commentary, Welles urged immediate action by the Truman administration. He reasoned that any solution to the problems of the Near East "must have force behind it" and that the force must come from the United States. Since the United Nations was in no position to offer a military solution to the problem of Palestine, Welles argued, it was up to the United States to do it.[48]

FEELING THE HEAT

By mid-August, the *Exodus* debacle, combined with mounting problems at home and abroad, convinced Britain's leadership to consider itself both isolated and virtuous, a position they were in at the time of the war. That is, in effect, what Prime Minister Clement Attlee said in a nationwide broadcast on August 10 when he described the reasons for Britain's precarious position in the postwar world. Colonial Secretary Arthur Creech-Jones, speaking in the House of Commons two days later, blamed the American and French press for the battering Britain's reputation was taking abroad. Their reporting of the *Exodus* incident, he charged, had provoked "a spate of malicious abuse and vilification," which had been egged on by a handful of American nationals with their own axe to grind.[49]

The trend in the British press was decidedly against the British cabinet's position on Palestine. The Jewish Agency saw press attitudes as a reflection of mounting exasperation over money and manpower shortages in Britain. The *Daily Telegraph* argued that Britain "could no longer continue its costly commitment to Palestine" and urged that "serious reductions in British forces begin with Palestine." The Eastern editor of *The Times* of London privately told Jewish Agency representative Abba Eban that British "public opinion would not let a chance of a settlement in Palestine to be missed." Gerald Barry, editor of the *News Chronicle*, promised to cooperate with the Jewish Agency in publicizing any "constructive report" of the U.N. committee of inquiry. He thought the British press would "watch vigilantly" to make sure a good settlement would not be missed. That was also the pledge Eban received from Elizabeth Monroe, the political editor of *The Economist*.[50]

The attitude of the Attlee government prevented it from ending the *Exodus* affair and led Jewish Agency representative Golda Meir to observe that British seemed convinced the struggle for a Jewish homeland was a conspiracy to embarrass Britain. The decision of the British cabinet on August 16 to send *Exodus* refugees to detention camps in British-occupied Germany played into the hands of Zionist propagandists. When Bevin cabled the decision to British ambassadors in Washington and Paris, they argued the action would unleash strident anti-British sentiment in the press and in world public opinion. Bevin replied that returning the refugees to Cyprus would be an admission of defeat. The refugees had sealed their fate, Bevin argued, when they failed to go ashore in France. It appears he hoped that at the last minute the French government or the Jewish Agency would urge the refugees to leave their ships at Port de Bouc. But Meir, speaking for the agency executive, answered that no Jew could tell another Jew to go anywhere but Palestine.[51]

The British ultimatum that Jewish immigrants had only twenty-four hours to disembark in France or face the trip to Germany provoked many in the American media. The *Nation* likened British action to that of the Nazis. *Newsweek*'s Toni Howard feared the immigrants would commit suicide before returning to detention camps. *Time* ran the refugees' plea that the world "should come to our Auschwitz!" The British demand was widely condemned by representatives of major Jewish agencies as well as members of Congress. Typical of the indignation was the charge by Louis Lipsky, chairman of the American Jewish Conference, that it was inconceivable the British understood the symbolic significance of what they were doing. "The proposal to send these unfortunate people back to the soil drenched with blood of their closest relatives and to places holding memories of hell," Lipsky charged, "is fraught with the gravest consequences."[52]

The press continued to give front page play to the *Exodus* story in the days leading up to their arrival in Hamburg. During the two week voyage, Zionists kept the story alive by a variety of strategies. They personally appealed to President Truman to intervene and end their "eleventh hour of suffering." They made the same request of the committee of inquiry, whose members were reportedly deadlocked in Geneva over the final disposition of Palestine. Zionists conducted a worldwide, day-long fast to protest the British action. They implored the full United Nations to stop "the illegal, inhuman and immoral action" of the British. British leaders contributed to the headlines when they made a final offer at Gibraltar to send Jews ashore with not a single one taking them up on it.[53]

With every passing day the drama was played for the benefit of the press and world opinion. British criticism in the Western press became more shrill, and members of the Truman administration were faced with the evolving conventional wisdom the British were at fault for the pathetic predicament of the *Exodus* refugees. Acting Secretary of State Robert A. Lovett told the *New York Times* his office was closely monitoring the situation and was "considerably concerned" over the "regrettable circumstances" the *Exodus* passengers faced. While mystery still surrounded the final decision of the committee of inquiry, which would be announced while the *Exodus* refugees were in transit to Germany, Associated Press reported the status of Europe's displaced persons would be a vital factor in the committee's final report.[54]

As the *Exodus* passengers neared Hamburg and the committee of inquiry struggled to find a consensus among its members, Zionists pressed their case. If the committee voted to partition Palestine, the Jewish Agency and AZEC were convinced the Truman administration would follow. The *Exodus* incident, they reasoned, could be portrayed as proof that only in a land of their own "could Jews be allowed to live as other men." State Department veterans were irritated British actions had strengthened this interpretation. They were certain neither the Attlee government not Zionist propagandists realized the consequences of what they were doing. Lovett feared that a committee of

inquiry decision to partition Palestine would create a situation threatening not
only American security interests but also the lives of those Jews who would be
asked to live in such a state.[55]

THE PARTITION RECOMMENDATION

In the minutes before their statutory deadline, the eleven members of
the United Nations Special Committee on Palestine finally agreed to disagree.
They filed a majority and a minority report, the first favoring the partitioning
of Palestine into separate Jewish and Arab states, and the latter recommending
the creation of a unitary, federated state. The first plan, endorsed by seven of
the delegates, was favored by members of the Jewish Agency, led by David
Ben-Gurion, who were convinced that a Jewish state in part of Palestine was
all that political conditions would permit. The minority report, signed by India,
Iran and Yugoslavia, with Australia abstaining, embraced Bevin's proposed
solution of an autonomous state ruled by an Arab majority linked to the British
commonwealth. The reaction to the committee's work was instant and
expected. Zionists were pleased; Arabs were outraged.[56]

The Zionist General Council, meeting in Zurich, passed a resolution
on a 50-16 vote welcoming the majority report as the basis for negotiations on
the a future Jewish state in Palestine. Silver, who had previously supported a
Jewish state in all of Palestine, voted with the majority. The American section
of the Jewish Agency, under Silver's leadership, was now given the
responsibility of representing the Zionist case before the United Nations when
it convened in the middle of September. The Arab states opposed the majority
report, but they also opposed each other. King Abdallah of Transjordan told
the *New York Times* he would not allow the creation of a Jewish state in
Palestine to prevent him from fashioning a Greater Syria, a kingdom in which
he alone would rule. Representatives of the Syrian, Saudi Arabian and
Egyptian governments indicated their firm opposition to both the partitioning
of Palestine and Abdallah's plan to keep it united under his rule.[57]

The committee of inquiry's majority report received warm and
widespread support in the American media. It was endorsed by the *New York
Herald-Tribune*, the *Washington Post* and the Scripps-Howard newspaper chain
to the delight of the nation's Zionists. The *New York Times* reiterated that it
"long had doubts about the wisdom of erecting a political state on the basis of
religious faith" but was now "ready to accept any favorable U.N. decision and
to work for the success of it." That work would necessarily include
constructing "public opinion favoring a just, peaceable and early settlement"
of the problem. Even the *Times'* veteran Washington correspondent Arthur
Krock admitted, "the world having conceded the soundness" of a Jewish
homeland, "the good faith of Washington" would be enlisted in making that

homeland a reality.[58]

This attitude was expressed by the nation's network commentators whose sentiments were summarized in a September 1 broadcast of Cecil Brown over Mutual Radio. Brown saw the way clear for a transformation of the Eastern Mediterranean into a beachhead for economic development and Western-style democracy. Spurred by United Nations sanction and American capital, Jewish farmers would make "the desert wastes grow where there had once been nothing but sand." Brown observed that "the record shows that the Jews can do that, and the record shows that the Arabs either cannot or will not do it."[59]

The British bitterly condemned the "injustice and unworkability" of the majority report. Bevin, still not seeing the situation for what it was, convinced himself that there could never be a settlement in Palestine that did not enjoy the cooperation of the British government and was not "an insult to its conscience." A subject of more immediate concern to the world's conscience was the fate of the 4,400 Jewish refugees, who were making their way during the first week of September to a landing at Hamburg. *Newsweek* reported them, "dazed and weary, laying in dejected heaps, where many wept and others slept in bunkless holds." Ruth Gruber reported in the *New York Herald-Tribune* that the sight in the hold was like "a charcoal drawing of an inferno."[60]

On September 4, the refugee transports passed Le Havre and sailed through the Strait of Dover. Associated Press reported the Jews aboard refused a final ultimatum by the British to disembark in Northern France. British authorities, in desperation, charged Zionists had kidnapped 200 Jewish children from Hungary and that they were aboard the refugee ships now approaching Hamburg. In the meantime, Associated Press reported that more than 200 reporters and photographers had gathered in Hamburg to await the flotilla's arrival. British military police would do them no favors. They were under orders to keep the media as far away from the refugees as possible. Correspondents would be kept in two dockside pens and away from the passengers "to make sure there wasn't any trouble."[61]

A day before the first of the three ships arrived, British authorities tightened these restrictions. Correspondents would not be allowed within the area where the ship was to dock until two hours after it had been berthed. British public relations officer Colonel J. A. D. Lamont explained that press restrictions were in the interests of the passengers' safety. American and British photographers unanimously protested the arrangements. When they were told they would each be given a picture by the official photographer of the British War office they intensified their protest.[62]

British authorities failed to appreciate the significance of the public relations beating they were taking over the *Exodus*. Some Zionists, most notably Chaim Weizmann, failed to understand the latent power of public and press opinion when fixed on a protracted crisis. Weizmann's path for more than a generation had been quiet diplomacy with British leaders in achieving Zionist objectives. The unending spectacle of needless human suffering in the *Exodus* affair sickened him. The day before the scheduled landing of the refugees at Hamburg he pleaded with the Jewish Agency Executive to end the crisis. If the agency insisted "in starting an international row in Germany," Weizmann warned, the British would only harden their opposition to the U.N. partition recommendation and would "induce the Americans to adopt the same attitude." Weizmann's eleventh hour efforts to reach a compromise with Foreign Office officials in London was deeply resented within the Jewish Agency. Weizmann had no formal ties to the agency, he was told, and the final disposition of the *Exodus* passengers was "none of his business."[63]

On the morning of September 8, when the *Ocean Vigour* landed at Hamburg, Zionists all over the world began a two hour work stoppage in protest. The early editions of America's east coast papers reported the first of the 1,300 passengers aboard the *Ocean Vigour* left the ship with barely a struggle. Later editions reported there had been a token struggle, a few injuries but little else. The 1,400 passengers aboard the *Empire Rival* followed quietly, with British officers on the docks relieved at the "effortlessness of the endeavour." Any smiles, however, faded when the 1,500 passengers aboard the *Runnymeade Park* refused to be budged. What followed was a three hour battle captured by the world press in which scores of individuals were arrested and dozens injured, as British soldiers used batons and rubber truncheons the get the crowd moving.[64]

Media criticism of British actions, mild enough at the beginning of the incident, boiled over at Hamburg. It was not simply that Bevin's willfulness had antagonized nearly everyone in the days leading up to the landing but that press restrictions at the scene only deepened the distrust. "A blunder of the first magnitude," concluded *The Star* of London, long a Liberal voice in England. "A manifest blunder," agreed *The Daily Telegraph*, "made all the more asinine in its utter purposelessness." "No more stupid decision could have been made," argued *The Evening News*, if the government had long considered the matter. British conduct had "shocked world public opinion," lamented *The Manchester Guardian*; "The government has not so much credit left in the world that it can afford to squander it in acts of unpremeditated folly." The *News Chronicle* charged, "British conduct is moving rapidly to the ultimate stage of lunacy." It added that Bevin should have known that "no one but a fool would try to compel a Jew to go to Germany of all countries."[65]

The anger in the British press was reflected in America's Jewish press, with many of its major dailies and network commentators joining in a rhetorical attack on the British decision. "How Hitler would have enjoyed this!" cried the *Detroit Jewish Chronicle*, in a headline over a four column picture of refugees being dragged from their ships. "May every displaced person camp in Germany be burned to the ground," the *B'nai Brith Messenger* reported in offering a Rosh Hashana prayer, "and may the Lord curse those who forced Holocaust survivors to return to the soil of their murderers." A *New York Times* editorial charged the British government with "a grievous error of judgment, producing a grim and pitiful saga." NBC's Clifton Utley reported that as Jews were "herded into trains" they could be heard shouting, "We will take up the trek back to Palestine."[66]

The British decision to return the *Exodus* refugees to Germany had the effect of capturing world headlines at precisely the time that a world body was deciding the fate of Palestine and creating a public environment far more sympathetic to Zionist arguments. "Maybe we were wrong," admitted Harold Beeley, in a cabinet meeting called to assess the damage done to British interests as a result of its handling of the *Exodus* affair.[67] But the recognition came too late for the pounding the British were taking in the world press and the pressures that were now being directed at the Truman administration to endorse the U.N. committee's majority report before the organization convened to consider it.

The Truman administration was coming to the conclusion that time was running out on its vague neutrality toward a Jewish state. Developments in Geneva and Hamburg had shattered a summer-long silence in which the President sat uneasily on the sidelines. On September 4, Democratic Committee Chairman Robert Hannegan told Truman the time had come to tell the press the administration favored the majority report and would call for the immediate admission of 150,000 Jews into Palestine. Hannegan's argument was countered by Defense Secretary James V. Forrestal, who vigorously maintained that Jewish statehood threatened American security interests with the Arab states.[68] Forrestal may have had senior officials within the State Department with him, but Hannegan had the gathering steam of public and press opinion behind him. The next chapter will show how crucial that momentum was.

The effort to land 4,500 refugees in Palestine, first conceived nearly a year before, had by mid-September 1947 both failed and succeeded. Although its passengers failed to make it to the "Promised Land," the skillful manipulation of their plight by Zionist propagandists and the bungling of the whole affair by the British had created pressures for the resolution of the conflict that seemed to favor the Zionist argument that a Jewish state in Palestine was now needed. Members of the U.N. committee as well as the Jewish Agency believed the tragedy of Europe's displaced persons as dramatized in the *Exodus* incident, helped persuade committee members that homeless Jews in Europe should be free to make a home in Palestine. This conclusion stemmed not only from the ingenuity of the *Exodus* propaganda campaign but also from the direct intervention by members of the world press who arranged contact between U.N. committee members and a correspondent aboard the *Exodus*. The conventional wisdom developed in the press was greatly aided by the hard-headedness of British leaders, whose stubbornness suggested to a majority of U.N. committee members that Palestine needed a separate Jewish state.

On another front, AZEC's drive to capitalize on this positive press to get the Truman administration to take the lead on Jewish statehood was still on hold by summer's end. The President remained silent during the committee of inquiry's consideration of the future status of Palestine and for weeks after its partition recommendation. But it was a silence that could not last long. The spectacle of the *Exodus* affair and its successful management in the world press made it far easier for Truman to trust his personal and political instincts and override the State Department to endorse the creation of a Jewish state in Palestine.

NOTES

1. For more on the storytelling function of the press and the ways in which reporters and editors create interpretative frameworks that "make things mean" consider Walter Lippmann, *Public Opinion* (New York: Free Press, 1922), chapter 1, "The World Outside and the Pictures in Our Head," chapter 23, "The Nature of News," and chapter 24, "News and Truth." Herbert J. Gans, *Deciding What's News: A Study of CBS Evening News, NBC Nightly News, Newsweek and Time* (New York: Pantheon, 1979), chapter 2, "Values in the News," and chapter 6, "Objectivity, Values and Ideology." Gaye Tuchman, *Making News: A Study in the Construction of Reality* (New York: Free Press, 1978), chapter 1, "News as Frame," and chapter 5, "The Web of Facticity." Stuart Hall, "The Rediscovery of Ideology in Media Studies," in Michael Gurevitch, Tony Bennett, James Curran and Janet Woollacott, eds., *Culture, Society and the Media* (London: Metheun, 1982), pp. 63-88. Bernard Roscho, *Newsmaking* (Chicago: University of Chicago), pp. 14-18, 53-64 and 105-125. Edward Jay Epstein, *News from Nowhere: Television and the News* (New York: Random House, 1973), pp. 17-25, 37-43 and 182-199. Peter Dahlgren and Sumitra Chakrapani, "The Third World on TV News: Western Ways of Seeing the Other," in William C. Adams, ed., *Television Coverage of International Affairs* (Norwood: Ablex, 1982), pp. 45-65. Robert Darnton, "Writing News and Telling Stories," *Daedalus* 104, 1975, pp. 175-194.

2. *New York Times*, May 26, 1947, p. 22 and May 28, 1947, p. 1. *Foreign Relations of the United States 1947*, Volume 3 (Washington: U.S. Government Printing Office, 1976), pp. 224-230.

3. *New York Times*, June 6, 1947, p. 2.

4. *New York Times*, June 7, 1947, p. 5.

5. *Chicago Tribune*, July 11, 1947, p. 12. *U.S. News and World Report*, July 18, 1947, p. 19. *Nation* 165, July 12, 1947, p. 29 and July 26, 1947, p. 85. *New York Times*, July 15, 1947, p. 22.

6. See *New York Times*, June 8, 1947, Section E, p. 8; June 26, 1947, p. 22; July 20, 1947, p. 8 and Section E, p. 7; and July 23, 1947, p. 22. The second and third weeks in July also saw extensive coverage of the displaced persons issue in the *Baltimore Sun, Philadelphia Inquirer, New York Herald-Tribune,* and *Boston Globe. New York Times* editorial concern over the consequences of Soviet expansionism appears March 12, 1947, p. 22; March 13, 1947, p. 26; March 16, 1947, Section E, p. 8; March 23, 1947, Section E, p. 8; April 3, 1947, p. 24; April 7, 1947, p. 22; April 11, 1947, p. 24; April 14, 1947, p. 26; April 20, 1947, Section E, p. 8; April 23, 1947, p. 24; May 3, 1947, p. 16; May 25, 1947, Section E, p. 3; May 26, 1947, p. 22; June 3, 1947, p. 24; June 8, 1947, Section E, p. 12; June 14, 1947, p. 14; June 26, 1947, p. 22; and June 27, 1947, p. 20. See also, *Christianity and Crisis*, July 7, 1947, p. 8.

7. *New York Times*, June 25, 1947, p. 8 and June 30, 1947, pp. 1, 2 and 18. Also, *Nation 165*, July 26, 1947, p. 85. *Time*, July 7, 1947, p. 25. See also, *New York Times*, July 15, 1947, p. 22 and July 17, 1947, p. 6.

8. *New York Herald-Tribune*, March 25, 1947, p. 5. *New York Times*, April 18, 1947, p. 15; May 18, 1947, p. 1; and June 12, 1947, p. 10. *New York Herald-Tribune*, May 18, 1947, p. 1. *Washington Post*, May 18, 1947, p. 1. *St. Louis Post-Dispatch*, May 18, 1947, p. 1. *Chicago Times*, May 18, 1947, p. 1. For extensive coverage, see also, the *Baltimore Sun, Boston Globe* and *Philadelphia Inquirer* of May 18, 1947.

9. *New York Times*, June 9, 1947, p. 11; June 11, 1947, p. 23 and June 17, 1947, p. 52. Also, *Newsweek*, September 15, 1947, p. 30.

10. Foreign Office. 371/61813 and 371/61814. The Public Record Office. Also, *New York Times*, May 18, 1947, p. 1.

11. *New York Times*, June 23, 1947, p. 1; June 26, 1947, p. 7; June 30, 1947, p. 1; July 13, 1947, p. 1; and July 14, 1947, p. 1. Also, *New York Herald-Tribune*, June 29, 1947, p. 1. *Washington Post*, July 13, 1947, p. 1. *Boston Herald*, July 13, 1947, p. 1. *Time*, July 14, 1947, p. 26. *Chicago Tribune*, July 14, 1947, p. 5 and July 15, 1947, p. 3.

12. Michael J. Cohen, *The Rise of Israel*, Volume 30, *The Holocaust and Illegal Immigration* (New York: Garland, 1987), p. 348, which includes a record of the British cabinet meeting dated May 1, 1947.

13. David C. Holly, *Exodus 1947* (Boston: Little, Brown, 1969), pp. 3-12 and 288-292. John S. Grauel, *Grauel* (Freehold, N.J.: Ivory House, 1982), p. 47. My thanks to Mr. and Mrs. George Grauel for bringing to my attention John Grauel's autobiography.

14. Bernard Postal and Henry W. Levy, *And the Hills Shouted for Joy: The Day Israel Was Born* (New York: David McKay, 1973), pp. 140-141. Michael Bar-Zohar, *The Armed Prophet: A Biography of Ben-Gurion* (London: Arthur Barker, 1966), p. 99. Jorge Garcia-Granados, *The Birth of Israel: The Drama as I Saw It* (New York: Knopf, 1949), pp. 173-174. Holly, p. 208. *New York Times*, July 19, 1947, pp.

1 and 5. Grauel, p. 2.

15. Harold Manson File. 4-1-2. AZEC Files. The Temple. Cleveland, Ohio. Also, Carl Hermann Voss, *The Palestine Problem Today: Israel and Its Neighbors* (Boston: Beacon Press, 1953), p. 22. *New York Times*, July 19, 1947, p. 5. *Baltimore Sun*, July 14, 1947, p. 1 and July 19, 1947, p. 1. Grauel, pp. 59 and 73. Garcia-Granados, pp. 174-175. *Washington Post*, July 17, 1947, p. 1.

16. Foreign Office. 371/61815. July 12, 1947. Public Record Office. Also, Granados, p. 175. Grauel, p. 75.

17. Foreign Office. 371/61815. July 12, 1947. Public Record Office.

18. Nicholas Bethell, *The Palestine Triangle: The Struggle for the Holy Land, 1935-1948* (New York: Putnam, 1979), chapter 10, which includes Bethel's interview with Aranne.

19. *Ibid.*, p. 321 and 329-331. Also, Foreign Office. 371/61815. July 15, 1947. Public Record Office. *New York Times*, July 14, 1947, pp. 1 and 3 and July 16, 1947, p. 6.

20. Correspondence. Minutes: AZEC July 14, 1947. File 4-2. AZEC Files.

21. Granados, p. 178. Grauel, pp. 19 and 81. Holly, p. 208.

22. Holly, p. 216.

23. Grauel, pp. 87-88.

24. Holly, pp. 228 and 235.

25. *Ibid.*, pp. 247-249. Grauel, p. 89.

26. Holly, p. 253. Grauel, p. 92. Also, Abba Eban, *An Autobiography* (New York: Random House, 1977), p. 79. *Palestine Post*, July 19, 1947, p. 1. *New York Herald-Tribune*, July 19, 1947 p. 1.

27. *New York Times*, July 19, 1947, pp. 1 and 5. *New York Herald-Tribune*, July 19, 1947, p. 1. *Washington Post*, July 19, 1947, p. 1. *Philadelphia Inquirer*, July 19, 1947, p. 1. *Baltimore Sun*, July 19, 1947, p. 1.

28. Granados, pp. 172-184. Grauel, pp. 94-97. *Time*, July 28, 1947, p. 18.

29. *New York Times*, July 20, 1947, Section E, pp. 1 and 7. Also, *Nation* 165, August 2, 1947, p. 113. Cecil Brown Radio Script. August 22, 1947. Box 13. Folder 3. Cecil Brown Papers. State Historical Society of Wisconsin. Madison, Wisconsin. *Time*, July 28, 1947, pp. 17-18. *Chicago Tribune*, July 21, 1947, p. 1. *Chicago Times*, July 19, 1947, p. 12.

30. *New York Times*, July 19, 1947, p. 5. *New York Herald-Tribune*, July 19, 1947, pp. 1 and 5. *Kansas City Jewish Chronicle*, July 25, 1947, pp. 1 and 3. *The Jewish Advocate* (Boston), July 25, 1947, pp. 1, 3 and 4. *The American Hebrew* (New York), July 25, 1947, pp. 2 and 7. *Detroit Jewish Chronicle*, July 25, 1947, pp. 1 and 2.

31. *Palestine Post*, July 20, 1947, pp. 1 and 3. Foreign Office. 371/61816. July 20, 1947. Public Record Office.

32. Foreign Office. 371/61816. July 22, 1947. Public Record Office. Also, *P.M.* (New York), July 23, 1947, p. 1. And, press release of the American Zionist Emergency Council. July 23, 1947. File 1-4-6. AZEC Files. *Washington Post*, July 23, 1947, p. 1. *Chicago Tribune*, July 25, 1947, p. 13. AZEC used the *Washington Post* editorial in advertisements appearing in several major American cities. See AZEC. File 1-4-6.

33. *Palestine Post*, July 24, 1947, pp. 1, 2 and 4. Also, Foreign Office. 371/61818. July 23, 1947. Public Record Office.

34. *New York Times*, July 22, 1947, pp. 1 and 3. *New York Herald-Tribune*, July 22, 1947, p. 1. *Washington Post*, July 22, 1947, p. 1. *Chicago Tribune*, July 22, 1947, p. 1.

35. Memorandum from Aubrey (Abba) Eban to Jewish Agency, dated August 5, 1947. File Z4/10381. Central Zionist Archives. Jerusalem, Israel.

36. *New York Herald-Tribune*, July 29, 1947, p. 1. *New York Times*, July 29, 1947, pp. 1 and 13.

37. *Palestine Post*, July 30, 1947, pp. 1 and 2.

38. *Palestine Post*, August 1, 1947, pp. 2 and 4. For background, see Major R. D. Wilson, *Cordon and Search: With the Sixth Airborne Division in Palestine* (London: Aldershot, Gale and Polden, 1949), pp. 132-133. *London Daily Express*, August 1, 1947, pp. 1 and 2. *The Times* (of London), August 1, 1947, p. 1.

39. *New York Herald-Tribune*, August 1, 1947, p. 1. *New York Times*, August 1, 1947, p. 1. Bethell, pp. 338-340.

40. *New York Times*, August 1, 1947, pp. 1 and 6. *The Manchester Guardian*, August 1, 1947, p. 1. *Morecambe Visitor* (Lancashire), August 3, 1947, pp. 1 and 5.

41. *New York Times*, August 2, 1947, pp. 1 and 6; August 3, 1947, p. 34; and August 4, 1947, p. 1. Also, *New York Herald-Tribune*, August 4, 1947, pp. 1 and 10.

42. *Nation* 165, August 9, 1947, p. 134. *Time*, August 11, 1947, p. 34. Brown Radio Script. August 25, 1947. Brown Papers. Box 13. Folder 4. *New York Herald-Tribune*, July 23, 1947, p. 1. *Detroit Jewish Chronicle*, August 8, 1947, p. 4. *The National Jewish Post*, August 8, 1947, p. 1. *B'nai Brith Messenger* (Los Angeles), August 8, 1947, pp. 1 and 4.

43. *New York Times*, July 29, 1947, p. 13 and August 1, 1947, p. 4. *Boston Herald*, July 29, 1947, pp. 2 and 22. *New York Herald-Tribune*, July 30, 1947, pp. 1 and 3.

44. Foreign Office. 371/61819. July 30, 1947. Public Record Office.

45. Bethell, pp. 335-336. Although it appears physical intimidation was not often used to keep passengers aboard the ship, the threat of social ostracisim was. Thirty-one of the ship's 4,400 passengers eventually accepted the French invitation to go ashore.

46. *New York Times*, August 3, 1947, p. 6. *Franc-Tireur*, August 8, 1947, pp. 3 and 13.

47. Press release. American Christian Palestine Committee. August 11, 1947. File 1-1-2. AZEC Files.

48. *New York Herald-Tribune*, August 12, 1947, p. 11. Broadcast by Sumner Welles over W.O.L.-radio. New York City. 7:45-8:00 p.m. File 1-4-42. AZEC Files.

49. *The Times* (of London), August 11, 1947, pp. 1 and August 13, 1947, p. 1. *The Daily Telegraph*, August 11, 1947, pp. 1 and 3. *London Evening Standard*, August 13, 1947, pp. 1 and 5.

50. *The Daily Telegraph*, August 5, 1947, pp. 1 and 11. Also, Memorandum from Aubrey (Abba) Eban to Jewish Agency, dated August 5, 1947. "Report on Visit

to London." File Z4/10381. Central Zionist Archives. Jerusalem, Israel.

51. Marie Syrkin, *Golda Meir: Woman with a Cause* (London: Victor Gollancz, 1964), pp. 161-162. See also, Henry M. Christman, *This Is Our Strength: Selected Papers of Golda Meir* (New York: Macmillan, 1962), pp. 29-47. Golda Meir, *My Life* (New York: Putnam, 1975), pp. 201-210. Colonial Office. August 16, 1947. 537/2312. Public Record Office. And, note from Meyerson to Bevin. August 20, 1947. Colonial Office. 537/2294. Public Record Office. Meir believed Bevin's anti-Semitism unwittingly facilitated propaganda efforts to push the *Exodus* affair to a dramatic conclusion. See Meir, *My Life*, p. 201.

52. *Nation* 165, August 23, 1947, p. 183. *Newsweek*, September 15, 1947, p. 29. *Time*, September 1, 1947, p. 18.

53. *New York Times*, August 22, 1947, pp. 1 and 4; August 23, 1947, p. 1; August 24, 1947, p. 25; August 25, 1947, p. 1; and August 27, 1947, p. 9. Also, *Washington Post*, August 22, 1947, pp. 1 and 12. *Baltimore Sun*, August 25, 1947, p. 1. *New York Herald-Tribune*, August 27, 1947, p. 1.

54. *New York Times*, August 28, 1947, p. 10. The speculation by the Associated Press is confirmed in Granados, pp. 172-173 and 210-213. See also, Eban, pp. 79-83.

55. *Detroit Jewish Chronicle*, August 29, 1947, p. 4. *B'nai Brith Messenger* (Los Angeles), August 29, 1947, pp. 1 and 4. *The New Palestine News Reporter Issue*, August 29, 1947, p. 1. And, memo from Harry Shapiro to local emergency committees, August 29, 1947. File 1-4-17. AZEC Files. Also, Walter Millis, ed., *The Forrestal Diaries* (New York: Viking, 1951), p. 306, containing Forrestal's notes of August 29, 1947 cabinet meeting.

56. *New York Times*, September 1, 1947, pp. 1 and 3. *New York Herald-Tribune*, September 1, 1947, pp. 1 and 5. *Washington Post*, September 1, 1947, p. 1.

57. *New York Times*, September 1, 1947, p. 3.

58. *The New Palestine*, September 12, 1947, p. 9. *New York Times*, September 1, 1947, p. 18 and September 3, 1947, p. 6.

59. Brown Radio Script. September 1, 1947. Brown Papers. Box 13. Folder 4. Also, Clifton Utley Radio Scripts. August 31, 1947 and September 5, 1947. Box 49. Folders 1 and 2. Clifton Utley Papers. Joseph Harsch Radio Script. August 31, 1947. Box 11. Folder 4. Joseph Harsch Radio Scripts. State Historical Society of Wisconsin. Madison, Wisconsin.

60. "Palestine" memo by the Secretary of State for Foreign Affairs. September 18, 1947. Cabinet Meeting. 129/21. Confidential Annex. Public Record Office. A cabinet committee formed to investigate British "refoulement" (the deportation of immigrants back to their port of departure) noted that although "His Majesty's Government has incurred considerable odium" over the *Exodus* incident, particularly in the United States, it was to be hoped that many would yet "recognize the rectitude of His Majesty's Government's actions and approve" of them. See draft memorandum from Commander W. Evershed, "Refoulement: Future Policy." Foreign Office. 371/61825. September 3, 1947. Public Record Office. See also, *Newsweek*, September 1, 1947, p. 32. *Time*, September 1, 1947, p. 18.

61. *New York Times*, September 5, 1947, p. 5 and September 6, 1947, p. 5.

62. *New York Times*, September 7, 1947, pp. 1 and 7.

63. Letter from Chaim Weizmann to Jewish Agency (of London). September 6, 1947, cited in Barnet Litvinoff, *The Letters and Papers of Chaim Weizmann*, Volume 23 (Jerusalem: Israel Universities, 1980), pp. 4-7.

64. *New York Herald-Tribune*, September 8, 1947, p. 1. *Baltimore Sun*, September 8, 1947, p. 1 and September 9, 1947, p. 1. *Boston Herald*, September 9, 1947, p. 1. *New York Times*, September 10, 1947, p. 1. *Washington Post*, September 10, 1947, p. 1.

65. *The Star* (of London), September 8, 1947, p. 11. *The Daily Telegraph*, September 8, 1947, p. 9. *The Evening News*, September 8, 1947, p. 12. *Manchester Guardian*, September 8, 1947, pp. 3 and 6. *The News Chronicle*, September 8, 1947, pp. 1 and 7.

66. *Detroit Jewish Chronicle*, September 19, 1947, p. 1. *B'nai Brith Messenger* (Los Angeles), September 12, 1947, p. 4. *New York Times*, September 11, 1947, p. 26. And, Utley Radio Script. September 8, 1947. Box 49. Folder 2. Utley Papers.

67. Cabinet Meeting. 129/21. Confidential Annex. Public Record Office.

68. Millis, pp. 310-322.

Four

The Decision to Partition,
September 1947–November 1947

The six months following the end of the *Exodus* drama and the recommendation of the United Nations committee to partition Palestine saw the triumph and then the apparent dashing of Zionist efforts to create a Jewish state. The vote within the U.N. General Assembly in November, 1947 to establish separate Arab and Jewish states in Palestine recognized the irreconcilability of national differences within the region and the necessity of ending the bloody British mandate over the territory while finding a safe haven for the dispossessed of Europe. If that conventional wisdom had been sustained, the Zionists would have had their state in mid-May 1948 with hardly a backward look. But as this study has suggested, the "taken for granted" that frames and ultimately sustains policy initiatives resides within a rhetorical realm of the politically possible and is struggled over by those determined to exert power over the dominant interpretation guiding and justifying political action.

In the case of Palestine, the British government, the Arab states and the U.S. State Department sought to shift the prevailing logic guiding policymakers in the weeks following the partition recommendation. The American media was a strategic site where this war was waged and the media itself became a contested prize in the competition. Media on both sides of the Atlantic embraced partition when finding sanctuary for Holocaust survivors and ending colonialism was the issue. But when Arab states openly resisted the partition recommendation and threatened to turn Palestine into a killing field, regional security dominated world headlines and conversations among Western leaders. This interpretation of events seemed to fit rapidly deteriorating East-West relations.

American Zionists had long fought interpreting events in Palestine in terms of rising Cold War tensions. So long as the region was perceived as a

place of Great Power competition, Zionists could not overcome the argument
that a Jewish state meant a military struggle between Arabs and Jews in which
Moscow would be the big winner. This view was what the State Department
had argued since the British turned the problem of Palestine over to the United
Nations. In the weeks leading up to the final vote on partition, each party to
the dispute intensified its mass mediated campaign hoping to win public
opinion and the mind of Harry Truman in support of their cause.

TRUMAN AS CHRISTIAN AND ZIONIST

Harry Truman grew up in a religious culture that saw the Jewish
return to the Holy Land as the fulfillment of scriptural prophecy.[1] While this
did not make him the nation's leading Zionist during the fall of 1947, it did
provide the background for the ensuing battle over Harry Truman's mind and
heart. Truman historians have found the President particularly susceptible to
pressure from one direction or another because of his relative lack of
experience in foreign policy matters and his tendency to often act before
considering the long range consequences of those actions.[2] This reading of
Truman led those on both sides of the Palestine issue to think of him as more
controlled by events and the interpretation of events than in control of either.[3]

The millenarian sentiment that "God had preserved the Jewish people
so that in the end of days they might be saved," dates back to colonial New
England.[4] As developed in Nineteenth Century America by Jewish and
Christian theologians as well as their allies in the secular press, the return of
the Jewish people to Palestine was a necessary precondition before Gentiles
attained "the fullness of time" predicted by the prophets and Christ returned
in glory to end the age and claim His own. The culmination of Christian
agitation for Jewish restoration during the Victorian era was the proclamation
presented to President Benjamin Harrison on March 5, 1891 calling for an
"early conference" to consider the plight of Russian Jews and to "alleviate
their suffering condition" by considering their claims to Palestine as their
"ancient home." Signing the document were editors and publishers of some of
the country's most prestigious papers as well as a cross section of political,
business and religious leaders.[5]

By century's end, a millenarian minority developed in the Lutheran,
Episcopal, Presbyterian, Dutch Reformed and Baptist communities.
Millenarian Christians were quick to embrace Theodore Herzl's *Judenstaat* and
the results of the First Zionist Congress, which called for a homeland for the
Jewish people. These arguments found expression in the *Prophetic Times*, a
monthly periodical propagating millenarian views among interested
churchgoers and prophecy conference speakers. Fundamentalists, those within
the church who rejected its drift to humanism and higher criticism, saw Jewish

restoration in Palestine as a proof the *Bible* was literally true. It was this eschatology that dominated the Southern Baptists, the church family into which Truman was born and to which he returned at the age of eighteen.[6]

Though an irregular churchgoer, who once remarked that the best services tended to be the briefest, Truman was long proud of his connection to the Baptist Church. Truman married a childhood sweetheart who was Episcopalian and they raised their only child as an Episcopalian, but Truman steadfastly maintained his lifelong membership in the Grandview, Missouri, Baptist Church. "I am a Baptist myself," Truman told church leaders in January, 1948, "and I am not a Baptist because my mother and father and grandparents were Baptists." All denominations were aiming at bringing into being God's kingdom on earth, Truman believed, but Baptists had evolved "a democratic approach to church government" which made every member aware "he was his brother's keeper." Truman maintained that being a Baptist gave him not only spiritual direction and comfort but a code of conduct that animated his political life.[7]

In post-Presidential remarks, Truman cultivated the impression his support for a Jewish state flowed from his reading of the *Bible* and his humanitarian concern for the "Jewish survivors of Hitlerism." Presidential aide Clark Clifford recalls Truman sometimes cited *Deuteronomy* 1:8, as a historical basis for the Jewish claim to Palestine. The text urges the Israelites to "go in and take possession of the land which the Lord hath sworn unto your fathers, to Abraham, to Isaac, and to Jacob." While critics have pointed out the distinct political advantages in Truman's attitude, there is no reason to suppose these remarks completely disingenuous. Nor is their reason to doubt the tears that Truman reportedly shed were real tears when at the close of his Presidency he was told by Israeli Prime Minister David Ben-Gurion that Truman had won "an immortal place in Jewish history." Truman's emotional identification with the fate of the Jewish people was something more than electoral convenience. On the one year anniversary of the U.N. vote to establish a Jewish state and three weeks after an election that had seen Truman lose traditional Jewish Democratic strongholds in New York, Pennsylvania and Michigan, Truman wrote a long and remarkable letter to Israeli President Chaim Weizmann. In it, Truman said he was "struck by the common experience" of the two men and how they had emerged victorious "over bitter and resourceful opponents" after being "abandoned as lost and forlorn causes." Truman said he was "elated" by Israel's "remarkable progress" and felt certain "what she had received at the hands of the world was less than her due."[8]

According to childhood friends and early letters, Truman seemed to share many of the racial attitudes characteristic of life in a small Southern border town at the turn of the century. He admitted to "hating" Asians and disliking "Niggers" and "Bohunks." He wrote bride-to-be Bess Wallace that

U.S. immigration policy was responsible for making life difficult for "good, white Americans." The struggle of the "white man" to make "a decent living," he told Bess, would be made easier if the Negroes were returned to Africa and "yellow men" to Asia.[9]

Truman's attitude toward Jews was complex. When he sailed with his Army unit for France in March, 1918 he found New York City a "kike" town. Later he would remark that a poker playing companion "screamed like a Jewish merchant" and that a campaign worker had been so obnoxious he would "cut the smart Hebrew loose." This, however, must be contrasted to Truman's long and warm relationship with Jews, beginning with the Viner family of Independence, Missouri, when as a boy he ran Sabbath errands for them, and his friendship with Jews during his Army days. Truman's coterie included Eddie Jacobson, Herman Rosenberg, Charley Hipsch and other poker playing partners, giving Truman the camp nickname of "Trumanheimer."[10]

Truman particularly admired Jacobson's tenacity and determination to make good against long odds. During the war the two ran a canteen together and after the war opened a clothing store in Kansas City, which failed during the economic downturn of 1920-1921. What followed was a fifteen year struggle to repay a $35,000 debt and a relationship made closer by Jacobson's personal bankruptcy in 1925. Although under no legal obligation thereafter to retire the debt of the haberdashery, Jacobson saw it as his "moral responsibility." The generosity was not lost on Truman. As a Democratic Party worker and local judge, Truman and his wife were regular visitors in the Jacobson home. Truman's order to his Senate staff, beginning in 1935, was that he was available to see Jacobson whenever the latter came calling. This policy was maintained throughout Truman's time as Vice President and President.[11]

During the months leading up to Truman's decision to support partition and favor the creation of Israel, Jacobson was a frequent visitor at the White House, serving as the Zionists' point man in dealings with the President. Jacobson was welcomed into the Oval Office on January 29, 1948 with B'nai Brith President Frank Goldman, and Jacobson's personal intercession won Chaim Weizmann a private audience with Truman on March 18, 1948. Jacobson always insisted, however, that Truman's decision on Palestine had less to do with personal friendship and everything to do with what he thought best for the country.[12] While Truman's tortured path on Palestine supports this assertion, the President's personal affection for a particular Jew and his Biblical backgrounding in the history of the Jewish people created conditions that facilitated Truman's support for Jewish statehood in the critical months leading up to independence.

In addition to Truman's predisposition to sympathize with the Jewish homeland movement as a consequence of religious training and personal acquaintance, one must examine the central place Truman gave religious values in presidential decision-making. Whereas most modern presidents have accommodated important religious interests while maintaining an official "neutrality" on specific religious issues, Truman saw his religious philosophy as basic to his political philosophy. "The fundamental basis of government is the *Bible*," Truman believed. Sound government was rooted in a code of ethics first found in the Sermon on the Mount. There was a strong relationship between a man's religion and a man's politics, Truman wrote State Department veteran John Foster Dulles. Spiritual values could survive "only as long as men are ready and willing to take action to preserve them." A government was only righteous, Truman claimed, when its public acts "bore witness" to the fundamental fact of existence "that God is the way of truth and peace."[13]

That the presidency was a mission field for Truman, cut both ways for Zionists in the fall of 1947. On the one hand it nurtured the notion in Truman's mind that a homeland in Palestine was "justice" for the Jews and a fulfillment of their historical pilgrimage. But this understanding was subordinated to the postwar crusade of containing Communism. The difference between American and the Soviet Union, Truman was convinced, was "the difference between a people with a moral code and a people without one." Truman told a White House gathering, "We believe in God and Jesus Christ. We believe in keeping our engagements. We believe in telling the truth. There is a system of thought growing up in the world that believes in none of these things." For that reason, the United States needed to assume the leadership in the world that God intended it to assume in 1920. America's primary postwar obligation, Truman believed, was to "cooperate with other nations in creating peace and preserving peace in the world." That would allow the United States to fulfill its Godly mission in defending "spiritual values and the moral code against the vast forces of evil that seek to destroy them."[14]

Truman's tendency to see a Christian mission for the United States in the postwar world meant he would avoid those initiatives, including support for a Jewish state in Palestine, if he perceived the policy would facilitate Soviet postwar expansionism. This awareness was at the heart of the State Department's continuing claim that partitioning Palestine would lead to civil war and welcome Soviet "meddling." As the U.N. General Assembly prepared to convene in September, 1947 with Palestine at the top of its agenda, Truman hoped to resolve the problem of Palestine while adding to the U.N.'s stature without permitting Soviet gains. The "very essence of religion" and the only hope for preserving the fragile postwar peace, Truman seemed convinced, was in making sure that the United Nations worked. Nurturing the growth and development of the infant organization was a fundamental goal of American foreign policy. The U.N. charter might not create "a new heaven and a new earth," he wrote the chairman of the National Council of Churches, but it would work to feed, clothe and house the poor of the world and in so doing, "fulfill Christ's command contained in the fifth, sixth and seventh chapters of the gospel of St. Matthew."[15]

THE COLD WAR COMES TO THE UNITED NATIONS

The weeks leading up to the partition vote were a time in which each of the interested parties to the Palestine dispute exerted a maximum effort to persuade world public opinion and Harry Truman on the salience of its cause. The opening of the U.N.'s fall session was preceded by a "United Nations Week" celebrated across America, an event extolling the virtues of the world body and recognizing it as "the chosen instrument of world public opinion." The General Assembly, wrote *New York Times* editor Anne O'Hare McCormick, "is the world's greatest sounding board and world sentiment is bigger than any of the big powers."[16]

The complexities of the widening public debate over the future of Palestine would put McCormick's simple statement to the test. It would take two-thirds of the United Nations' fifty-six voting members to pass either the majority or the minority reports on Palestine. Failure of either report to muster the votes would return the issue to committee, something Zionists were desperate to avoid. So the thrust of their fall offensive was to argue that world sentiment had already spoken through the majority report and that neither Arab threats nor British obfuscation should prevent other nations, most especially the United States, from embracing its findings.

The Zionist argument successfully exploited the high regard in which the American public held the United Nations. Public support in the United States for a body like the United Nations had been slow in coming, despite its careful cultivation by the U.S. State Department. Two years before the outbreak of World War II, only one American in four favored U.S. participation in any such organization. By the time America entered the war, the number had risen to one in three. By the end of the war, it was three in four. State Department planners saw the United Nations as an important tool in forging collective security and in enhancing American postwar world leadership. Leading up to the Dumbarton Oaks conference the State Department conducted a major media campaign designed to educate the public on the organization's practical necessity.[17]

The department's initiative was also an effort to link its tarnished reputation after the war with the bright prospects of an international organization officially dedicated to the promotion of peaceful relations among nations. Certain historians have pointed out that while the State Department talked a good line, the reality of its relationship with the United Nations was far more restrained. The department publicly associated itself with the U.N.'s idealistic internationalism, while seeking to solve world problems on the basis of national interests. John Foster Dulles, who was a delegate to the Dumbarton Oaks conference and a member of the U.S. delegation to the United Nations, summarized the attitude of the State Department when he warned that "yearning for a world of fellowship and love" needed to be backed up by U.S. military might if it was to prevent "the triumph of Russian power and ideology" in the postwar world.[18]

President Truman and Secretary of State George C. Marshall's message to the nation in advance of the U.N.'s consideration of Palestine was that administration policy would be governed by a determined commitment to make the organization work. Marshall told a nationwide broadcast audience that "support for the United Nations is the cornerstone of American foreign policy." The *New York Times'* editorial policy saw the situation similarly. The United Nations not only enjoyed the overwhelming support of Americans, it concluded, but had "the confidence of mankind."[19]

When Marshall spoke before the General Assembly to open its fall session, his position on Palestine carried a double meaning to the media. State Department veteran Dean Rusk believes Marshall wanted to find a solution in Palestine with which Jews and Arabs could live, without strengthening ties between Moscow and the Arab states. The press interpreted Marshall's statement that the U.S. government attached "very great weight" to the findings of the committee of inquiry as a clear indication that Washington was poised to endorse the majority report and partition. But privately, Marshall was giving members of the American delegation as well as the press a very different impression. "Adoption of the majority report," he warned them, "would mean very violent Arab reaction." Above all, the United States should avoid any appearance of leading the partition fight, for this would "actively arouse the Arabs," bringing about their "rapprochement with the Soviet Union."[20]

The makeup of the American delegation to the United Nations reinforced this ambiguity. Ambassador Warren Austin shared Marshall's reticence on the desirability of a Jewish state in Palestine. He did not see how it was possible to carve out of an area already too small for a state a still smaller state. Austin believed such a state would have to defend itself "with bayonets forever, until extinguished in blood." The Arabs, he was certain, would never be willing to have such a state "aimed at their heart." But other members of the delegation disagreed. And the press took Marshall's appointment of pro-partitionists Eleanor Roosevelt, John Hilldring and John Foster Dulles to the American U.N. team as an indication Washington would support the majority report.[21]

The *New York Times* was having a hard time understanding why Washington continued to hesitate before announcing its support for partition. Leading Congressional Republicans and Democrats were nearly uniform in their support of the majority report. Years of careful cultivation by American Zionists was now paying dividends. With the nation's leading papers and radio commentators on board, Abba Hillel Silver and his colleagues at the American Zionist Emergency Council considered it only a matter of time before Truman signed on.[22]

An explosion, however, of East-West animosity during the opening hours of the U.N. General Assembly vastly complicated Zionist plans. First, Marshall charged Yugoslavia, Bulgaria and Albania, without naming them, of having violated the U.N. charter in their "acts of aggression" against Greece. The Soviet response by Andrei Vishinsky, the country's deputy foreign minister, was made before the General Assembly on September 18. The *New York Times* considered Vishinsky's attack on "America's appetite for world domination" an unexpected sensation, "the vehemence of which left its listeners stunned and heartsick." Response in the American press was no less vituperative. The *New York Herald-Tribune* called Vishinsky's address "nihilistic" and the *Philadelphia Inquirer* charged it represented a "staggering blow" to hopes of cooperating with the Soviet bloc at the United Nations. That sentiment was echoed in the *St. Paul Pioneer Press*, which thought Vishinsky's speech "all but destroys what hope may have existed that Russia might yet come back within the community of world cooperation."[23]

The freezing in Cold War relations could not have come at a worse time for Zionists. Silver's public relations campaign had been counting on the ability of the Soviet Union and the United States not only to work together in behalf of the majority report but also to urge their allies to support it. Vishinsky's outburst, instead, rekindled the Cold War mentality of America's prestige press, which doubted the possibility the two nations could work together to lower tensions in the postwar world. The attitude was captured by the *Times'* Anne O'Hare McCormick who believed the United States was "up against a state of mind which regards every dissenter as an enemy."[24]

As the United Nations prepared to consider the work of its committee of inquiry, Zionists were forced to take another look at their position. The sudden souring of American-Soviet relations raised the possibility Washington might oppose partition simply because the Soviets supported it. Equally damaging was the opposition by Arab states to the partition plan and their widely publicized promise that passage of the majority report would mean war. Zionists saw Britain cultivating the public impression the Arabs would be swept into Russia's open arms if it came to that. Britain's September 26 statement at the United Nations refusing to impose any settlement on the region, confirmed the worrying impression in the media that only the United Nations could prevent Palestine from sliding into chaos if partition was voted.[25]

TRYING TO RECAST CONVENTIONAL WISDOM

The British announcement that it would not impose partition gave Loy Henderson, the State Department's chief of Near East Affairs, a pretext to urge Marshall to revise the partition scheme. Henderson told Marshall that it was the view "of nearly every member of the foreign service and the State Department" that American strategic interests would suffer when Palestine erupted into violence. Henderson's hope was that a carefully constructed media campaign might sensitize the American people to the dangerous consequences of partition while defeating Zionist claims that the United Nations was already committed to partition.[26]

Henderson's task was a formidable one. With only days remaining before the administration announced its position on the majority report, eighty-five percent of all Americans indicated their support for the United Nations. Eighty-two percent were agreeing with the administration's own line---that it was "very important" to make the United Nations a success. This meant opposition to the majority report could not be perceived as opposition to the United Nations if it was to be politically palatable. By emphasizing the "impracticability" of partition, Henderson hoped to have the force of public opinion on his side. Polling showed that three in four Americans by October, 1947 were convinced the Soviet Union was out to rule the world and to wipe out Christianity. At the same time, only three percent of all those surveyed said that they supported sending U.S. troops to Palestine to police partition.[27] The task for opponents of partition was to seize on these fears, constructing a conventional wisdom through the press, that emphasized the prospects of a Great Power collision over a partitioned Palestine.

The Arab states were making headlines that appeared to underline Henderson's warning. A representative of the Arab League told the media that partition meant war in the Middle East, "probably sooner than later." The warning was renewed four days later at a meeting in Baghdad of foreign ministers of the Arab states. On September 20, the political committee of the Arab League told the Associated Press in Cairo all Arabs realized "the dangers threatening Palestine" and would offer "every support and sacrifice." The Arab League's warning two days later was even darker. Its representative in London told Associated Press that Arabs would break "all economic and cultural ties" to the United States and Europe if they backed partition.[28]

Defense Secretary James V. Forrestal wanted the Truman administration to take the Arab threats seriously. He reiterated Henderson's assertion that America's strategic interests were clearly on the side of maintaining a free and uninterrupted flow of oil from the Middle East. Forrestal supported Henderson's assertion that the mass media needed to be used to make this point unavoidably clear to the American people. Truman, however, remained unconvinced. He still sought to reconcile Zionist aspirations with the strategic difficulties they might create. He suggested to New York Senator Robert Wagner that "partition of Palestine with economic union" of its Arab and Jewish communities "seemed the most practical way for the United Nations to go."[29]

Truman's sensitivity to public opinion and his natural sympathy for the Jewish state movement was now mitigated by his growing anger over AZEC pressure tactics. He told Wagner that as President he would not be bullied by letter writing campaigns and political threats. Such tactics, he warned, "only threatened the results Zionists sought." Truman observed in his *Memoirs* that, "I do not think that I ever had as much pressure and propaganda aimed at the White House as I had in this instance. The persistence of a few of the extreme Zionist leaders---actuated by political motives and engaging in political threats---disturbed and annoyed me." When a Chicago attorney wrote Truman demanding to know why his administration "preferred fascist Arab elements in opposition to the democractic loving Jewish people of Palestine," Truman blew up. He ordered his special assistant in minority affairs, David K. Niles, to answer the letter. "It is such drivel as this that makes anti-Semites," the President thundered. "I thought maybe that you had better answer it, because I might tell him what's good for him."[30]

The pressure on Truman was beginning to take its toll. On the eve of his administration's decision on partition, assistant press secretary Eben A. Ayers remembers coming into the Oval Office one Saturday morning to find the President asleep in his chair, with a pile of newspapers opened on the desk before him. "I feel like I could sleep til Monday," the usually upbeat Truman told him, "but I'm not about to do it." Zionists were in no mood to ease up. For Silver and AZEC "everything" was now at stake. A report by the *New York Times*' U.N. correspondent Thomas J. Hamilton that the Truman administration was "keeping an open mind" on its Palestine policy because of Arab threats, put the Zionists publicity mill into a panic. AZEC's executive director Harry Shapiro sent to the organization's 400 local chairmen a fact sheet challenging press reports that Arabs would "break with the West" if the United States supported partition. Local chairmen were to make the point that there was no substance to the Arab threats. Journalists and commentators needed to be aware that "these threats should not be taken at face value. Arabs have no army to be frightened of."[31]

Shapiro's initiative was designed to stem reports such as the one filed by H. V. Kaltenborn following the latter's "fact-finding mission" to Palestine. There the dean of America's network commentators had interviewed the Grand Mufti of Jerusalem, the Arab generally seen as leading the opposition to partition. Kaltenborn told his NBC listeners of the Mufti's charge that "six million Jews were dictating the political opinions of 135 million Americans who were not Jews." Kaltenborn replied that he told the Mufti "of the power of a militant minority in a democratic humanitarian country." The *New York Times*' Clifton Daniel had sharpened this image. Daniel reported that the Mufti's unexpected arrival at a strategy session of the Arab Higher Committee in Alia, Lebanon had "electrified the meeting." The Mufti's field commander, Fawzi el-Kuwukji, showed Daniel "a blotchy letter from a young recruit, written in blood," pledging death to the Zionists.[32]

Shapiro issued a release through AZEC's local councils designed to discredit the Mufti. It emphasized his collaboration with the Nazis during the war and demanded that the State Department release its file on him. Nationally syndicated columnist Drew Pearson cooperated by printing one of the documents in the Mufti's file that had been leaked to him by a State Department staffer. Mutual Radio's Cecil Brown amplified Pearson's charges. The Mufti and his nephew, Jama el-Husseini, were "political opportunists," Brown charged, who had been "pretty energetic in preventing democracy from getting root among the Arab people during the war." Their current opposition to partition and threat to align themselves with the Soviets was an attempt "at oil blackmail."[33]

This was the argument AZEC's ally, the Nation Associates, was making to U.N. Secretary General Trygve Lie. The organization, headed by Freda Kirchwey, publisher of *The Nation* magazine, had completed a seventy-five page study under the direction of Dr. Frank P. Graham, president of the University of North Carolina, discounting Arab warnings as "empty threats." The *New York Times* quoted Graham as saying the Arab states would not cancel their oil contracts with the West because the "feudal landlords" who ran those countries were "the sole beneficiaries of those enormous royalties." Kirchwey, born a Gentile, had converted to Zionism after a 1918 interview with Chaim Weizmann, which was one of her first assignments as "subeditor" for the eminently liberal *Nation*. Her infatuation with a plan to return Jews to Palestine to create a "broadly democratic" regime took on new urgency during the war. As owner, publisher and editor of *The Nation*, she became an aggressive advocate of Jewish immigration to Palestine. She publicized reports of Jewish extermination in 1943 and 1944 and linked the Jewish struggle to the "struggle for democracy," with the Jews becoming a symbol "of what fascism is attempting to destroy." Her support for Zionist objectives deepened in the spring of 1946 after meetings with Golda Meir and Chaim Weizmann. Kirchwey was treated like a celebrity and given a grand tour of the country. Afterward she reported on its "promising socialist future."[34]

Kirchwey's advocacy of a Jewish homeland took many forms. *Nation* articles castigated the allies on their "collapse of sympathy and their failure of imagination" in helping the Jews. The Nation Associates funded studies and Kirchwey frequently lectured in behalf of a Jewish state. "Only the combination of sun and open air, of communal living and mutual help," she claimed, "can wipe out the effects of long years of suffering and mental and physical torture." Kirchwey submitted a memorandum to the United Nations in its review of the Palestine problem. Weizmann, who considered Kirchwey's activity "of great value" to the Zionist cause, used Kirchwey's study as part of his own presentation before that body.[35]

Truman, however, was less receptive to Kirchwey's unsolicited advice. *The Nation* had resisted the Truman administration's anti-Soviet line and rejected the Truman Doctrine, calling it a 1947 version of "Manifest Destiny." The struggles in Greece and Turkey were "indigenous to those countries," Kirchwey insisted. When Kirchwey through a friend, David Niles, attempted to make Truman personally aware of British plans to frustrate partition, Truman turned a deaf ear. When Kirchwey attacked those within the State Department aiding and abetting the British and attempted to relay this message through the Navy Department to Truman aboard his yacht, the *U.S.S. Williamsburg*, the acting clerk at the White House refused to send the cable. When Kirchwey then charged Truman with "capitulating to the Arabs," she succeeded in alienating Eleanor Roosevelt, one of *The Nation*'s strongest supporters within the Democratic Party. As a member of America's U.N. delegation and a leader in the fight for a Jewish state, Roosevelt did not think it appropriate "to be affiliated with any group making such irresponsible charges" against the President.[36]

If Kirchwey's two-fisted approach to Truman did AZEC little good, other approaches gave high visibility to Zionist claims that U.S. support for partition would strike a blow for postwar world order. The American Christian Palestine Committee and members of the U.S. Congress rushed wires and telegrams to President Truman and Secretary Marshall arguing America's leadership in the world required support for the United Nations and its majority report on Jewish statehood. This alone, they contended, would let the United Nations avoid the fate that befell the League of Nations.[37]

By October 5, the *New York Times* reckoned that the Truman administration could no longer delay its decision on partition. Edwin L. James reported that although Arab sources were privately indicating the Russian delegate would support their case, there was no indication of it. In the meantime, the British were unable to stop the flow of illegal immigrants to Palestine. "Americans should be able to understand the reason for their flight," a *Times* editorial argued. "The mental agony, the uncertainty, and the growing helplessness" of Europe's refugee population could no longer be ignored.[38]

The day before the United States announced its position, Zionists feared they had lost the battle. The Jewish Telegraph Agency reported that Arab states had lined up several nations within the British Commonwealth against the majority report. For the report to receive the necessary two-thirds majority, the United States and the Soviet Union would have to endorse it and convince their allies to do the same. Boris Smolar, the owner of the agency, worried that East-West tensions would prevent cooperation. Smolar's pessimism was captured in a *Detroit Jewish Chronicle* editorial cartoon. It showed Secretary Marshall embracing a robed Grand Mufti below a headline asking, "What's Going On?"[39]

The eagerly awaited statement by Herschel V. Johnson, deputy U.S. representative to the United Nations, was hardly a ringing endorsement of the majority plan. The *New York Times* trumpeted it in a three line, four column front page headline, while saving for the small print the conditions the United States attached to its position. The Arab state envisioned by the partition plan would have to be expanded; Britain would have to assume the responsibility of preparing the way for partition; and under no circumstances would the United States be drawn into providing troops to enforce a partition plan. Zionists acclaimed the decision as "American statesmanship at its best and noblest." Arabs saw it sewing "seeds of conflict." The British were "taken by surprise." The *New York Times* thought it "fair and reasonable."[40] Time would tell that it raised more questions than it answered.

ATTEMPTING TO UNDO WHAT'S DONE

Reaction to the American decision to support partition was immediate and far-reaching. Hamilton in the *Times* predicted that "delegates who had held back waiting for the great powers to show their hands" were now sure to act. When China quickly announced its support for partition, Arab resentment deepened. The Arab Higher Committee of Palestine released a statement to United Press calling the United States the Arabs' "number one enemy." It claimed it would look for friends elsewhere, including the Soviet bloc. But that was hardly possible when twenty-four hours later the Soviet Union announced its support for the partition plan. The decision took both British and American delegates by surprise. Previous to that statement, they had feared the Soviets would oppose partition to befriend the Arabs. Now they were certain the Russians had endorsed partition so the Red Army could enforce it.[41]

The American Zionist Emergency Council now felt it had "the best fighting chance ever" to bring a Jewish state into being but realized there were still problems. Silver pointed out that victory was hardly assured. He observed the administration endorsement was qualified, a point not lost on the *New York Times'* James Reston. Reston noted that Truman would never get the American people to go along with committing regular U.S. troops to enforce partition and there was no indication he wanted to. That was the problem cited by Anne O'Hare McCormick in her "Abroad" column. Since the United States was insisting the British enforce partition, and London had already refused, it raised the "spectre of regional chaos" unless an international force was quickly organized.[42]

The Near East division of the State Department seized on this difficulty in attempting to reverse the administration's decision on partition. It warned that for any international force to be viable, it would have to contain American troops, and this meant there would be Soviet troops in Palestine as well. In a cable on October 17, Gordon P. Merriam, the chief of the division of Near Eastern Affairs, told Robert McClintock, an expert on U.N. affairs, that the department needed to "convince public opinion that the majority report is impossible, impracticable and dangerous." Loy Henderson was also taking this approach. He was convinced that once the public understood partition could not be enforced without putting the Red Army in Palestine, support for partition would evaporate. He urged the department to move matters along by putting out the story that Soviet undercover agents, posing as Jewish refugees, were already penetrating Palestine. They would serve, Henderson suggested it be pointed out, as a Soviet beachhead in the Near East.[43]

The *Times* resisted Henderson's intrigues. It continued to play partition as support for the United Nations and justice for the Jew. Hamilton reported that the initial excitement created by the Arabs' massing of troops near the frontiers of Palestine had subsided. He observed that "if both the United States and the Soviet Union really insist upon partition, that solution will almost inevitably be accepted." The *Times* editorial board was admittedly skeptical about American-Soviet cooperation in Palestine, but it held out the hope the region might yet "be removed from the zone of conflicting power politics."[44]

American Zionists were doing everything in their power to nurture just such an impression. AZEC's Eliahu Ben-Horin, joined by veteran Boston newspaper editor Frank Buxton, and members of the Anglo-American Committee of Inquiry, which had investigated the Palestine problem in 1946, sent an open letter to the *New York Times* declaring the emptiness of Arab threats. The State Department and Arab leadership, committee members charged, wanted the American media to believe partition would result in war when the Arab states were in no position to fight one. That was also the message of Anglo-American Commission member Richard Crossman and former undersecretary of state Sumner Welles. Both men had extensive experience in journalism, Crossman in England, and Welles as a syndicated columnist in the United States. Each argued that cooperation between East and West over Palestine could serve as a turning point in Soviet-American relations.[45]

On November 2, 1947, Palestine fell into an eerie silence. It was the thirtieth anniversary of the Balfour Declaration, the proclamation of the British government during World War I to work for the establishment in Palestine of a national homeland for the Jewish people. The Arabs conducted a two hour general strike as a "symbolic protest." Meanwhile, the Jews of Palestine looked to Washington and New York, where all sides were now bracing for a final vote on the region's future.[46]

To the final minute the State Department agitated for a reversal of the U.S. position on partition. George F. Kennan of the Policy Planning Staff reported to Marshall that while the danger of imminent war with the Soviet Union had been "vastly exaggerated" by the press, there was no doubt "the world situation is still dominated" by the effort of the Russians "to extend their virtual dominance over all, or as much as possible, of the Eurasian land mass." Forrestal concurred and forcefully argued at a cabinet meeting on November 7 for an immediate reversal of the American stand. Marshall was persuaded. He now saw the Middle East as a "tinderbox" that would go up in flames if partition were pushed.[47]

Zionists attempted to smash the department initiative by discrediting the department in the national press. *Collier's* began printing a series of articles by former Treasury Secretary Henry Morgenthau charging that in 1942 the State Department "suppressed vital information" that would have led to the "liberation of Jews kept in Hitler's death camps." Morgenthau, who had taken over the reigns of the United Jewish Appeal's campaign to assist the displaced Jews of Europe, was convinced that the department through "sabotage, procrastination and hostility" had thwarted all efforts to rescue detainees during and since the war. His allegations were immediately picked up by the Jewish press, which urged "American public opinion" to "demand a Congressional investigation." The *New York Times* gave space to former Governor Herbert Lehman, who extended Morgenthau's theme. Lehman, who had served as director of the United Nations Relief and Rehabilitation Administration, claimed that only by facilitating "the immediate immigration of at least 150,000 European Jewish refugees into Palestine" could the United States begin to repay its debt to the victims of "persecution and hatred and bestiality."[48]

The State Department's charges and the Zionists' counter-charges helped to create the final frame in which America's Palestine policy was wrestled over in the days leading up to ultimate disposition of the matter in the U.N. General Assembly. It was an intense and bitter contest between rivals intimately aware of the other's determination to establish the conventional wisdom on Palestine. Foggy Bottom invoked the Red Menace; Zionists remembered the Holocaust. And each attempted to play to public opinion by claiming the United Nations was or ought to be on their side. Although Truman resented Zionist hardball tactics, he resented the State Department's cockiness even more. And in the days leading up to the partition vote this would become a major factor.

TRUMAN AND THE "STRIPED PANTS BOYS"

Truman did not appreciate what he considered the Near East desk's effort to overturn his Palestine policy. On November 10, Henderson, acting like a candidate on the campaign trail, complained to the Academy of Political Science in New York that partitioning Palestine "menaced world peace." Henderson's remarks, which were widely reported, included the charge that Moscow was launching "a diplomatic, press and radio campaign" to undermine American interests in the region. Once the Soviet Union was in possession of the Middle East, Henderson argued, it would be in a position to "decide the destinies of at least three continents and to cast a dark shadow over the whole world for many years to come."[49]

Shortly after Henderson's remarks, the State Department, without telling Truman, demanded proponents of the Jewish state make last minute territorial concessions or risk American support. The Zionist counter-attack was led by the President's Special Counsel Clark M. Clifford. A St. Louis lawyer who had entered White House service as Assistant Naval Aide, Clifford had under the sponsorship of Roosevelt and Truman speechwriter Judge Sam Rosenman, risen to the post of legal aide and political confidant of the President. He shared Truman's wariness in dealings with the State Department and was particularly irritated by Henderson's determination to link Communism with Zionism while going over the head of the President. "The department's attitude contained the inference," Clifford observed, "that the only correct position was the one they advanced." Clifford facilitated Chaim Weizmann's Oval Office meeting with Truman on November 19 in which Weizmann successfully argued that amputation of the Negev desert from the proposed Jewish state would deny it an outlet to the Red Sea and the trading routes to Asia and Africa. Truman was so perturbed that the department "was attempting to make an end run around him" that he picked up a telephone and personally ordered Hershel Johnson to stick by the majority report without killing amendments. Truman then requested General Hilldring of the U.N. delegation report to him directly of any further efforts to bypass the President's authority.[50]

Truman ordered Henderson to stop his efforts to overturn the administration's policy on Palestine. Henderson replied that "propaganda and demagogic talk in the press" had gotten the administration into a hole. He showed the President a report from the Central Intelligence Agency which supported his claim that Soviet provocateurs would likely manipulate partition "to provoke conflict in Palestine and great unrest throughout the Arab world." Henderson claimed, in light of these facts, he was only advocating "a more mature approach to the problem."[51]

Henderson, however, would lose this round. The President had made up his mind. Henderson brooded that it should have been Marshall and not he to have made this case to the President. But Marshall was tired of the whole affair. "I realized that Marshall was not happy with the role that history was calling him to play," Henderson later observed. "He said he would be grateful if I took up matters relating to Palestine with the undersecretary rather than him. Palestine had become, he said, more of an internal than an international problem and had to be faced in a way quite different than most foreign affairs problems." Without Marshall, Henderson believed the department would be unable to defeat Clifford and Niles in the battle for press and public opinion.[52]

What Henderson's calculations missed was Truman's allergy to Near East "careerists" who incessantly articulated the "British line" on Palestine. Truman found them arrogant, held them in contempt and was sure the sentiment was reciprocated. Truman was certain the department's senior members saw themselves as the true caretakers of the nation's foreign policy, and presidents, who came and went, as just temporary nuisances. He resented what he considered their patronizing attitude on Palestine. "The striped pants warned me, in effect, to watch my step," he told Stephen Wise, a veteran Zionist, shortly after Truman took office. "They thought I really didn't understand what was going on over there." Truman was convinced department "pros" openly resisted the "meddling" of elected executive leadership. He wrote his sister that he "had thought when General Marshall went over there he'd set them right," but Marshall had been too busy. He felt he was "hampered all the time by a lack of cooperation within the middle and lower levels of the State Department." Some of that opposition, he was convinced, stemmed from the department's anti-Semitism. "They were an anti-Semitic bunch over there," he observed, before adding with a touch of irony, "they put the Jews in the same category as Chinamen and Negroes."[53]

Truman's irritation with the State Department and its Near East desk also reflected his lingering prejudice against stylistic differences he saw as pretentious. State Department bureaucrats had "the social approach," he found, "the striped pants approach." They made a show of being experts. "An expert's a fellow who's afraid to learn anything new because then he won't be an expert anymore," Truman remarked. "The career fellows in the State Department thought they ought to make policy, but as long as I was President, I'd see to it that I made policy. Their job was to carry it out."[54]

Truman's colleagues at the State Department suggest that Truman may have been speaking for the benefit of the historical record, and that in fact he gave wide latitude to the State Department on Palestine. State Department veteran Dean Acheson was convinced "Truman looked principally to the Department of State in determining foreign policy and---except where force was necessary---exclusively in carrying it out." That is what Acheson's successor as undersecretary, Robert Lovett, liked about Truman. "Roosevelt wanted to play every instrument in the band, and that's a good way to get a split lip." Truman, Lovett believed, respected the department's judgment. As Marshall's predecessor as Secretary of State James F. Byrnes put it, Truman realized department personnel were not "striped pants cookie pushers." They were seasoned professionals who carried out the President's foreign policy, and not their own.[55]

The collision of egos between Truman and certain staffers at the State Department served to make Henderson's and Forrestal's job of changing the President's mind on partition more difficult. The Armageddon that department analysts predicted if Palestine was partitioned seemed like hyperbole in light of American-Soviet cooperation on the question. The press had turned a deaf ear to department complaints that allowing Jews into Palestine would overrun the region with Communists or that partition would push the Arabs into Soviet arms. U.N. Secretary General Trygve Lie also promoted the majority report because he "badly needed an achievement for the United Nations that would give it some resonance in world opinion."[56] Lie and Zionists would have their way because public and press opinion made it easy for Truman to follow his emotional instincts in supporting a Jewish state.

THE VOTE

The final vote at the United Nations on partition was a cliffhanger. Even though the majority report was approved in committee days before the voting by a twenty-five to thirteen margin, there were seventeen abstentions, with the Philippines and Paraguay voting present. The *New York Times* reported that "a partition victory is near," but Zionists were not so certain. Silver ordered AZEC's local committees to mount a last ditch effort in the final hours of the fight. When word came that the Philippines, Haiti and Greece had "fallen away" from supporting the majority report, Silver urged public leaders and the masses alike "to converge on the government and induce the President to assert the authority of his administration on reluctant delegates."[57]

Thomas J. Hamilton, reporting from Flushing Meadow, described tension within the assembly hall and the corridors leading to it as "acute." Last minute switching on both sides had left proponents of partition "puzzled and doubting" they had enough votes to win. On the evening of November 27, with the final vote forty-eight hours away, Clifford discussed the matter with the Philippine Ambassador to the United Nations, Michael Elizalde. The following day, Clifford reported to the President and the White House staff that Philippine support for the majority report was likely. Hamilton's head count indicated the vote would be "very close" and might well depend on strenuous U.S. efforts "to win over the undecided."[58]

On the morning of November 29, the United States formally urged other nations to support its lead and approve the majority report. Hamilton reported that Haiti, which originally supported partition, and then opposed it, would vote with the majority. Paraguay would do the same. As Hamilton was filing his report, the President was boarding a special train, along with an entourage of 300 people who were going to Philadelphia to watch the Army-Navy football game. The President was told it appeared certain the United Nations would now vote for partition. Assistant Press Secretary Eben Ayers noted in his diary that the game in Philadelphia "hadn't been much of a match," certainly nothing compared to the high drama of Flushing Meadow. There, on a vote of thirty-three to thirteen with ten abstentions, the U.N. General Assembly approved the majority report partitioning Palestine into separate Jewish and Arab states, while calling upon the inhabitants of Palestine and the international community "to take such steps as may be necessary on their part to put this plan into effect."[59]

"Thanks be to God!" *The New Palestine* proclaimed in an editorial following announcement of the U.N. vote. After a wait of 1,877 years, on the sixteenth day of Kislev in the Jewish year 5708, the Jewish people were restored to their land. The state of New Judea, which Rome had destroyed in the year 70 of the Christian era would be reborn and its flag would fly next to the flags of other nations. "Nothing can now deny us our Zionist ideal!" the paper told its readers. "Victory at last!" Harry Shapiro wired the chairmen of AZEC's local emergency committees. A lifetime's dream had come true. The great moment in history had arrived, and they had helped bring it to pass. Now at last the Jewish people would have the opportunity to live in dignity and respect among other nations of the world. "While struggles and hardships remain ahead," Shapiro told them, "now has come a time to celebrate our achievement."[60]

The *New York Times* reported the decision in a three line, four column headline, above a story that described "the electric thrill of the atmosphere" that built up before the decision was announced. Newspapers and news agencies throughout the country reported their switchboards were jammed with calls from people seeking the latest information. The U.N. switchboard became so overloaded with calls that it blew a fuse and was knocked out of commission for thirty-four minutes. "On the floor," the *Times* reported, "delegates seemed well aware they were participating in a history-making occasion." When the votes were in, Jews on both sides of the Atlantic erupted in celebration. The *New York Times* saw the result as a vindication of the stand the United Nations had taken and suggested that if it had not been for the uncertainty of enforcement, the vote would have been even greater in support of Jewish statehood.[61]

Silver saw the vote in similar terms. He considered it a reflection of world public opinion which Zionists had assiduously built and finally canalized in support of the majority report. The result had not been all Zionists had hoped for, but it was "all that a committee representing the world was prepared to give us." And it was enough to end a history of "galuth," a period of dispersion and acute suffering for the Jewish people.[62]

The success of Zionist agitation, as Samuel Halperin has pointed out in his study of American Zionism, was that its message matched the pre-existing inclinations of a growing audience. It was an audience that had lived through the tragedy of the war, its aftermath and revelations of the Holocaust, as well as the continuing spectacle of hundreds of thousands of displaced persons living in detention camps throughout Europe. This created conditions in which public opinion could be mobilized to support what a majority of members within a U.N. committee had already gone on record as saying---that a settlement of the Palestine controversy necessarily needed to include a resolution of the displaced persons problem. Once that linkage was made and the United Nations appeared to be committing itself to partition, the force of American public opinion was mobilized to endorse the action.[63]

In the two generations since the partition vote, much scholarly attention has been directed at the political reasons behind President Truman's decision to support a Jewish homeland in Palestine.[64] Several Zionists have contributed to the notion that Truman acted to win Jewish votes.[65] What this crude arithmetic fails to take into account is the political climate in which the President reached his decision and the role the mass media played in helping to create that climate. When Henry Cabot Lodge backed a Jewish commonwealth in 1922, the *New York Times* charged him with political opportunism. But when Harry Truman announced his support for Jewish statehood in the fall of 1947, the *Times* considered his decision consistent with world public opinion. It was not simply that the *Times*, which as late as February, 1947 opposed a sovereign state based on a religious faith, had changed or even that world public opinion had changed but that Zionists had effectively exploited this change.

Zionists were greatly aided in their quest by the American mass media, which had been a place of bitter competition between Zionists and the State Department for many months. When the media failed to embrace Henderson's claim that partition equalled a Soviet victory, the department was unable to show how the United States could support the United Nations without supporting its partition plan. Truman, of course, was a major player at the table. He did not see the Soviet threat in Palestine as Henderson saw it, and this distinction allowed him to follow his natural instincts in the matter.

"The simple fact was that our policy in Palestine was an American policy," he wrote in his *Memoirs*, "rather than an Arab policy or a Jewish policy. It was American because it was based on the desire to see promises kept and human misery relieved."[66] That Truman later saw the decision over

Palestine within this frame of reference, rather than those argued by the British or the Arabs or the American diplomatic community, owed much to the power of interpretation as well as historical amnesia in the conduct of foreign policy and in the recollection of that conduct. For the struggle to define the conventional wisdom on Palestine was hardly over. A sudden deterioration in East-West relations would rewrite geopolitical logic for Truman and lead to his about face on Palestine, even though he refused to call it an about face then or afterwards. The freeze in American-Soviet relations created conditions made to order for State Department opponents of partition. They had long been proficient in the language of the Cold War, and suddenly the international temperature suited them. They saw their opportunity, seized it, and to the horror of Zionists, seemed to bring the mass media and Truman along with them.

NOTES

1. For an analysis of millenarian sentiment in the Southern Baptist Church see Hertzel Fishman, *American Protestantism and a Jewish State* (Detroit: Wayne State University, 1973), pp. 94-95. Also, Isidore S. Meyer, ed., *Early of Zionism in America* (New York: Arno Press, 1977), pp. 55-76. Ernest R. Sandeen, *The Roots of Fundamentalism: British and American Millenarianism, 1800-1930* (Chicago: University of Chicago, 1970), pp. 4-13. Moshe Davis, ed., *Christian Protagonists for Jewish Restoration* (New York: Arno Press, 1977), p. 2. Michael Pragai, *Faith and Fulfillment: Christians and the Return to the Promised Land* (London: Vallentine, Mitchel, 1985), pp. 10-15.

2. Zvi Ganin, *Truman, American Jewry and Israel, 1945-1948* (New York: Holmes and Meier, 1979), pp. 178-179. Michael J. Cohen, *Palestine to Israel: From Mandate to Independence* (New York: Frank Cass, 1988), pp. 215-216. Michael J. Cohen, *Truman and Israel* (Berkeley: University of California, 1990), pp. 275-281. Ian J. Bickerton, "President Truman's Recognition of Israel," *American Jewish Historical Quarterly* 58, 1968, p. 199. John Snetsinger, *Truman, the Jewish Vote and the Creation of the State of Israel* (Stanford: Hoover Institution Press, 1974), pp. 137-140. Robert Donovan, *Conflict and Crisis: The Presidency of Harry S. Truman, 1945-1948* (New York: W. W. Norton, 1977), pp. 386-387. Evan M. Wilson, *Decision on Palestine---How the U.S. Came to Recognize Israel* (Stanford: Hoover Instituion Press, 1979), pp. 137-138 and 149-154.

3. Ganin, pp. 141-142. Cohen, *Truman and Israel*, pp. 24, 82, 151 and 203. For background, see Geoffrey S. Smith, "Harry, We Hardly Knew You: Revisionism, Politics and Diplomacy, 1945-1954," *American Political Science Review* 70, 1976, pp. 560-583. Athan G. Theoharis, *The Truman Presidency: The Origins of the Imperial Presidency and the National Security State* (Stanfordville, N.Y.: Earl M. Coleman Publishers, 1979), introduction. Raymond G. O'Connor, "Harry S. Truman: New Dimensions of Power," in Eugene E. Robinson, ed., *Powers of the President in*

Foreign Affairs (San Francisco: Commonwealth Club of California, 1966), pp. 51-52. Robert Griffith, "Truman and the Historians: The Reconstruction of Postwar American History," *Wisconsin Magazine of History* 59, 1975, pp. 20-50. Donald R. McCoy, "Harry S. Truman: Personality, Politics and Presidency," *Presidential Studies Quarterly* 12, 1982, pp. 216-225.

4. Ira V. Brown, "Watchers for the Second Coming: The Millenarian Tradition in America," *Mississippi Valley Historical Review* 39, 1952, pp. 441-458. Lee M. Friedman, *Jewish Pioneers and Patriots* (New York: Macmillan, 1943), pp. 153-159. Alan Heimert, *Religion and the American Mind* (Cambridge: Harvard University, 1966), pp. 66-67. Moshe Davis, ed., *Israel: Its Role in Civilization* (New York: Harper, 1956), p. 252.

5. Meyer, pp. 56-58. Fishman, p. 18. Sandeen, p. 106. Davis, *Israel*, p. 256. Davis, *Protagonists*, pp. 2-4. David Rausch, *Zionism Within Early American Fundamentalism* (New York: Edwin Mellen Press, 1979), pp. 85-89.

6. Fishman, pp. 94-95. Rausch, pp. 89-97 and 128-129.

7. See Truman's letter to Bess Truman, dated July 12, 1945, in Robert H. Ferrell, *Dear Bess: The Letters from Harry to Bess Truman, 1910-1959* (New York: W. W. Norton, 1983), p. 517. Merlin Gustafson, "The Religion of a President," *Journal of Church and State* 10, 1968, p. 380. See also Truman's remarks before the nation's Baptists on January 21, 1948 in Papers of Harry S. Truman. White House Official Reporter. Working Papers. Public Statements of the President. Box 30. Harry S. Truman Library. Independence, Missouri.

8. Merle Miller, *Plain Speaking: An Oral Biography of Harry S. Truman* (New York: Putnam, 1973), pp. 214-215. Harry S. Truman, *Memoirs: Years of Trial and Hope* (Garden City: Doubleday, 1956), p. 132. Also, Clark M. Clifford, "Annals of Government: The Truman Years," in *The New Yorker*, March 25, 1991, p. 61. Clark M. Clifford, "Recognizing Israel," *American Heritage* 28, 1977, p. 11. And, letter from Harry S. Truman to Chaim Weizmann, dated November 29, 1948. Weizmann Archives. Rehovoth, Israel.

9. Letter from Harry to Bess Truman, dated June 22, 1911, in Ferrell, pp. 39 and 52.

10. Letters from Harry to Bess Truman, dated March 27, 1918; June 30, 1935; and August 30, 1940; in Ferrell, pp. 254, 366 and 443. See also, Oral History Interview: Sarah Peltzman, pp. 3-8. Harry S. Truman Library. Independence, Missouri. Letter from Harry to Bess Truman, dated February 23, 1918, in Ferrell, p. 246. Frank J. Adler, *Roots in a Moving Stream: The Centennial History of Congregation B'nai Jehudah of Kansas City, 1870-1970* (Kansas City: The Temple, Congregation B'nai Jehudah, 1972), pp. 198-203.

11. Adler, pp. 198-225. Cohen, *Truman and Israel*, pp. 10-17. Harry S. Truman, *Memoirs: Year of Decisions* (New York: Doubleday, 1955), p. 135. See also, Eddie Jacobson's interview with Jonathan Daniels, on September 27 and September 28, 1949, interview number 3466. Jonathan Daniels Papers. Southern Historical Collection. University of North Carolina. Chapel Hill, North Carolina.

12. Papers of Harry S. Truman. Official File. 204 Misc. Box 773. Folder 5. See also, Margaret Truman, *Harry S. Truman* (New York: William Morrow, 1973), p. 387. H. Truman, *Memoirs: Years of Trial and Hope*, p. 162. Also, Adler, p. 223.

13. Merlin Gustafson, "The Religion of a President," *Journal of Church and State* 10, 1968, pp. 379-387. Merlin Gustafson, "The Religious Role of the President," *Midwest Journal of Political Science* 4, 1970, pp. 708-709. Harry S. Truman, *Mr. Citizen* (New York: Bernard Geis Associates, 1953), p. 135. Also, Papers of Harry S. Truman. White House Official Reporter. Working Papers. Public Statements of the President. Box 30. This box contains notes of Truman's January 31, 1948 meeting with the nation's Baptists and his May 13, 1948 Rose Garden address to the Alumni Association of North American Colleges. See also, letter from Harry S. Truman to John Foster Dulles, chairman of the Committee on Peace, Federal Council of Churches, dated November 6, 1945, in File PPF 33. Harry S. Truman Library. Independence, Missouri. Also, see Truman's speech to Washington Pilgrimage of America Churchmen, given at the National City Christian Church, on September 28, 1951, in File PPF 200. Truman Library.

14. H. Truman, *Mr. Citizen*, p. 137. Frank McNaughton and Walter Hehmeyer, *This Man Truman* (New York: McGraw-Hill, 1945), pp. 178-179. See also, Truman's speech at the New York Presbyterian Church, on April 3, 1951, in File PPF 21. Truman Library.

15. See Truman's speech before the Federal Council of Churches, Columbus, Ohio, March 6, 1946, in PPF 200. Truman Library. Also, Letter from Harry Truman to Lem T. Jones, Chairman of the United Churchmen, United Council of Churches, dated October 5, 1951, in File PPF 5573. Truman Library.

16. *New York Times*, September 15, 1947, pp. 1 and 16.

17. The polls were conducted by the American Institute of Public Opinion and appear in Michael Leigh, *Mobilizing Consent: Public Opinion and American Foreign Policy, 1937-1947* (Westport: Greenwood Press, 1976), pp. 99-101 and 104-105.

18. *Ibid.*, pp. 101-104. Gabriel Kolko, *The Politics of War: World and U.S. Foreign Policy, 1943-1945* (New York: Random House, 1968), pp. 482-483. Ronald W. Pruessen, *John Foster Dulles: The Road to Power* (New York: Free Press, 1982), p. 290.

19. *New York Times*, January 1, 1948, p. 1; September 15, 1947, p. 3; and February 3, 1948, p. 24.

20. Letter from Dean Rusk to Clark Clifford, dated April 29, 1977, and made available to the author by Mr. Rusk. Also, *New York Times*, September 18, 1947, pp. 1 and 24. And, *Foreign Relations of the United States 1947*, Volume 5 (Washington: Government Printing Office, 1975), pp. 1147-1151.

21. *New York Herald-Tribune*, September 8, 1947, p. 1. Also, *New York Times*, September 25, 1947, pp. 1 and 6. John Hilldring, the State Department's assistant secretary for occupied areas, was appointed to the U.N. delegation at the urging of David K. Niles. Hilldring was sympathetic to the Zionist cause through his experience in the displaced persons camps, and Niles advocated his appointment to balance the advice American U.N. delegates were getting from Loy Henderson and George Wadsworth, the U.S. ambassador to Syria. See Memo from Niles to Truman, copied to Robert A. Lovett, dated August 6, 1947. Presidential Secretary File. Box 184. Truman Library.

22. *New York Times*, September 15, 1947, p. 4; September 22, 1947, p. 5; and September 25, 1947, pp. 1 and 6. *New York Herald-Tribune*, September 24, 1947,

pp. 3 and 5 and September 25, 1947, pp. 5 and 6. *Philadelphia Inquirer*, September 17, 1947, p. 4. Also, Correspondence. Minutes: AZEC. September 17, 1947. File 4-2. AZEC Files. The Temple. Cleveland, Ohio.

23. *New York Times*, September 15, 1947, pp. 3 and 16 and September 19, 1947, pp. 1 and 22. *New York Herald-Tribune*, September 19, 1947, p. 11. *Philadelphia Inquirer*, September 19, 1947, p. 14. *St. Paul Pioneer Press*, September 19, 1947, p. 9.

24. *New York Times*, September 20, 1947, p. 14.

25. *New York Times*, September 27, 1947, pp. 1 and 2.

26. *FRUS 1947*, 5, pp. 1153-1158. See also, Oral History Interview: Loy W. Henderson, p. 126. Truman Library.

27. Hazel Gaudet Erskine, "The Cold War: Report from the Polls," *Public Opinion Quarterly* 25, 1961, pp. 308-309. George H. Gallup, *The Gallup Poll: Public Opinion, 1935-1971* (New York: Random House, 1972), pp. 682 and 687.

28. *New York Times*, September 20, 1947, p. 10 and September 23, 1947, p. 1. *New York Herald-Tribune*, September 21, 1947, p. 24. The Grand Mufti's newspaper, *Al-Wahda*, published on September 22, 1947 indicates divisions within Arab ranks. On p. 1, the Mufti urges King Abdallah of Transjordan to stop all his talk of a Greater Syrian Kingdom under the King's leadership. The Mufti urged Abdallah to concentrate his energies on preventing the Jewish state from coming into existence.

29. Walter Millis, ed., *The Forrestal Diaries* (New York: Viking Press, 1951), p. 322, contains Forrestal's notes of September 29, 1947 cabinet meeting. See also, H. Truman, *Trial and Hope*, pp. 156-158.

30. H. Truman, *Trial and Hope*, pp. 158-160. Also, letter from Joseph J. Abbell to Harry Truman, dated August 19, 1947. Note from Truman to David K. Niles, dated August 23, 1947. Papers of David K. Niles. Civil Rights and Minorities. Jewish Affairs. Box 27. Folder 5. Truman Library.

31. Diary entry. November 15, 1947. Papers of Eben A. Ayers. Box 16. Folder 4. Truman Library. And, *New York Times*, September 25, 1947, p. 1. Memorandum titled, "Is There Any Substance to Arab Threats of a Break with the West?" Undated. File 1-4-17. AZEC Files. In the same folder, Harry Shapiro, AZEC's executive director, instructs local chapters to create the impression that Arab armies were "picturesque, but ill-trained and ill-equipped." See also, Correspondence. Minutes: AZEC. September 17, 1947. File 4-2. AZEC Files.

32. K. V. Kaltenborn Radio Scripts. September 15, 23 and 26, 1947. Also, October 1, 1947. Box 183. Folders 2 and 3. H. V. Kaltenborn Papers. State Historical Society of Wisconsin. Madison, Wisconsin. Also, *New York Times*, October 6, 1947, p. 4.

33. Correspondence. Minutes: AZEC. September 17, 1947. File 4-2. AZEC Files. Also, Cecil Brown Radio Scripts. September 29, 1947. Box 14. Folder 1. Cecil Brown Papers. State Historical Society of Wisconsin.

34. *New York Times*, October 6, 1947, p. 4. Also, Sara Alpern, *Freda Kirchwey: A Woman of the Nation* (Cambridge: Harvard University, 1987), pp. vii, 32, 139-140 and 196. *The Nation* 162, June 22, 1946, pp. 737-739.

35. Letter from Chaim Weizmann to Moshe Shertok, dated April 19, 1948, in Barnet Litvinoff, ed., *The Letters and Papers of Chaim Weizmann*, Volume 23

(Jerusalem: Israel Universities, 1980), p. 110.

36. *The Nation* 164, March 22, 1947, pp. 317-318; May 31, 1947, p. 647; and June 21, 1947, pp. 731-732. Also, letters from Kirchwey to David K. Niles, dated December 5, 1947 and February 27, 1948. Papers of David K. Niles. Israel File. Box 30. Folder 2. For Truman's irritation with Kirchwey, see correspondence of February 25, 1948 in Truman Papers. Official File. 204 Misc. Box 774. Folder 2. Truman Library. And, Alpern, p. 198.

37. *B'nai Brith Messenger* (Los Angeles), October 3, 1947, pp. 1 and 4. *The New Palestine*, September 26, 1947, p. 8. *The Jewish Advocate* (Boston), September 25, 1947, p. 8. Also, press release from the American Christian Palestine Committee, dated September 29, 1947. File 1-4-2. AZEC Files.

38. *New York Times*, October 5, 1947, Section E, pp. 3 and 8.

39. *Kansas City Jewish Chronicle*, October 19, 1947, p. 2. *Detroit Jewish Chronicle*, October 10, 1947, p. 2.

40. *New York Times*, October 12, 1947, pp. 1, 63, 64 and Section E, p. 8. Also, *The Sunday Times* (of London), October 12, 1947, p. 1.

41. *New York Times*, October 13, 1947, pp. 1 and 8. And, Henderson Oral History Interview, p. 126. Truman Library. Clark Clifford, "Factors Influencing President Truman's Decision to Support Partition and Recognize the State of Israel," a speech delivered to the American Historical Association, December 28, 1976, in Washington, D.C. and made available to the author by Mr. Clifford. See also, *FRUS 1947*, 5, pp. 1173-1180.

42. Correspondence. Minutes: AZEC. October 13, 1947. File 4-2. AZEC Files. *New York Times*, September 13, 1947, pp. 1 and 22.

43. Note from Merriam to McClintock, dated October 17, 1947. Robert McClintock Reference File. M1175. Roll 8. National Archives. McClintock appears to be dubious concerning Merriam's initiative. On the bottom of the note he has written: "Weekly Public Opinion Mail Analysis for October 13-17 states that of the 761 letters received by the department on Palestine, 726 support the UNSCOP report and only two protested it." See also, *FRUS 1947*, 5, pp. 1196-1198. And Henderson Oral History Interview, pp. 126-128.

44. *New York Times*, October 15, 1947, p. 26 and October 19, 1947, Section E, p. 4.

45. *New York Times*, October 14, 1947, p. 3.

46. *Palestine Post*, November 3, 1947, pp. 1, 3 and 14.

47. *Foreign Relations of the United States 1947*, Volume one (Washington: Government Printing Office, 1975), pp. 772-777. Also, Millis, p. 341, which includes Forrestal's notes of November 7, 1947 cabinet meeting.

48. *Collier's*, October 25, 1947, pp. 24-25. *Detriot Jewish Chronicle*, October 31, 1947, p. 4. *The Jewish Advocate* (Boston), November 6, 1947, p. 10. *Kansas City Jewish Chronicle*, October 31, 1947, p. 2. *B'nai Brith Messenger* (Los Angeles), October 31, 1947, p. 1. *New York Times*, November 4, 1947, p. 16.

49. Department of State, *Bulletin* 17, November 10, 1947.

50. Telegram from Shapiro to AZEC local committee chairmen, dated November 19, 1947. File 1-4-17. AZEC Files. Clifford, "Factors Influencing," pp. 8-9. Abba Eban, *An Autobiography* (New York: Random House, 1977), pp. 94-95.

Robert S. Allen and William V. Shannon, *The Truman Merry Go Round* (New York: Vanguard, 1950), p. 26.

51. Clifford, "Factors Influencing," p. 9. C.I.A. Report. "Review of the World Situation." National Security Council Meeting. November 19, 1947. Presidential Secretary File. Box 203. Truman Library. Henderson Oral History Interview, pp. 57 and 126-127.

52. Henderson Oral History Interview, pp. 130-131.

53. Miller, p. 214. Also, Truman Papers. Memoirs. Foreign Policy. Palestine. Post-Presidential. Truman Library. And, M. Truman, p. 389.

54. Miller, p. 216.

55. Dean Acheson, *Present at the Creation: My Years in the State Department* (New York: W. W. Norton, 1969), pp. 734-735. Oral History Interview: Robert A. Lovett, pp. 12-16. Truman Library. James F. Byrnes, *Speaking Frankly* (New York: Harper, 1947), p. 247.

56. Eban, pp. 90-91.

57. *New York Times*, November 26, 1947, pp. 1 and 4. Correspondence. Minutes: AZEC. December 11, 1947. File 4-2. AZEC Files.

58. Diary entry. November 28, 1947. Papers of Eben A. Ayers. Box 16. Folder 4. Ayers Papers. Truman Library. Eban, pp. 95-96. *New York Times*, November 27, 1947, pp. 1 and 14 and November 28, 1947, pp. 1 and 10.

59. *New York Times*, November 29, 1947, pp. 1 and 2. Also, Diary entries. November 28; November 29; and December 2, 1947. Ayers Papers. Box 16. Folder 4. Ayers Papers. Walter Laquer and Barry Rubin, eds., *The Arab-Israeli Reader: A Documentary History of the Middle East Conflict* (New York: Facts on File, 1985), pp. 113-122.

60. *The New Palestine*, November 30, 1947, p. 4. Also, telegram from Shapiro to local emergency committee chairmen, dated November 29, 1947. File 1-4-17. AZEC Files.

61. *New York Times*, November 29, 1947, p. 2 and November 30, 1947, p. 1 and Section E, p. 10. *New York Herald-Tribune*, November 29, 1947, p. 1. *Palestine Post*, December 1, 1947, pp. 1-4.

62. Correspondence. Minutes: AZEC. December 11, 1947. File 4-2. AZEC Files.

63. Samuel Halperin, *The Political World of American Zionism* (Detroit: Wayne State University, 1961), pp. 12-16.

64. Snetsinger, pp. 65-71. Wilson, pp. 51-56. Fred J. Khouri, *The Arab-Israeli Dilemma* (Syracuse: Syracuse University, 1968), chapter three. Robert P. Stevens, *American Zionism and U.S. Foreign Policy* (New York: Pageant Press, 1962), pp. 210-219. Frank E. Manuel, *The Realities of American-Palestinian Relations* (Washington: Public Affairs Press, 1949), pp. 275-300 and 358-361.

65. Letter from Emanuel Neumann to Rabbi Leon I. Feuer, dated June 28, 1965. Misc. File. American Jewish Archives. Cincinnati, Ohio. See also, letter from Feuer to Jacob R. Marcus, undated. Misc. File. American Jewish Archives.

66. Truman, *Trial and Hope*, pp. 156-157.

Five

War Scare Month and the Reversal on Partition, December 1947–March 1948

The winter of 1948 found a freeze in East-West relations that led to a warming in State Department prospects that a Jewish state in Palestine might yet be prevented. When NBC news reported on the evening of January 22, 1948 that "present Russian policy will lead inevitably to another world war," the Gallup Poll was showing that three in four Americans agreed with this assessment. The State Department exploited this vision of reality in March to reverse American policy on partition and apparently shatter the Zionist vision of a Jewish homeland on the eve of its realization.

The year-long linkage between a Jewish state in Palestine and the fear of Great Power fighting reached its climax during three days in March. President Truman's dramatic appearance on March 17 before a Joint Session of the U.S. Congress, in which he called for a return to the draft, was praised in the press as "one of the most important statements in American history." But his decision announced forty-eight hours later to abandon support for partitioning Palestine was widely panned as "the climax to a series of moves which has seldom been matched for ineptness in the handling of any international issue by an American administration."

Praise and scorn were linked in the mind of the media to what was commonly seen as the danger of imminent war with the Soviet Union and the need for America to be seen as morally courageous and militarily prepared to prevent that war from happening. Truman's apparent "boldness" in standing up to the Soviets now needed to be reconciled with his "lack of moral guts" in appeasing the Arabs. Truman's special counsel Clark Clifford fully understood the President's predicament. How could American leadership in preserving the fragile postwar peace be taken seriously, he told Truman, if it was perceived as "caving in to idle Arab threats."

An anxious and greatly attentive public combined with a mobilized press would make the State Department's March, 1948 reversal of the President's Palestine policy a Pyrrhic victory. Clearly, America's foreign policy "experts" defeated Zionists and their White House allies in reversing American policy on partition. But the triumph was short-lived and illusory. For it exposed the President and his administration to the long held doubt that he was up to the challenge of leading the Free World in the crisis it now faced. That this view was held, owed much to the department's fundamental failure to convince public opinion and the press that the switch on partition was not an act of diplomatic "cowardice," but "courage."

The State Department's winter-long offensive to change Harry Truman's mind on partition was greatly aided by escalating violence in Palestine and Zionist uncertainties and divisions over what to do about it. Zionists achieved their greatest propaganda success with the *Exodus*, when a dramatic news event focused international attention on Jewish homelessness and apparent helplessness. But when the Jewish underground used smuggled arms from America to meet violence with violence in Palestine, Zionist propaganda could no longer claim the moral high ground. These events amplified the State Department's argument that bloodshed in Palestine encouraged Soviet expansionism, threatened Western security interests and risked more Jewish lives. This logic, by March, 1948, proved persuasive to the President. In reluctantly pulling the plug on partition, he thought he was doing the right thing for reasons the American people could be made to understand. But as this chapter will show, Truman's strategy failed and that led to the making and unmaking of American Cold War policymaking in Palestine.

TRUMAN AND THE *TIMES*

The days following the U.N. vote to partition Palestine saw an intensification of Arab-Jewish violence in the region as well as efforts to shape the media's coverage of that violence. The competition to control press treatment of developments in Palestine can best be seen in the active courting of the *New York Times* by Zionists and members of the Truman administration. Each group considered the *Times* crucial to the construction of public opinion that sustained foreign policy initiatives.[1] The *Times* saw itself as the natural custodian of foreign policymaking, superintending the all important link between policymakers and the public and assuring public participation in decisions affecting the national destiny.[2]

Times editorial policy in the winter of 1948 was rooted in the conviction of its publisher and editors that the paper was more than a mere purveyor of the government's foreign policy initiatives; it was also a molder of the informed judgments of its readers. *New York Times* publisher Arthur

Hays Sulzberger viewed these readers as "intelligent Americans who desire information rather than entertainment" and who saw "in this critical period of our nation's history the need for responsible journalism" rooted in the time-tested values of Americanism.[3] The paper prided itself on its intimate contacts with members of the Truman administration, who fed the paper's appetite for exclusivity. Arthur Krock claimed Secretary of State George Marshall sought his advice on how to respond to President Truman's request that Marshall make a public statement indicating America's national security would not be compromised by the creation of a Jewish state in Palestine. The publisher's nephew and the paper's chief foreign correspondent, C. L. Sulzberger, had a similar experience with Truman on November 4, 1947. In a private Oval Office interview, Truman asked Sulzberger what he thought chances were of war with Russia. Sulzberger refused to commit himself. "I tried to keep him answering rather than asking questions," Sulzberger reported.[4]

The *Times'* editorial staff did not hold Truman in particularly high regard. Sulzberger found him "very sincere and quite self-confident" while displaying "a rather rural knowledge of the world." Sulzberger saw Truman's understanding of Soviet tactics in the Middle East as "naive and simple-minded." Sulzberger agreed with the analysis of the State Department's Charles "Chip" Bohlen and the U.S. Ambassador to the Soviet Union, Bedell Smith, that "Russia would push hard for gains in every field" and that developments in the Middle East could lead to a Great Power confrontation throughout Europe, which would see the Russians on the English Channel within a week. That was essentially the same message Sulzberger got in his meeting with Truman, who pointed to a map of the Middle East, China and Germany and reportedly asked Sulzberger where World War III would begin.[5]

Times diplomatic correspondent James Reston shared Sulzberger's misgivings about Truman and believed the President failed to work with the press in winning support for his policies. Reston was continuously critical of Truman's failure to lead the administration's public relations fight to sell its postwar foreign policy. He thought Truman particularly ill-advised in allowing his administration to appear double-minded on Palestine. Reston argued that Truman should have forced his subordinates to accept his partition policy or resign. The appearance of Presidential indecision, Reston felt, allowed members of the media to keep the controversy alive by serving as a sounding board for those taking differing positions on the issue.[6]

Reston believed that Truman's problems with the press on Palestine were compounded by his presidential style. At news conferences, Reston observed, Truman "decapitated you and then grinned." That was also the opinion of the *Times* Washington correspondent Arthur Krock. Krock noted that Franklin Roosevelt gave the impression of wanting the news of his administration presented in the most favorable light, but Truman's attitude seemed to be "take it or leave it." One veteran White House watcher wrote that Truman came across as a "backwoods preacher laying down the law" to the press. This appearance of "arrogance and obstinacy alienated both the Congress and the public" and made more difficult Truman's efforts to win press approval for his policy switch on Palestine.[7]

If the *Times* editorial staff was sour on Truman, the sentiment was not reciprocated. Several reporters who covered the Truman White House were convinced the *Times* had an influence over the President unlike any other paper. W. McNeil Lowry, chief of the Washington bureau for Cox newspapers, believed Truman saw the *Times* as his most important channel of informed public opinion. Jack Bell, veteran Washington correspondent for Associated Press, thought "the *Times* was the Bible for the President" when it came to knowing the mood of the country and in reaching elite opinion within it. This impression created more than a little enmity between *Times* reporters and those from other papers that covered the White House. "The *New York Times* always had it easier," remembered Walter Trohan, executive director of the Washington bureau of perhaps Truman's least favorite newspaper, the *Chicago Tribune*.[8]

Members of Truman's White House press office confirm that Truman was particularly sensitive to what appeared in the pages of the *New York Times*. They indicate it was not unusual for them to receive a wakeup call at six or 6:15 in the morning, in which Truman would say, "What's this story in the *New York Times*, what is this all about, where did this come from?" Members of the President's staff observed that Truman always appeared "very anxious to know through the press what the people were interested in and wanted to know." Visitors to the President's office generally saw at least seven newspapers on the table behind his desk. Truman frequently admitted to a life-long devotion to newspaper reading, which, by his own estimate, involved the reading of "at least a dozen papers every day."[9]

Truman's morning staff meetings at eight routinely involved summaries of news items he may have missed. These were generally presented by George Elsey, the administrative assistant to White House counsel Clark Clifford. It was also at these meetings that President press secretary Charles Ross briefed Truman on problems that might arise in his dealings with reporters. Elsey suggests that on days of press conferences, Ross might bate Truman at these meetings with dozens of questions with other members of the President's staff joining in.[10]

Even when Truman travelled he was not far away from his newspapers. They would be flown to him by special messenger. One analyst of Truman's relationship to the press found that he read newspapers "extensively, intensively and regularly" because he had "a genuine respect for the general influence of the press on public thinking." This analyst found that during Truman's eight years in the Presidency, he made 644 significant references to the press in public and private talks. During his private talk with Sulzberger, Truman showed bitter indignation with the "sabotage press" that had failed to accurately portray his policies to the American people. Part of Truman's love-hate relationship with the press, Krock was convinced, grew from the complexity of the man. "His character curiously combined pettiness with greatest," Krock observed. He could make momentous decisions "with an iron backbone," yet did not suffer his critics well.[11]

"I think the general impression was that Mr. Truman was extremely hostile to his critics," Bell concluded. "He always had a chip on his shoulder." This impression, Elsey maintained, grew from Truman's tendency to sometimes behave as private citizen and not the President of the United States. Ross' biographer saw him as the greatest restraint on Truman's frequently impulsive attitudes toward the media. But Ross appeared to neither understand the demand of the press for a constant feeding of spot news nor the strategies for selling the President and his policies to the American people. Ross, who served for years as Washington bureau chief of the *St. Louis Post-Dispatch* and was a boyhood friend of Truman, shared his boss' distrust for some reporters and Truman's overall impatience with the press.[12]

Truman's criticism of the press, however, did not extend to the *New York Times*, which advocated the broad outlines of his foreign policy while leading the fight in the nation's press for quick passage of the European Recovery Program. It was a relationship of mutual benefits. Truman had in the *Times* a powerful ally in his effort to win public and Congressional support for the costly Marshall Plan. The *Times* had in Truman access to one of the chief architects of the postwar world. If the *Times*' editorial staff privately questioned Truman's management style, it most often supported him on the big issues of war and peace.[13]

The *Times*' cooperation was an outgrowth of the senior Sulzberger's sense that by articulating the President's foreign policy to its readership, the paper molded opinion in a manner required by successful policymaking. Sulzberger saw this function at the heart of what he called "responsible journalism." As developed by Lester Markel, the paper's Sunday editor, the *Times*' primary objective at the beginning of the Cold War was "to gain for American policies the support of public opinion at home and abroad." Reston similarly saw the role of the *Times* "in the present world struggle" was to help large numbers of people to see "the changes and convulsions in the world in which America must operate."[14]

In the matter of foreign policy there seemed little misunderstanding between Truman and the *Times*. Each realized the President was at the center of the stage, and the *Times* was at its edge. Initiative rested with the President. He alone would be held responsible for the results of American foreign policy.

Insofar as it was able, the *Times* would support the President's Cold War policy and his support for a partitioned Palestine. This partnership between the Truman and the *Times* in crafting postwar foreign policy was clearly not a collaboration of equal partners, but it was a collaboration nevertheless. Truman understood that no initiative of his could be sustained in the absence of public support.[15] For its part, the *Times* was prepared to endorse administration policy in supporting the United Nations and opposing Communist expansion because that was the paper's policy as well.

As for Palestine, the *Times*' long opposition to a Jewish state ended when the United Nations voted on November 29, 1947, to partition Palestine. When violence gained ground in Palestine in the weeks which followed, Truman changed his mind on partition, and American Zionists, watching developments with mounting horror, were doing everything in their power to make sure the *Times* did not change its editorial position as well.

TIMES REPORTING ON PALESTINE

Analysis of the *New York Times* in the fifty days following the U.N. vote to partition Palestine shows the degree to which developments in that region had moved to the center of the world stage. The *Times* ran eighteen separate stories on the partition issue the day after the General Assembly action, and 360 stories in the seven weeks that followed, an average of more than seven stories per day. On all but two of those days, events in Palestine, or related developments in Washington, New York, London or Moscow, commanded front page attention. The bulk of the *Times* reporting was done by Sam Pope Brewer, stationed in Palestine; Dana Adams Schmidt, who filed stories out of Beirut and Damascus; Gene Currivan, who reported out of Cairo; and Thomas Hamilton, who reported on developments at the United Nations. Their reporting in December and January was dominated by the violence in Palestine that greeted the U.N. decision to partition and by the efforts within that organization to put an end to the bloodletting. The effect of this coverage was to give fodder to those within the Truman administration seeking to reverse the President's position on partition.[16]

Defense Secretary James Forrestal initiated the Truman administration's reconsideration of its Palestine policy, and he used a *New York Times* editorial to do it. At a staff meeting with the President on the morning of December 1, Forrestal cited a *Times* editorial of the previous day that warned of "the wisdom of erecting a political state on the basis of a religious faith." Forrestal argued that American support for partition was "fraught with great danger for the future security of this country." What Forrestal failed to mention, and what Truman probably recognized if he followed his daily ritual of reading the *Times*, was that the paper had actually endorsed the partition decision. While the *Times* reiterated its long held reservations about the efficacy of a Jewish state in the midst of an Arab population, it was prepared to yield to world public opinion as expressed in the two-thirds vote at the United Nations. The paper's position during the stormy winter of 1948 remained the same. The Security Council, it insisted, should be given the necessary means to enforce its decision if the credibility of the United Nations was to stand.[17]

The American Zionist Emergency Council welcomed the *Times'* editorial position but strongly objected to the way it reported events in Palestine. What raised Zionist ire was the *Times'* heavy reporting of casualty figures out of Palestine. They feared that it would create the impression that violence there was out of control and that partition could not be implemented without international military might. Some within AZEC were convinced that the *Times*, long an opponent of a Jewish state, was captive to "subtle British and Arab propaganda" advanced by the State Department. AZEC's executive committee feared that a continuation of the *Times* preoccupation with Palestinian violence would "stalemate the situation" and lead to a reversal in America's partition stand.[18]

By the second week in December, casualties in Palestine rose to over 200, with the *Times* reporting the predictions of Arab spokesmen that partition would lead to a holy war in the region. When Tel Aviv was attacked and Jerusalem was torn by rioting and arson, the *Times* reported that the Arabs seemed to be making good on their threat. Thereafter, *Times'* three column front page headlines reported that Palestine strife had widened, with Brewer reporting that much of the country was under the grip of "pillage, arson and assault. War cries were seen as rising in the surrounding Arab world," he added, "with bloodshed likely to spread throughout the region."[19]

Opponents of partition within the administration, led by Forrestal and Loy Henderson, head of the State Department's Near East desk, seized on the *Times* reports in an effort to change President Truman's mind on the wisdom of supporting a Jewish state in Palestine. The two men saw exploiting press attention to the deepening violence in Palestine as crucial to winning their case. The *Times* and other prestige papers, they reasoned, could now be made to see that the General Assembly action endorsing partition was only advisory and that for partition to take place it must be demonstrated to be "just and workable." These papers could succeed in creating a climate in public opinion, Forrestal and Henderson agreed, which would make it easier for Truman to reconsider his policy.[20]

Forrestal and Henderson were heartened by public opinion polls showing that while six in ten Americans followed the U.N. debate over partitioning Palestine, an even greater number, nine in ten, were aware of the violence in the region. Those polled by a margin of two to one sympathized more with the Jews than the Arabs in that conflict, but by a margin of three to one, Americans said they opposed sending American troops to the Middle East to police partition.[21] If the State Department was to reverse the trend in opinion supporting partition, it must show that enforcement required the stationing of American troops in Palestine.

To the extent that the *Times* concentrated on reporting the violence in Palestine it served the State Department's purpose in arguing that partition could not be imposed without force. But to the extent that the *Times* portrayed Palestine as a test case for the United Nations, in which member states were obligated to enforce the General Assembly action, it played into Zionist hands. Complicating the calculations of each side was the *Times* early determination to play the story of Palestine in the context of the Cold War. The paper's editors worried that while Communist expansion in Western Europe might have reached its outer limits in Western Europe, its goals in Palestine might be achieved without firing a shot. The paper's skepticism was only heightened when Soviet Deputy Foreign Minister Andrei Gromyko told it that "the Soviet Union has no direct interest or other interest in Palestine."[22]

C. L. Sulzberger, reporting from London, fed the paper's fears that Palestine might be next on the Kremlin's shopping list. Sulzberger's private meeting with Prime Minister Clement Attlee convinced him that Truman did not appreciate the danger of Soviet designs on the Near East. Attlee thought Truman a captive of Jewish interest groups and told Sulzberger that U.S. endorsement for partition would allow the Soviets to penetrate Palestine through a U.N. policing force. Sulzberger received the same warning in his private session with Foreign Secretary Ernest Bevin. Bevin was "mystified" by Truman's utter inability to lead the Free World at a time when the chances of a shooting war increased daily.[23]

"THE MOST NON-SENSICAL STORIES"

As the winter deepened and the violence in Palestine intensified, American Zionists found themselves divided and on the defensive, with AZEC's media specialist Eliahu Ben-Horin wondering what could be done to douse "the most non-sensical stories" daily appearing in the press. Casualties, which had risen to 200 by the second week in December, climbed to 300 killed by Christmas Day. The *Times* reported that violence was "random and indiscriminate." AZEC did not know how to stem such assertions. Its leader, Rabbi Abba Hillel Silver, was in Palestine and unable to coordinate an American media campaign. Some within AZEC believed reports of an emergency in Palestine would play to Arab propaganda and eventually lead not to U.N. enforcement but U.N. recision of its partition plan. Another bloc, headed by Benjamin Netanyahu, argued that the dangers now facing the Jews of Palestine could not be minimized. Netanyahu argued that if the Jews "could not now completely repel attacks of bands, how could it later face armies?" He urged the organization to immediately take the *Times* and other major papers into its confidence and urge the arming of Palestinian Jews and the U.N. policing of partition.[24]

While the AZEC executive committee waited for consultations with the Jewish Agency on how to proceed, factions within AZEC proceeded independently. Executive Director Harry Shapiro urged local committee chairmen to speak to editors of their towns' papers whose headlines "exaggerated the seriousness of the situation by suggesting the Arab world is in flames." Such reports had a negative impact on American public opinion, where in the coming months, Shapiro believed, "the fate of Palestine will be decided." The Jewish wire services, however, were reporting Netanyahu's line, which was picked up in the Jewish press. Lebanese and Syrian troops were reported massing on the Palestine border "for a possible invasion of the Holy Land," the Jewish Telegraph was reporting. Palcor reported that Jewish defense forces were "girding for an all-out attack." That was the message that Jewish readers were getting---that without immediate action by the United States, the "security of New Judea was at risk."[25]

Further complicating AZEC's handling of the crisis was the *Times* front page conviction that "hordes of Red Fifth Columnists" were exploiting the violence in Palestine. The *Times* cited authoritative British sources in claiming "hand-picked Communists or fellow travelers" with links to the Jewish underground were attempting to install a Communist state in Palestine. The Jewish Agency in Palestine immediately denied the story as "a malicious slander" and deplored the *Times'* willingness to unwittingly aid "a British smear campaign against Jewish refugees and the Zionist movement." Whitehall's strategy, the agency claimed, was designed to reverse American policy "by reversing American public opinion's support of partition."[26]

The *Times* continued to give front page play to the deteriorating situation in Palestine when New York City police and customs agents on January 4, 1948 seized thirty-two tons of explosives believed bound for Palestine. The *Times* reported the State Department and the Federal Bureau of Investigation were investigating those responsible for the shipments. The *Times'* fear that the Jewish underground, aided by American Jews, was pushing Palestine into the Communist camp escalated when federal agents seized 50,000 pounds of T.N.T. at a New Jersey farm and arrested eight men charged with plotting to ship the cargo to Palestine.[27]

AZEC and the Jewish press deeply resented the *Times'* suggestion that "Reds" aided by American Zionists were "moving on the Mediterranean." They argued that analysis pieces, filed by Drew Middleton in London, which spoke of "the historic tendency of the Russian Empire to push southward," only put the problems of Palestine in a false light. The Jewish press charged that "while most American newspapers have the good sense" to ignore "Red Menace" stories, the editors of the *Times* seemed determined "to smear the Zionist movement with red paint."[28]

The *Times* handling of the story, however, was soon reflected by several of the nation's leading commentators, along with the unsettling theme that a lack of patriotism by American Jews threatened Western vital security interests in Palestine. H. V. Kaltenborn told his NBC listeners that American Jews "bore the responsibility" for the gathering storm in the Eastern Mediterranean. Even AZEC ally Joseph Harsch of the *Christian Science Monitor* warned his CBS listeners that "losing Palestine would mean Russia could strangle American interests not only in the Mediterranean but throughout the Western world."[29]

These stories, embroidered by charges from the Arab Higher Committee in Palestine that the American Jewish community was prepared to see the Middle East go Communist to get its state in Palestine, played well to latent American anti-Semitism. During the years of World War II, more than one American in four described the Jew as less patriotic than other Americans. After the war, that statistic had hardly changed. Up until the war, Americans thought by a three to one margin that the persecution of Jews in Europe was either partly or entirely the Jews fault. At war's end, Americans by a four to one margin said that knowledge of the mass killings of Jews had not changed their attitudes toward Jews in the United States. Three in five still thought the German people should not be blamed for what had happened to the Jews. When asked what national, religious or racial group within the United States posed the greatest threat to the country, respondents chose Jews over any other group.[30]

American Jewish leaders contributed to this suspicion and received wide play in the *New York Times* in doing so. Lessing Rosenwald, president of the American Council for Judaism, charged that American Jews "should consider it their duty to state where their first loyalty lies." At a national conference to consider the impact of a Jewish state on American Jews, the *Times* quoted Baltimore Rabbi Morris S. Lazaron as calling for "an uncompromising fight to stem Jewish nationalism" and to oppose its program, which he considered "an effort to impose its judgment on all Jewish people and in doing so to attack the unity of the Jewish people."[31]

The Jewish press blamed Sulzberger's long opposition to a Jewish state for keeping the controversy over Jewish patriotism alive. It charged the *Times* was serving as an accomplice in a conspiracy hatched "by the bloody hand of Henderson" and the "skilled hands of the masters of Ten Downing Street" to overturn the will of the international community on partition. Joseph M. Proskauer, president of the American Jewish Committee, an organization long opposed to the creation of a Jewish state, wrote the *Times* an open letter, charging the paper fueled fears of those suspicious of Jewish motives. The country needed to know that "the Jews of America suffer from no political schizophrenia," the letter said. "We are not split personalities." American Jews were "first and foremost Americans, profoundly interested in developments in Palestine."[32]

PULLING BACK FROM PARTITION

During the third week in January, 1948, Zionists urged the Truman administration to arm the Jews of Palestine and to empower the United Nations to carry out partition. The President did not publicly retreat from his partition stand but reiterated his opposition to sending American troops to Palestine to police partition. The *Times'* Arthur Krock thought Truman's reticence stemmed from his awareness that America could not match Soviet manpower in the Eastern Mediterranean or anywhere in Europe. Truman's rapid demilitarization of U.S. forces after the war had been "the greatest mistake of his Presidency" and now he was paying for it. Krock writes that in a personal meeting with Truman, the President conceded that fact. Secretary of State Marshall told members of the Senate Foreign Relations Committee that the administration recognized "the way of life we have known is literally hanging in the balance." But Secretary of the Army Kenneth Royall's estimate was that it would take $2.25 billion and the immediate training of 160,000 troops if the United States was to field a force to match the Soviets.[33]

The *Times* viewed developments in Palestine with alarm. The paper's London correspondent Benjamin Welles reported that the British government had agreed to sell up to $25 million in arms to the Arab states, while the United States led an international embargo in arms sales to the Jews. Thomas Hamilton, reporting from Lake Success, predicted that fear of Soviet expansionism would gut efforts within the U.N. Security Council to establish a police force to carry out partition. The paper charged in an editorial that "post war is not peace." It viewed Palestine "as a test case" of whether the will of the international community would be allowed to work or whether chaos would invite "Soviet imperialism."[34]

As Palestine's casualty total surpassed 1,000, the press fed on Truman's failure to clarify the administration's position. Press secretary Charles Ross had to defend the President from charges in *Look* magazine that Truman was failing to take the American people into his confidence in the construction of the country's foreign policy. Truman's press conference claim that his administration supported U.N. partition plan but would not commit troops to its enforcement exasperated many in the press and exposed their lingering doubts over Truman's ability to lead the nation. Increasingly, members of the press, both publicly and privately, began to blame Truman for what they saw as a drift in American foreign policy.[35]

Truman's reading of the fighting in Palestine seemed to substantiate State Department warnings that the Soviet Union would be the only winner when Palestine was partitioned. The Arab Higher Committee was committed to establishing a national administration over Palestine the day the British terminated their mandate. Various parts of Palestine, the U.S. representative in Jerusalem reported, would be annexed to bordering states. At a cabinet meeting, Marshall told Truman that arms were pouring into Palestine "at an increasing rate and young Arabs were undergoing rigid training." Forrestal warned that the conflict would inevitably curtail oil production in the region and without the oil "the Marshall Plan would not succeed." Forrestal told the President the United States "could not fight a war" or "even maintain the tempo of its peacetime economy without Middle Eastern oil." Forrestal not only asked Truman to see the problem in these terms, but to get these facts "to the people at once" so that they would support a new proposal postponing partition.[36]

Forrestal's case was greatly aided by a report from George F. Kennan, the Director of the Policy Planning Staff, who recommended the immediate abandonment of partition as "unworkable." Kennan charged that while Zionists had skillfully "manipulated" public sentiment in support of their objectives, continuation of the administration's current policy would only antagonize the Arabs. The Middle East was an area "of great strategic significance to the United States," Kennan argued, and Washington could not be seen "as declaring war on the Arab world."[37]

Kennan's claims were countered by U.N. Secretary General Trygve Lie. Anxious that the United Nations not appear impotent in its first postwar crisis, Lie publicly committed the United Nations to enforce "by whatever means are necessary" the recommendations of its Security Council. Lie's remarks were printed in their entirety by the *New York Times* and coincided with that paper's own conviction that the partitioning of Palestine should go forward because "it represents the will of the vast majority of the members of the United Nations." *Times* editors were not unaware that "the Mediterranean Sea, the ancient center of civilization" had become "a new strategic focus in the cold war between the United States and Russia." Whoever controlled the region, the *Times* was convinced, would "profoundly influence the entire global picture." That was why the moment called for a commitment by the President in letting the United Nations do its will in preserving the peace of Palestine.[38]

The demand that Truman do something to stem the violence in Palestine intensified in early February when Karel Lipiscky, the chairman of the United Nations Palestine Commission, formally asked the Security Council for an international force to implement the partition plan. The *Times* criticized British efforts to obstruct partition by vetoing the formation of any militia force, a move the *Times* saw "threatening the success of the United Nations." The British Colonial Office attempted to deny the charge even while continuing to secretly arm Arab security forces throughout Palestine. Eleanor Roosevelt, a member of the U.S. United Nations delegation and a strong backer of partition, was alarmed by the *Times* report. She told Truman she feared Britain was risking the fate of the United Nations to prolong its preeminency in the Eastern Mediterranean. Truman wrote back reassuringly that he was well aware of British/Soviet competition in that part of the world but that the United Nations had already taken the matter out of their hands.[39]

Privately, Truman was anything but certain about whether to proceed on partition. When George Wadsworth, the American Ambassador to Iraq, asked Truman, at Henderson's urging, to assure the Arab states the United States would not "act unilaterally" in sending troops to Palestine, Truman reportedly interrupted him "with a categorical ejaculation of concurrence." Henderson asked Dean Rusk, the Director of the State Department's Office of the United Nations, to persuade the President that unless he abandoned partition "general chaos will reign in Palestine" by mid-April. But Rusk believed that as long as the public perceived the future of the United Nations to be bound to the future of Palestine, it would be difficult for Truman to reverse course.[40]

Rusk's conclusion was also shared by Sumner Welles, the former Undersecretary of State, who by mid-February 1948, had begun a second career as author, syndicated columnist and radio commentator, as well as unofficial advisor to AZEC. Welles noted on February 17 that support for the United Nations had been "the cornerstone of American foreign policy since the war." Now, as that body faced its first real postwar test, "the United States was nowhere to be found." Welles warned that the United Nations would "fail" without U.S. leadership and "the establishment of a peaceful world order will vanish with it." Welles privately warned AZEC representatives that Truman's ultimate decision on Palestine would not be governed by "principles but perceptions of what was politically possible." That was why Welles urged AZEC's local councils "to keep the pressure up to deny the State Department the public support it sought."[41]

CZECHOSLOVAKIA AND WAR SCARE MONTH

It would be difficult to exaggerate the shock in the United States and in much of the West following the Communist takeover of Czechoslovakia on February 25, 1948, nor the impact this had on accelerating fears of war with the Soviet Union. The debate over America's Palestine policy became absorbed within this fearfulness, and opponents of partition successfully exploited it in changing Harry Truman's mind on the efficacy of a Jewish state in Palestine. What made the Communist takeover in Czechoslovakia so shocking to many Americans was that they were little prepared for it. By the time the media caught up to the story, a major war panic was beginning to build, a scare the media helped to promote.

The Czechoslovakian crisis was precipitated by Communist attempts in early February, 1948 to control police forces in and around Prague. Western diplomats on the scene worried that the country's fragile democratic coalition would not hold. Media attention, however, remained minimal, with troubles in the Eastern Mediterranean dominating international news. It was not until the day before President Eduard Benes surrendered the government to Communist control that the troubles in Czechoslovakia merited anything more than a one column headline in the *New York Times*. A *Times* editorial urged Benes and democratic forces within the country "to stand firm against Communist usurpation" and "totalitarianism of the Russian variety." When it became clear two days later that Benes had bowed to Communist pressure and that Communist forces under Premier Clement Gottwald had taken control of the country, reaction in the West was overwhelming. British and French leaders were reportedly "shocked" by what had happened and feared "for the future of Western Europe." A *Times* editorial warned that "the Communist seizure of Czechoslovakia rounded out a new Russian empire with a tremendous additional war potential."[42]

The war scare dominated the pages of the *New York Times*. James Reston believed the "Red threat would spur movement for a Western security pact." When Soviet leader Joseph Stalin "demanded" a defense agreement with Finland on February 27, the British were reported as certain the Soviet step was designed "to rule Finland." The *Times* now referred to the "Russian tide," comparing it to the "imperialistic mission" of Nazi Germany in 1939. Senate Foreign Relations Committee Chairman Arthur Vandenberg urged speedy passage of the Marshall Plan "to avert a Third World War." The *Times* saw the "Russo-Communist steamroller driving ruthlessly across Eastern and Central Europe and a large part of Asia, crushing beneath it the last vestige of freedom."[43]

The death, either by suicide or murder, of Jan Masaryk, the non-Communist Czech foreign minister, provoked widespread moral revulsion in the West. Secretary of State Marshall argued that it showed "the reign of terror" the postwar world was in for. Former British Prime Minister Winston Churchill could see "the menace of war rolling toward the West." The United Nations became caught up in the controversy when the head of the Czechoslovak mission charged that Moscow had had a direct hand in installing the Communist regime in Prague. Italy, France and Palestine were seen as next on Moscow's shopping list.[44]

Defense Secretary Forrestal began a round of highly publicized meetings with the Joint Chiefs of Staff to plan the nation's war readiness. At the same time, he scheduled a series of meetings with representatives of the nation's news media to come up with a plan of voluntary censorship to prevent military secrets from falling into the hands of the enemy. The *Times* reluctantly endorsed the plan with Hanson Baldwin reporting that "the United States is clearly at war with Russia." Though First Amendment freedoms would have to be preserved, Baldwin suggested that circumstances might well warrant Justice Department and Federal Bureau of Investigation involvement in protecting national security from press leaks.[45]

Certain historians have argued that the Truman administration helped whip up a war scare during the winter of 1948 to create a climate which would dispose the Congress to support its European Recovery Plan. But one might just as readily argue that national leaders on both sides of the Atlantic and their interested publics were genuinely worried by what they saw happening in Czechoslovakia and had reason to interpret events as a possible replay of 1939. Speculation in the media attempted to identify what would be the next act of Soviet aggression to plunge the world into war. Former Secretary of State James Byrnes and retiring General of the Army Dwight Eisenhower told reporters they believed if conflict came it would be as a result of developments in the Mediterranean.[46]

THE RETREAT FROM PARTITION

As an official silence settled over the White House, the Jewish press blamed "State Department termites" for America's uncertain policy on Palestine. "A totalitarian cell" had developed within the "inner sanctums" of the State Department, the Jewish press now charged. Its purpose was to "brazenly circumvent every effort by the American people and the Truman administration to help the Jews of Palestine." The angry reaction followed weeks of bloodletting in Palestine producing more than three thousand casualties along with AZEC's reluctant assessment that prospects for a Jewish state were now in jeopardy. With the United Nations deadlocked over a plan to enforce its partition plan, the Arab Higher Committee boldly told the U.N. Secretary General that the only way to erect a Jewish state would be "to wipe out every Arab---man, woman and child."[47]

Washington's silence on the violence in Palestine convinced many in the media that a major policy reevaluation was underway. Mutual Radio's Cecil Brown regretted that the administration's Palestine policy "had become a prisoner of the Cold War" and predicted the President's fear of the Soviet Union would lead to a repudiation of the U.N.'s partition plan. Neither

Truman nor Marshall were doing anything to dispel the idea that a policy switch was coming. At separate February press conferences they refused to clarify the American position on Palestine.[48]

Formal reconsideration of the American policy had been underway since the middle of February and took on increased urgency as the death toll mounted. The Arab press was doing all it could to deepen the international impression that partition would be a very bloody business. Cairo newspapers made much of the Egyptian government's training of "volunteers" for the front and the granting of six month leaves for men and army officers prepared to fight for an Arab Palestine. Images of military preparedness began to dominate Arab newspapers. Within those pages, Arab governments competed with one another in self-praise for their support of the coming military campaign. Egyptian leaders claimed they had sent one million pounds, forty-six percent of the total raised, for the armed forces of Palestine. Arab snipers were photographed firing on Jewish targets from the walls of Jerusalem's Old City. The Western press quoted representatives of the Arab Higher Committee predicting "the extermination of the Zionists."[49]

When the Arab League announced that it would fight any U.N. police force sent to Palestine, a *New York Times* editorial urged the President to break his official silence and tell the Arab states "that they are challenging the authority, the prestige and the very right to exist of the United Nations." That was also the argument Truman's Special Counsel Clark Clifford was making. Clifford warned Truman that the media were now blaming the administration for not taking action in support of the United Nations. Truman, who had just received a report from the National Security Council indicating it would take 160,000 or more troops to enforce partition, told Clifford he had done everything but mobilize troops to signal his support for partition, and he was not about to do that.[50]

The Truman administration billed Ambassador Warren Austin's February 24 speech before the U.N. General Assembly as a clarification of its position on partition. That proved to be a mistake since the speech raised more questions than it answered concerning America's willingness to stand by the U.N.'s partition plan. The State Department hoped that the press would get the message "in plain English" that the United Nations lacked the enforcement powers to impose partition on belligerents. This view reflected Marshall's conviction that "Palestine was not ready for self-government." But Truman, who approved the outline of Austin's speech, warned that nothing the ambassador said should be construed in the press "as a recission on our part from the position we took in the General Assembly." The result was a double-minded message that half-sounded as though the administration was dumping the partition plan despite its pledge not to do so.[51]

Media criticism of the Austin speech was strident. James Reston, citing U.N. sources, predicted that if Austin's suggestion was followed, partition would never be enforced. The *Washington Star* criticized the President for his "lack of clarity and candor." No one could now be certain, the *Star* charged, whether American troops would be committed to Palestine. Joseph and Stewart Alsop, syndicated columnists who opposed partition, saw Truman as a "wriggling president" whose "indecision will certainly bring division at home, loss of face abroad and eventual use of force anyway." The *U.S. News and World Report* reflected the degree to which the administration initiative had failed to quiet its critics or console its friends. "The United States was going to have to pay the costs of enforcing peace in the end," it reported. Why had the administration "pretended it could evade the responsibility" now?[52]

Truman saw himself in a no win predicament. He wrote his long-time friend Eddie Jacobson, "the situation has been a headache for me for two and a half years. The Jews are so emotional and the Arabs are so difficult to talk with that it is almost impossible to get anything done. The two have expected a Big Stick approach on our part and have naturally been disappointed when we can't do that. I hope it will work out alright, but I have about come to the conclusion that the situation is not soluble as presently set up."[53]

What helped the President to finally make up his mind were reports from the State Department's Policy Planning Staff and the Central Intelligence Agency. They concluded that partition was unworkable and that continuing American support for it would open the region to Soviet penetration. As the evidence mounted, the State Department awaited Truman's decision and kept its cards close to its vest. Nothing was to be said publicly to indicate the reversal in policy that department veterans now considered only a matter of time. This action further frustrated media efforts to get at the administration's policy, and it enhanced the public image of an administration whose foreign policy was in a state of paralysis.[54]

Even members of the Truman administration recognized the veracity of press criticism and fretted over its possible effects. Special Counsel Clark Clifford told Truman it was "inconceivable" the United States would now back away from partition after publicly endorsing it only weeks before. Clifford did not see how the action could be defended in the nation's press. He feared that the official silence on partition had "eroded public confidence in the United Nations and the United States commitment to it." The definite impression in the press, he feared, was that "we have no foreign policy, that we do not know where we are going, that the President and the State Department are bewildered, and that the United States, instead of furnishing leadership in the world is drifting helplessly." Clifford's aide, George Elsey, who daily monitored press coverage for the White House, believed the *Washington Star* put it correctly when it observed the United States was now "in the position of having issued the partition decree and of having taken no steps to enforce it."[55]

Even the State Department was growing restless under the strain of press criticism. When the *New York Times* quoted legal experts at the U.N. Secretariat who claimed the Security Council did have the authority to partition Palestine by force, Dean Rusk's aide Robert McClintock feared that would only add "to the unfortunate public impression that the United States and the United Nations were at odds over its powers." Rusk was forced to agree. McClintock noted that the *New York Herald-Tribune* quoted U.N. Secretary General Trygve Lie claiming that Arab states opposed to partition were in violation of a U.N. order. McClintock asked Rusk how it would be possible for the United States not to be seen as aiding the violator.[56]

Truman never appreciated the unsolicited advice of what he called the "sabotage press," but his public silence on Palestine exposed him to such criticism. Duke Shoop, one of Truman least favorite reporters, noted in the March 14 *Boston Herald*, that "everyone in Washington is asking, where is President Truman getting such bad advice on Palestine?" Another Boston paper charged that what Truman now needed "was a good dose of moral guts!" The Alsops under the title, "Time Bomb," did a column charging "there is no American policy on Palestine." An editorial cartoon in the *Chicago Daily News* showed Palestine as a land mine drifting dangerously at sea. Daniel Bishop in the *St. Louis Star-Times* extended the metaphor. His cartoon showed a nervous Uncle Sam in a rudderless rowboat about to go over a treacherous falls marked "World War III."[57] Syndicated columnist Drew Pearson reported a conversation between Truman and *New York Post* publisher Ted Thackerey charging that Truman angrily pounded his Oval Office desk while "shouting that New York Jews were disloyal to the country." At Truman's press conference two days later, the President called Pearson "a liar out of the whole cloth" and further inflamed the situation.[58]

Truman understood the weakness of his own position and the consequences in remaining silent on Palestine much longer. After leaving office he observed that "the most dangerous course a President can follow in time of crisis is to defer making decisions until they are forced on him." Truman noted that when events get out of hand they "take control of the President, and he is compelled to overcome situations which he should have prevented." Truman acknowledged that when a President finds himself in that situation "he is no longer a leader but an improviser who is driven to action out of expediency or weakness."[59] And that was to clearly become Truman's fate when he finally acted to put the problem of Palestine behind him.

SEIZING DEFEAT FROM VICTORY

March's war scare and the controversy over Palestine reached their climax in the same moment, an historic coincidence of considerable consequence as the President prepared to deal with each crisis. While American diplomats sounded out the British on a plan calling for a U.N. trusteeship of Palestine to blunt Soviet penetration in the region, finishing touches were put on a March 17 speech the President would deliver before a joint session of the Congress. In the address, Truman called for a return to the draft to meet the "critical nature" of the challenge facing the United States. It was now clear, Truman announced, that the Soviet Union and its agents were "a growing menace dedicated to a ruthless course of action" that had already killed democracy in Czechoslovakia and threatened to do the same from Finland to the Eastern Mediterranean. Only by strengthening the nation's armed forces, Truman said, could the United States hope to prevent war.[60]

Truman's speech provoked an overwhelmingly positive reaction in the nation's media. It gave him the most favorable coverage he had received on any issue in months. Only twelve days before, Arthur Krock in the *New York Times* had speculated the rapid decline in the President's popularity might mean he would not seek another term. Following his speech, the *Times* devoted a three line, seven column front page headline reporting Truman's dramatic appearance before Congress and in an editorial praised the President "for his national call to action." Other elite papers were no less effusive. The *Los Angeles Times* saw it as the most effective speech Truman had ever made and "one of the most important statements of history." The *Atlanta Constitution* urged the Congress to meet the President's challenge. Even the *Kansas City Star*, never a Truman admirer, admitted he had made "a reasoned and effective plea to preserve peace by stopping Russian aggression." The paper thought Truman's plea involved risk, but observed, "failure to act involves even greater risk." The *New Orleans Times-Picayune* claimed to speak for the nation when it urged strong leadership in Washington to overcome "the pressure of menacing events and their threat to our national safety and free institutions."[61]

The day after his speech, as President Truman prepared to leave Washington for a long weekend away from the pressures of his office, he agreed to a request from his old friend, Eddie Jacobson, that he see Chaim Weizmann. Weizmann had been flown to Washington by the Jewish Agency in hopes his last minute intercession with the President might prevent a reversal of the administration's on partition. At their meeting in the Oval Office, Truman reassured Weizmann of his continuing support for partition and told him the following day Ambassador Austin would make a statement to the Security Council to that effect.[62] Thus mollified, Weizmann must have been shocked when he opened the evening newspapers the next day to discover the speech Austin made was regarded by the press as a "sellout" on partition in favor of a U.N. trusteeship over Palestine. Undoubtedly, Truman was surprised also, for reading it in the press is how he found out about it too.

In only two days, the President seized defeat from the jaws of victory. After being scolded by the media for his failure to make his intentions on Palestine clear to the American people, he had won a ringing endorsement for his decisive stand against what was widely perceived as a dangerous Soviet threat. The shift on Palestine, however, announced hastily by Austin at the United Nations, while Truman and Marshall were out of Washington, created a furor in the media, and plunged Truman into one of the darkest moments of his Presidency.

Truman knew that when a President failed to show initiative, the initiative would pass to others, and he would be forced to manage a crisis while perceived as an ineffectual leader. That is precisely how the media now portrayed the President following what it saw as the fiasco over Palestine. The *Times*, fresh from praising the President's "boldness" in dealing with the Soviets, now editorially rebuked his timidity with the Arabs and his moral abandonment of the United Nations.[63] The rest of the nation's prestige press was no less muted. They agreed with the assessment Clifford had given the President that the United States had "crossed the Rubicon" when it championed partition in November, 1947, and now there was no turning back.

The State Department had twin objectives at the beginning of the winter of 1948. The first was to reverse the American position on the position of Palestine, and the second was to modify public opinion enough to make the change stick. The department succeeded on the former count but, as events would show, not the latter. In winning the battle for Palestine during war scare month, the department would soon learn how completely it had lost the war.

NOTES

1. Meyer Berger, *The Story of the New York Times, 1851-1951* (New York: Simon and Schuster, 1951), see the foreward written by Arthur Hays Sulzberger, written in 1951, and pp. 474-476. Also, Lester Markel, *Public Opinion and Foreign Policy* (New York: Harper and Row, 1949), pp. 3 and 34-35. Oral History Interview: W. McNeil Lowry, p. 66. Oral History Interview: Jack Bell, p. 72. Both interviews are in the Harry S. Truman Library. Independence, Missouri. Francis H. Heller, *The Truman White House: The Administration of the President, 1945-1953* (Lawrence: Regents Press of Kansas, 1980), p. 146. Correspondence. Minutes: American Zionist Emergency Council. October 13, 1947. File 4-2. AZEC Files. The Temple. Cleveland, Ohio.

2. Bruce J. Evensen, "Surrogate State Department? *Times* Coverage of Palestine, 1948," *Journalism Quarterly* 67, 1990, pp. 391-400.

3. Markel, pp. 44-45. Also, James Reston, *The Artillery of the Press* (New York: Harper and Row, 1967), introduction. Berger, 473-476 and 527-529.

4. Arthur Krock, *Memoirs: Sixty Years on the Firing Line* (New York: Funk and Wagnalls, 1948), p. 214. Cyrus L. Sulzberger, *A Long Row of Candles* (New York: Macmillan, 1969), pp. 362-363.

5. C. Sulzberger, pp. 361-365.

6. James Reston, "The Number One Voice," in Markel, ed., pp. 74-75. And Reston, *Artillery*, p. 75.

7. Reston, *Artillery*, p. 59. Krock, pp. 181-182. Douglas Cater, *Fourth Branch of Government* (Boston: Houghton Mifflin, 1959), pp. 36 and 42. Also, Louis Liebovich, "Failed White House Press Relations in the Early Months of the Truman Administration," p. 17, a paper delivered at the Midwestern Journalism Historians Conference at the University of Illinois, on April 11, 1987.

8. Lowry Oral History Interview, pp. 65-66. Bell Oral History Interview, p. 72. Oral History Interview: Walter Trohan, p. 70. Harry S. Truman Library. Independence, Missouri.

9. Heller, pp. 120, 146 and 164. C. Sulzberger, p. 364. Also, Transcript. 124th Press Conference. October 17, 1948. Press Conference File. Box 62. Harry S. Truman Library. Independence, Missouri.

10. Foreign Relations: Palestine. George Elsey Papers. Box 59. Also, Oral History Interview: Eben A. Ayers, p. 37. Oral History Interview: George Elsey, p. 77. Harry S. Truman Library. Independence, Missouri.

11. Herbert Lee Williams, "Truman and the Press: April 12, 1945---January 30, 1953," unpublished Ph.D. dissertation, University of Missouri, 1954, pp. 28 and 492-502. Also, Reston in Markel, p. 70. Reston cites Truman's daily attention to the news ticker installed in the White House press room and his receiving scraps of information from it through the course of his day as expressions of Truman's interest in the news. In Sulzberger, p. 364, Truman mentions the *New York Daily News*, the *Washington Times-Herald*, the *Chicago Tribune* and the Hearst newspapers as out to "sabotage" his administration. See also, Krock, p. 221.

12. Bell Oral History Interview, p. 47. Elsey Oral History Interview, p. 34. Also, Ronald T. Farrar, *Reluctant Servant: The Story of Charles G. Ross* (Columbia: University of Missouri, 1969), pp. 236-244.

13. Krock, pp. 234 and 264.

14. Berger, p. 476. Markel, pp. 4-5. Reston, *Artillery*, introduction.

15. There seems to be little to suggest that Truman was being disingenuous when he told a gathering of the American Society of Newspaper Editors on April 17, 1948 that "you editors have as great an influence on the welfare of this country as any other set of men in the country." Public Statements of the President. Working Papers. White House Official Reporter. Box 30. Papers of Harry S. Truman. Truman Library.

16. The Palestine story appeared in the *New York Times* for fifty consecutive days following the U.N.'s November 29, 1947 vote to partition Palestine. On all but three of those days, there were three stories or more pertaining to the issue. What irritated AZEC about this coverage were "specials" to the *Times* in which more than

half of all assertions went unattributed. This contributed to AZEC's criticism that the *Times* was not backing up its charge of "chaos" in Palestine with competent authority.

17. Walter Millis, ed., *The Forrestal Diaries* (New York: Viking Press, 1951), p. 346, Forrestal's diary entry for December 1, 1947. See also, *New York Times*, December 1, 1947, Section E, p. 10. An editorial calling for U.N. enforcement of the partition scheme appears on January 13, 1948, p. 24, where Palestine is described as "a critical test case for the United Nations."

18. Correspondence. Minutes: American Zionist Emergency Council. January 6, 1948. File 4-2. AZEC Files.

19. *New York Times*, December 2, 1947, p. 10; December 3, 1947, p. 1; December 4, 1947, pp. 1 and 5; and December 5, 1947, p. 1.

20. *Foreign Relations of the United States, 1948*, Volume 5 (Washington: Government Printing Office, 1976), pp. 581-583. See also, Millis, p. 362, Forrestal's diary entry of January 29, 1948.

21. Charles Herbert Stember, *Jews in the Mind of America* (New York: Basic Books, 1966), chapter 8, "The Impact of Israel on American Attitudes," especially pp. 174-180.

22. The violence in Palestine dominates the *Times'* coverage throughout December, 1947, with this spotlight almost equally shared by reports on U.N. enforcement during the latter half of January, 1948. It is at this time that Thomas Hamilton begins to report on difficulties the U.N. Special Committee on Palestine was experiencing in carrying out the recommendation of the General Assembly. See *New York Times*, December 3, 1947, p. 4; December 4, 1947, p. 8; December 9, 1947, p. 15; December 11, 1947, p. 18; December 12, 1947, p. 3; December 14, 1947, Section E, p. 1; and December 18, 1947, p. 6.

23. Sulzberger, diary entries of December 4 and December 5, 1947, pp. 370-372.

24. Correspondence. Minutes: American Zionist Emergency Council. Meetings of December 11, 1947, January 6, 1948 and January 11, 1948. AZEC Files. See also, letter from Leo Sack to Abba Hillel Silver, dated December 9, 1947. Harold Manson File. AZEC Files. Also, *New York Times*, December 18, 1947, p. 4; December 20, 1947, p. 8; December 21, 1947, Section E, pp. 1 and 4; and December 25, 1947, p. 1.

This sense of violence gone out of control can also be seen in the thrust of radio coverage as well. See Clifton Utley Radio Script. December 23, 1947. Box 49. Folder 4. Clifton Utley Papers. Cecil Brown Radio Scripts. December 22, December 24, December 25, December 29 and December 31, 1947. Box 15. Folder 1. Cecil Brown Papers. H. V. Kaltenborn Radio Scripts. December 24 and December 31, 1947. Box 183. Folder 4. H. V. Kaltenborn Papers. All scripts can be found in the State Historical Society of Wisconsin. Madison, Wisconsin.

25. Harry Shapiro to Committee Chairmen of the American Zionist Emergency Council. December 15, 1947. File 4-17. AZEC Files. Also, *B'nai Brith Messenger* (Los Angeles), December 12, 1947, pp. 1-2. *The Jewish Chronicle* (Kansas City), December 19, 1947, p. 1. *Detroit Jewish Chronicle*, December 12, 1947, p. 2 and December 19, 1947, pp. 1-2. *The American Hebrew*, December 19, 1947, p. 6.

26. *New York Times*, January 1, 1948, p. 1 and January 2, 1948, p. 7.

27. *New York Times*, January 5, 1948, pp. 1 and 3; January 6, 1948, pp. 1 and 7; January 7, 1948, p. 5; and January 9, 1948, p. 1.

28. *B'nai Brith Messenger* (Los Angeles), January 9, 1948, p. 2. *New York Times*, January 9, 1948, pp. 1, 14, 15 and 20 and January 10, 1948, p. 1.

29. Joseph Harsch Radio Scripts. January 4 and January 9, 1948. Box 12. Folder 1. Joseph Harsch Papers. Also, H. V. Kaltenborn Radio Script. January 5, 1948. Box 184. Folder 1. All scripts available in the State Historical Society of Wisconsin.

30. Stember, pp. 128, 138, 143-144 and 215-216.

31. *New York Times*, January 18, 1948, p. 28.

32. *Kansas City Jewish Chronicle*, January 16, 1948, p. 2. *Detroit Jewish Chronicle*, January 16, 1948, p. 2. *The Jewish Advocate* (Boston), January 9, 1948, p. 2 and January 16, 1948, p. 2. *New York Times*, January 25, 1948, Section E, p. 5.

33. *New York Times*, January 12, 1948, p. 4. Krock, p. 234. Also, U.S. Congress. Senate. Committee on Foreign Relations. Hearings on S-2202. "European Recovery Program," part 1. Eightieth Congress. Second Session. 1948. pp. 10-16, 30-36 and 444-454. January 8 and January 14, 1948.

34. *New York Times*, January 13, 1948, pp. 1, 6 and 26.

35. *New York Times*, January 8, 1948, p. 4. Also, letter from Charles Ross to Felix Jager, editor, *Look* magazine, dated January 14, 1948. Correspondence File. Box 2. Papers of Charles G. Ross. Truman Library. Transcript. 133rd News Conference. January 15, 1948. Press Conference File. Box 63. Truman Library. Bell Oral History Interview, p. 36. Oral History Interview: Charles J. Greene, pp. 6-7. Oral History Interview: Carroll H. Kenworthy, pp. 12-15. Oral History Interview: Robert L. Riggs, pp. 14-15. Oral History Interview: Raymond P. Brandt, pp. 25-29. Each of these reporters of the Truman White House express misgivings about Truman's ability to mobilize consent behind foreign policy initiatives. They are particularly critical of his failure at press conferences to speak to the broader outlines of policy. All interviews available at the Truman Library.

36. *FRUS 1948*, Volume 5, p. 543. Also, Millis, p. 359, Forrestal's diary entry for January 16, 1948 of cabinet meetings on that day.

37. *FRUS 1948*, Volume 5, pp. 547-554.

38. *New York Times*, January 10, 1948, p. 4 and January 18, 1948, Section E, p. 5. The *Times'* editorial position also coincides with the attitude of the reporter who covered the Arab states from Damascus and Beirut. See Dana Adams Schmidt, *Armageddon in the Middle East* (New York: John Day, 1974), p. 198, where Schmidt cites the "long-standing Soviet interest in the Middle East" going back to the Russo-German Pact of 1939.

39. *New York Times*, February 1, 1948, Section E, p. 3 and February 8, 1948, Section E, p. 10. Also, first monthly report of the United Nations Palestine Commission to the President of the Security Council. January 30, 1948. Arthur Creech-Jones Papers. Box 31. File 3. The analysis of Arab security strength can be found on p. 78. Rhodes House Library. Oxford, England. See also, letter cable from Arthur Creech-Jones to Sir Alan Cunninham, dated February 3, 1948. Creech-Jones Papers. Box 60. File 2. Rhodes House Library. And, United Nations General Assembly. Document A/A.C. 21/7. January 30, 1948. Also, Margaret Truman, *Harry S. Truman*

(New York: William Morrow, 1973), p. 385.

40. Letter from Dean Rusk to the author, dated May 15, 1987. Also, letter from Loy Henderson to Dean Rusk, dated November 20, 1977. Box 11. Loy Henderson Papers. Manuscript Division. Library of Congress. Washington, D. C. And, *FRUS 1948*, Volume 5, pp. 592-598 and 602-603.

41. *New York Herald-Tribune*, February 17, 1948, p. 6 Also, letter from Sumner Welles to Benjamin Akzin, dated February 7, 1948. File 1-4-1. AZEC Files. For background, see Sumner Welles, *We Need Not Fail* (Boston: Houghton Mifflin, 1948), pp. 85-86.

42. *New York Times*, February 2, 1948, p. 2; February 8, 1948, p. 6; February 14, 1948, p. 1; February 23, 1948, p. 1; February 24, 1948, p. 24; and February 26, 1948, pp. 1 and 22.

43. *New York Times*, February 27, 1948, p. 1; February 28, 1948, p. 1; February 29, 1948, Section E, p. 10; March 2, 1948, p. 1; and March 3, 1948, p. 22.

44. *New York Times*, March 7, 1948, p. 18 and March 11, 1948, pp. 1, 5, 6, 9 and 17.

45. *New York Times*, March 2, 1948, p. 18; March 3, 1948, p. 4; March 6, 1948, p. 6; and March 7, 1948, p. 12.

46. For a summary of the Revisionist literature on Truman and his use of the media in constructing the Cold War, see Thomas G. Paterson, "Presidential Foreign Policy, Public Opinion, and Congress: The Truman Years," *Diplomatic History* 3, 1979, pp. 1 and 2. Also, John Lewis Gaddis, "The Emerging Post-Revisionist Synthesis on the Origins of the Cold War," *Diplomatic History* 7, 1983, pp. 172-175. Michael Leigh, *Mobilizing Consent: Public Opinion and American Foreign Policy, 1937-1947* (Westport, Conn.: Greenwood Press, 1976), introduction. For background, see Michael Wala, "Selling the Marshall Plan to Aid European Recovery," *Diplomatic History* 10, 1986, pp. 247-265. Thomas G. Paterson, *Soviet-American Confrontation: Postwar Reconstruction and the Origins of the Cold War* (Baltimore: Johns Hopkins, 1973), pp. 101-130. *New York Times*, February 26, 1948, p. 1 and March 14, 1948, p. 1.

47. *B'nai Brith Messenger* (Los Angeles), January 30, 1948, p. 2. Also, First Report to the Security Council. "The Problem of Security in Palestine." United Nations General Assembly. Document A/A.C. 21/9. February 16, 1948. Cable from Sir Alan Cunningham to Arthur Creech-Jones, dated February 4, 1948. Letter from Arab Higher Committee to Secretary General, dated February 6, 1948. Creech-Jones Papers. Box 31. File 3. Rhodes House Library.

48. Cecil Brown Radio Script. February 2, 1948. Brown Papers. Box 15. Folder 3. Also, Press conference summary by Robert McClintock. Palestine Reference File of Dean Rusk and Robert McClintock. M1175 National Archives. Washington, D. C. For background, see *FRUS 1948*, Volume 5, pp. 525-526. Transcripts. Press Secretary Files. Box 63. Truman Library.

49. Millis, pp. 371-372, Forrestal's diary entry of February 12, 1948. *Musamarat al-Jeib* (Cairo), February 2, 1948, p. 1. *Al-Ahram* (Cairo), February 11, 1948, p. 1. *Al-Masri* (Cairo), February 11, 1948, p. 1. *Al-Musawwar* (Cairo), February 20, 1948, p. 1.

50. *New York Times*, February 17, 1948, p. 24. Also, Eben Ayers diary entry of February 17, 1948. Papers of Eben A. Ayers. Box 16. Folder 4. Harry S. Truman

Library. Independence, Missouri. Harry S. Truman, *Memoirs: Years of Trial and Hope* (Garden City: Doubleday, 1956), p. 159. *FRUS 1948*, Volume 5, pp. 632-633.

51. *FRUS 1948*, Volume 5, pp. 640, 645 and 649.

52. *New York Times*, February 25, 1948, p. 1. *Washington Star*, February 25, 1948, p. 1. The Alsops' nationally syndicated column of February 25, 1948 and the *U.S. News and World Report* article appear in the George Elsey Papers. Foreign Relations: Palestine. Box 60. Truman Library.

53. Letter from Harry Truman to Eddie Jacobson, dated February 25, 1948. Papers of Harry S. Truman. Official File. 204 Misc. Box 774. Folder 1. Truman Library.

54. *FRUS 1948*, Volume 5, pp. 665-667 and 674. See also, Oral History Interview: Loy Henderson, p. 130. Truman Library.

55. *FRUS 1948*, Volume 5, pp. 667, 674 and 690-695. And, Elsey Papers. Foreign Relations: Palestine. Box 60. Truman Library.

56. *FRUS 1948*, Volume 5, pp. 701 and 730.

57. Duke Shoop's article appears in the David K. Niles Papers. Israel File. Box 30. Folder 3. Truman Library. *The Jewish Advocate* (Boston), March 11, 1948, p. 2. The Alsops' March 12, 1948 column appears in the Elsey Papers. Foreign Relations: Palestine. Box 60. Truman Library. *Chicago Daily News*, February 20, 1948, p. 24. *St. Louis Star-Times*, March 12, 1948, p. 18.

58. See Eben Ayers diaries, pp. 38-39. Ayers Papers. Box 16. Folder 5. Truman Library. Also, M. Truman, p. 386. And, Transcripts. Presidential Secretary Files. Box 63. Truman Library.

59. Harry S. Truman, *Mr. Citizen* (New York: Bernard Geis, 1953), p. 261.

60. Department of State, *Bulletin* 18, March 17, 1948. *New York Times*, March 18, 1948, p. 4.

61. *New York Times*, March 7, 1948, Section E, p. 2. For an analysis of Truman's standing in the pre-election polls see Frederick Mosteller, Herbert Hyman, Philip J. McCarthy, Eli S. Marks and David B. Truman, *The Pre-Election Polls of 1948: Report to the Committee on Analysis of Pre-Election Polls and Forecasts* (New York: Social Science Research Council, 1949), pp. 18-27, 53, 80, 257 and 298-301. For a summary of the assumptions pollsters made that went into their calculations on presidential elections see Paul F. Lazarsfeld, Bernard Berelson and Hazel Gaudet, *The People's Choice: How the Voter Makes Up His Mind in a Presidential Campaign* (New York: Dell, Sloan and Pearce, 1944), pp. 2-3, 10, 20, 83-94 and 124-151.

Also, *New York Times*, March 18, 1948, pp. 1 and 26. *Los Angeles Times*, March 18, 1948, p. 22. *Atlanta Constitution*, March 18, 1948, p. 16. *Kansas City Star*, March 18, 1948, p. 16. *New Orleans Times-Picayune*, March 18, 1948, p. 16.

62. H. Truman, *Memoirs*, p. 162.

63. *New York Times*, March 21, 1948, Section E, p. 8.

Six

Reversing the Reversal: The Limits of Presidential Leadership and the Creation of Israel, March 1948–May 1948

The eight weeks between the U.S. reversal on partition and the establishment of Israel saw the culmination of a sixteen month struggle that began when the British government submitted the intractable problems of Palestine to world public opinion. In the months that followed, a variety of interested parties attempted to use the American mass media, and particularly the *New York Times*, to advance their cause. The media, reflecting the reticence of public opinion on a Jewish state in Palestine and public restlessness over deteriorating Soviet-American relations, took no leading role in the outcome of the debate then underway at the United Nations. Despite the *Times'* clarion call for the postwar press to take its role in foreign policymaking more seriously, *Times* editors embraced the administration line on Palestine, seeing the region as a site of Great Power competition, and later, as a test case for the infant United Nations.

The decision of a divided Truman administration to abandon partition in the middle of a major war scare reignited suspicion in Times Square and in the media generally over Truman's leadership qualities and his grasp of the presidency. At issue was the President's moral courage to insist that the will of the international community, as embodied in the U.N. partition plan, be carried out. If the President was seen appeasing the Arabs, critics charged, what message might that send to Moscow? The *Times* wondered whether Truman's untimely vacillation had killed his political future. It was among those papers that believed the firestorm following the switch on partition might lead to Truman's withdrawal from the presidential primaries.

In analyzing media coverage of the Truman administration's policy shift on Palestine along with the administration's hasty and eventually failed efforts at damage control, this chapter probes the limits of presidential leadership. The media could have accepted the administration's explanation for its reversal, but it did not. Truman could have stuck by his guns, despite press and public outrage, but he did not. Instead, he quietly reversed himself on reversal and allowed his aides to blame the brouhaha on "those striped pants conspirators" in the State Department.

The President liked to say that the buck stopped at his desk and that he took responsibility for the tough decisions of his presidency. But in the case of Palestine, Truman was not above distancing himself from an unpopular decision that he rationalized as the State Department's doing. After his presidency, Truman and his advisers liked to claim that Truman led, rather than allowed himself to be led, by the vagaries of public opinion in conducting the nation's foreign policy. But the public outcry over the policy switch on Palestine finds an embattled President greatly anxious over press coverage of the issue and eager to prevent what he feared would be the public perception and political consequences of that coverage.

March 19, 1948 was the date Truman finally lost control of his Palestine policy, largely because he could not contain press reaction to his decision to indefinitely postpone partition in favor of a U.N. trusteeship over Palestine. It was a reaction sustained by the widespread public impression that the United Nations would be crucial in preserving peace in the postwar world and that the United States had stabbed the organization in the back by abandoning its partition scheme. This notion was reinforced by leaders in Congress and representatives at the United Nations who interpreted the American action in the same way.

In the days leading up to Israeli independence, the media advanced and reflected the widely shared sense that the President had made the wrong decision on Palestine and for the wrong reasons. As a result, the media helped to focus public indignation on the President and helped to create the political climate within which he abruptly recognized, minutes after its announcement, the nation of Israel. The loser in that decision was the State Department, which had succeeded in reversing the American stand on partition, while failing to defeat how that action was publicly interpreted. It served as a painful lesson to department veterans and the President on the force of an aroused press when harnessed to a war-wary public at the beginning of the Cold War.

CUTTING THE PRESIDENT'S THROAT

The forty-eight hours following U.S. Ambassador Warren Austin's March 19 speech shows how badly the Truman administration had misread public and press sentiment on partition. The days that followed made even clearer the Zionist determination to create a state regardless of the American position. A surge of public and press support strengthened Zionist resolve to insist on immediate partition and nothing less. Zionist insistence, in turn, strengthened claims in the American press that a Jewish state would come into existence May 15, 1948, with or without the endorsement of President Truman or the State Department.

Truman appears to have been genuinely surprised and greatly irritated by the specifics of Austin's speech and the storm it provoked in the press. On his March 20 calendar he wrote, "The State Department pulled the rug out from under me today." Truman, in Key West, had approved Austin's statement but apparently did not read Austin's speech before it was given. "This morning I find the State Department has reversed my Palestine policy. The first I knew about it is what I see in the paper! Isn't that hell!" After promising Zionist leader Chaim Weizmann that there would be no reversal on partition, Truman realized he was now "in the position of a liar and a double-crosser." He brooded that there were "people on the third and fourth levels of the State Department who have always wanted to cut my throat" and that he had "never been so low in my life." Truman wrote his sister that career men at the State Department had "tried by every means at their command to upset my plans" and had "completely balled up the Palestine situation." Someday soon, he claimed, he would get even with those "striped pants conspirators."[1]

The White House press office thought the State Department had purposely embarrassed the President with the timing of Austin's speech coming just a day after Truman's conciliatory meeting with Weizmann. But since Truman told Weizmann the speech was coming, it appears more likely that Truman's Special Counsel Clark Clifford is right in claiming the department scrapped some important conditions Truman attached to trusteeship to make it appear the administration was repudiating partition. Truman's Press Secretary Charles Ross noted since "the reversal was without warning to the public" it placed Truman "in the most embarrassing position in his presidential career." The March 20 mood at the White House was "like a wake," the usually upbeat assistant press secretary Eben Ayers wrote in his diary. Newspapers all over the country had carried front page stories on the policy switch. The *New York Times* alone ran ten separate stories on the decision and gave wide play to Congressional critics who charged the action was "shameful" and "the most terrible sellout of the common man since Munich."[2]

Ayers wrote that "telegrams began coming in charging the President with betrayal and worse." The State Department was covering its tracks by telling the Associated Press the Austin speech was made "on the direct authority of the President." At his morning staff meeting on March 21, Truman denied the charge. "He seemed shocked and depressed," Ayers thought. Truman canceled his cabinet meeting for the following afternoon pending an investigation. "The President commented something about feeling blue," Ayers recorded. "The political effect may be terrificly bad." "What a dilemma," Ross wrote in his diary. To admit Truman was unaware of the details of Austin's speech would "make the President out to be both vacillating and ignorant." The goal now was "to salvage all we can from an impossible situation" and to avoid "the truth from getting into the newspaper or in radio speculation." Truman told Ross he was going to "fight it out," but there was no denying these were "dark political days."[3]

The White House staff and the State Department spent the next twenty-four hours in damage control and not a little finger pointing. Truman blamed the middle ranks of the State Department. Clifford fingered Secretary of State George Marshall. The President replied he could not believe that Marshall was responsible. Austin claimed the State Department had given him the go ahead on the speech, but Undersecretary Robert Lovett, like Marshall, was out of the city and could not be reached.[4] Dean Rusk, the director of the department's Office of U.N. Affairs, attempted to put out the fire by scheduling a background briefing for the press, which the White House abruptly cancelled. Instead, Ross and Ayers met with Rusk, along with Clifford and Matthew Connelly from the White House staff. Together they drafted a statement Marshall would give that evening from Los Angeles. The press was to be told that they were incorrect in charging the United States had changed its fundamental position on Palestine. "A temporary trusteeship," Marshall told reporters, "should be established in Palestine in order to maintain the peace." The trusteeship would be ended "as soon as a peaceful solution could be found."[5]

The administration's hasty efforts to curb press criticism only stimulated it. The *New York Times* was making much of the fact that the U.S. delegation to the United Nations was unaware of the policy shift until the very last minute. It portrayed an administration that was in disarray, that did not understand its own policy. Both the policy and Truman, its apparent architect, becomes objects of ridicule. Mutual Radio's Cecil Brown charged the switch "mortally wounded the United Nations and reflected America's gutless fear of Russia." This fear had led to "the abandoning of our moral position as the champion of democracy." Clifton Utley told his NBC listeners that the decision to abandon partition would not have the desired effect of keeping the Soviets out of Palestine and would lead directly to their capturing Italy. The *Washington Times-Herald* and the *Wall Street Journal* elaborated on this theme. The *Times-Herald* focused on the damage the decision had done to Truman's personal prestige. It concurred with the powerful chairman of the House Ways and Means Committee, North Carolina's Robert "Muley" Doughton, when he said, "Just as the Republicans were getting set to kill him off next November, up comes Truman and commits suicide on them." The *Journal* claimed the President had only himself to blame for not being more forthright. If the President had committed political suicide with his decision, the *Journal* observed, it was because he had not taken the American people into his confidence when deciding the future fate of Palestine.[6]

Similar sentiments can be found throughout the media in the days immediately following the controversial decision to support trusteeship. Marquis Childs, who had argued in his column for reconsideration of partition, now saw the administration's decision to do precisely that as a "revolving, perpetuating mistake." Childs saw the President's "lack of candor" taking the nation, American allies and "Truman's own administration" by surprise.[7] The media demanded the President explain his position to the American people. The *New York Times* quoted backers of the President saying they hoped he would clarify the confusion soon. The *Washington Post*, long worried about the "great disparity between Mr. Truman's experience and the responsibilities thrust upon him," claimed Truman needed to explain how trusteeship "made any sense" when it required more troops to enforce than partition.[8]

Press attacks were fed by those within the Truman administration who favored abandonment of the trusteeship scheme. As a result, leaks began popping up on the afternoon of March 21 faster than either the White House or its press office could plug them. At a morning briefing with reporters on March 22, Ross categorically denied Clifford was about to resign over the administration's Palestine policy and would be replaced by Truman speechwriter Sam Rosenman. Ross got Truman to cancel a cabinet meeting on the controversy seeing it as "a terrible mistake" likely to be "built up in the press as a crisis meeting." Then Marshall's secret testimony before an executive session of the Senate Foreign Relations Committee was leaked to the media and became front page news the following day in the *New York Times*, which reported the committee rejected Marshall's explanation of the incident.[9]

Behind the scenes Marshall told State Department veteran Charles E. Bohlen that the poor timing of the Austin speech opened the President up to what he was attempting most to avoid ---"a political blast from the press." Reports the department was getting from the field made matters worse. The department solicited the opinion of Middle East correspondents who were convinced "to a man that the Jews would set up their state in any event." Marshall was told that reporters were now convinced that in light of the administration decision "bloodshed will increase tremendously with Jews desperate and Arabs feeling new strength."[10]

A TRUMAN PRESS CONFERENCE

Truman's switch on Palestine led to charges he had victimized the United Nations, raised old questions concerning his fitness to be President and now new questions over whether he would be his party's nominee in the fall election. Not since 1912, wrote Arthur Krock in the March 28 Sunday edition of the *New York Times*, had an incumbent faced such opposition to a second term. In Krock's mind, Truman was nationally perceived as "an ineffectual leader." The bungling over Palestine, Krock observed, was the latest indication the President might be out of his depth. It convinced many that "Truman cannot succeed himself, whether or not he remains in the field."[11]

The *Times'* handling of the President's predicament focused on his failure to face up to the major challenges of foreign policy and the impact that failure was having on America and her allies. The *Times'* Thomas Hamilton, analyzing the week's developments at Lake Success, concluded that morale at the United Nations "sagged badly" following the U.S. switch on Palestine. U.N. Secretary General Trygve Lie deepened this impression when he told the *Times* the prestige of the United Nations had suffered as a result of the American about face on partition. The *Times* excoriated Truman for his failure to lead at a time of international crisis. His Palestine policy was "as badly bungled, as confused, and as inconsistent as any policy could be."[12]

Reporters of the period believe Truman understood the consequences to foreign policymaking if the perception persisted that he was unable to lead the nation. Raymond Brandt, the long-time chief of the Washington bureau for the *St. Louis Post-Dispatch*, said Truman tried to overcome this impression by "cultivating the working press, the reporters." Robert Nixon, a former employee of the State Department, who covered the Truman White House for International News Service, thought Truman went out of his way to get a good press from the country's three wire service reporters because he understood their interpretations of his actions would be transmitted nationally. Edward Folliard, the White House correspondent for the *Washington Post*, believed Truman knew he would never change the editorial position of publishers but hoped he might influence the way a reporter interpreted the news he covered.[13]

Truman's problem with Palestine, reporters noted, was that his leadership style, particularly his misuse of the press conference, did little to further his interpretation of events. A second problem was his staff. "Truman had no inborn finesse," observed Jack Bell, the Associated Press' chief political writer. Bell points out that Press Secretary Charles Ross "hadn't written a story in years" after a long tenure as news analyst on the *St. Louis Post-Dispatch*. As a result, Ross did not understand the demands of news reporters to interpret the significance of breaking events. "Everybody loved Charlie," Bell noted, "but he wasn't worth a damn in the practical aspects of the job." Gould Lincoln, reporter and columnist for the *Washington Star* and Charles Greene, Washington bureau chief of the *New York Daily News*, thought the same was true for Ross' aide Eben A. Ayers. "Ayers was terrible," Brandt agreed. "He had no access to anybody." Robert Riggs, chief Washington correspondent for the *Louisville Courier-Journal*, thought the failure of his staff contributed to Truman's problems with the press and left the impression "Truman was not always in command."[14]

Never was Truman's lack of command clearer than his March 25 press conference at which he attempted to sell the new policy on Palestine. Reporters covering the White House had long been disappointed with Truman's terseness at such meetings. "He very rarely used the press conference as much of a tool to get his ideas across to the public or the Congress," observed Carroll Kenworthy, editor of the foreign department at United Press. Robert Walsh, a reporter for the *Washington Star*, thought Truman "hurt his image" by "being so abrupt" with reporters. Truman's own press handlers thought the same thing. They realized that when the President and the press met "it was to do battle."[15]

The battle was joined, however, before the President ever stepped into the ring with reporters. A meeting between State Department personnel and White House aides, chaired by Truman, disintegrated into name calling. The department's Near East point man, Loy Henderson, who was the chief architect of the administration's switch on Palestine, found himself "cross examined" by Truman's Special Counsel Clark Clifford and Minority Affairs Aide David Niles. Henderson wanted a sustained publicity campaign to sell the new policy to the American people. Clifford's intense opposition to this idea, Henderson believed, "was designed to humiliate me and break me down in the presence of the President." Marshall suggested the situation might be diffused if the State Department could announce a truce in Palestine. Ayers wanted the President to announce one at his news conference. Marshall reportedly "glowered" at him and said negotiations between the warring factions would take another week.[16]

The President had Clifford prepare a statement he could give to the press "that would adapt the trusteeship proposal to partition." Clifford's staff worked through the night, but its draft hardly satisfied the 172 reporters who filed into the President's Oval Office and spilled out into the adjoining hallway to hear the President's explanation. It was the largest number the press office had ever seen. Truman read from Clifford's statement in a high voice. "Partition could not be carried out by peaceful means," the President told reporters, "and we could not impose this solution on the people of Palestine by the use of American troops." Since large scale fighting would be the "inevitable" result of partition now, trusteeship was an effort to "fill the vacuum" soon to be created by the end of the British mandate.[17]

What then followed was a "barrage from the press," which Truman handled in his typically abrupt fashion. The President was asked if his statement meant the United States was not prepared to send troops to Palestine. He answered, "Our policy is to back up the United Nations in the trusteeship by every means necessary." Did that mean the United States would commit forces to Palestine? "The first thing to do is to restore peace there," he answered, "to try and see if we can get an arrangement that will stop the bloodshed." But what if trusteeship had to be imposed by force? He did not believe that would be necessary. Then did that mean he still favored partition? "That is what I am trying to say here as plain as I can," he answered.[18]

The President's press conference of March 25 failed to reconcile how the United States could support the United Nations "to the limit" without a commitment to send troops to Palestine. Twice in the news conference Truman refused to make such a commitment, saying instead, "we will cross that bridge when we come to it."[19] But in the minds of many in the media that bridge had been crossed on November 29, 1947, when the United States voted with the majority to support the U.N. decision to partition Palestine. Truman's failure now to stand by a pledge he had made then spoke volumes to a press and public increasingly fearful that strong leadership alone would prevent a shooting war from starting with the Soviets.

A VACUUM OF LEADERSHIP

Truman's press conference failed to silence his critics on Palestine and created an even greater vacuum in leadership, which the media, seeing a good story, did everything to exploit. The story that emerged from the March 25 news conference was that the administration lacked a sense of direction or the nerve to carry its policy forward. Truman's failure to deal successfully with the implications of his policy enlarged the impression that he had none, or at minimum, was operating in the absence of principles that ought to have guided that policy. That was the message Secretary General Lie gave the *Times*. Lie considered the U.S. reversal a "rebuff to the United Nations" and felt so personally betrayed that he considered resigning his post.[20]

Truman's isolation was deepened when none of the major players in the Palestine controversy rallied to his cause. The *Times*' Thomas Hamilton reported that the President's new position had alienated both Jewish and Arab representatives. The British cabinet, after reading the text of Truman's press conference, refused to consider extending their costly stay in Palestine. The American Zionist Emergency Council's Abba Hillel Silver told the Security Council that meant the Jews would declare their state in Palestine on May 15, the date of the British withdrawal. The President, Clifford observed, found himself in the unenviable spot of defending a policy he did not fully support, before a public and press now hardening in their opposition to it. The *Times* could not believe Truman's miscalculation. Competent authority had recognized since November that the United Nations would have to back up its partition plan with the threat of force. Was the President, the *Times* asked, only discovering that now?[21]

The *Times*' greatest fear was that the U.S. position on Palestine had "pitifully weakened" the United Nations and isolated the United States at a time in which joint action by the world community was needed "to overcome the threat of war." Syndicated columnists Joseph and Stewart Alsop concurred. The unfolding of American policy on Palestine stood "as a chilling object lesson on how not to make foreign policy." *Time* saw it as a "comic opera performance which had done little credit to the greatest power on earth." Henderson still hoped to reverse this trend in opinion through a concerted media campaign designed to give Truman a "breathing space in implementing trusteeship." But Marshall was reluctant to push the department's cause in the press. He did not like the "politics of diplomacy" and told Henderson there was little reason to think the department could campaign for a policy the President obviously did not fully support.[22]

Marshall's reluctance to launch a publicity campaign in behalf of trusteeship exposed Henderson to an intense political heat the White House did nothing to lessen. Clifford, Ayers, Niles and White House aide Matthew Connelly were quick to blame Henderson for the mess Truman was now in. They encouraged a letter writing campaign and press reports demanding Henderson's resignation. Henderson was attacked in the Congress, amid demands he be transferred to another assignment. The Jewish press attempted to broaden the conspiracy by demanding the resignations of Henderson's "agents"---Defense Secretary James Forrestal and Chief of Staff Admiral William Leahy. AZEC stepped up its pressure on trusteeship through mass marches in scores of American cities and a national day of prayer. AZEC's executive noted "the widely perceived lack of leadership in Washington" had made work with America's churches, media, labor and veterans groups that much easier.[23]

By early April the White House was working to extricate Truman from a policy they increasingly blamed on Henderson. The strategy nearly backfired when the editor of the *New York Herald-Tribune* asked Ross to confirm its story that Marshall had "double-crossed the President on Palestine." While many elements in the story were accurate, it exposed the White House to one of its greatest fears, that pushing the break between Truman and the State Department too strongly would result in the resignation of Marshall. The White House reasoned that Marshall was the one indispensable man in the cabinet, not only because Truman deeply admired him but because his prestige as a great war hero gave administration Cold War policymaking a certain standing in the press. Ross succeeded in getting the *Herald-Tribune* to spike the story of a breach between Truman and Marshall, claiming that "publication would do great harm to national security."[24]

The President's Palestine policy, wrote *New York Times* editor Anne O'Hare McCormick, had provoked serious concern throughout the nation because it called into question the President's capacity to lead the West in a dangerous postwar world. The fall of Czechoslovakia to Communism, the

threat to Italy and France, the collapse of Britain and the crisis over the future
of Berlin, convinced McCormick that "the next few weeks and months will be
decisive in the history of the world." That was what worried the *Times*'
Washington correspondent Arthur Krock. The decline in Truman's prestige,
Krock warned, "weakened the effectiveness of American foreign policy." A
region by region analysis of the decline in Truman's personal appeal convinced
Krock that the mishandling of the administration's Palestine policy may have
made Truman unelectable. On the third anniversary of when Truman took
office, Krock observed the President had dissipitated "an atmosphere of
bipartisan good feeling" and seemed destined to serve out his term as a lame
duck.[25]

THE MOMENTUM OF EVENTS

By mid-April, the weight of public opposition to the American
reversal on partition all but ended administration efforts to carry out that
policy. Having been rebuffed by Marshall, Henderson described to
Undersecretary Robert Lovett a high profile media campaign designed to
resuscitate the trusteeship scheme. It would begin with President Truman's
announcement that he was going "to devote a major portion of his time and
energy to the Palestine problem." That would be followed by a highly
publicized conference with leaders of Congress and the Jewish community.
Henderson urged aggressive use "of the press, radio and public addresses" in
an offensive designed to "gain the support of the American people."[26]

Henderson's campaign was never launched. The White House was
instead trying to distance the President from the unpopular plan. The dilemma
the White House staff faced was that it could not publicly claim the policy
switch on Palestine was solely the State Department's idea without making it
appear Truman did not know what his own administration was doing. That
would play to press criticism that Truman could not exert leadership even
within his own administration and might risk a nasty rupture between Marshall
and Truman. Army Day speeches by the Army Chief of Staff, the Secretary
of the Air Force, the Chief of Naval Operations and the Commanding General
of the Strategic Air Command denouncing the Soviet Union as a menace to
basic American freedoms only heightened the call in the American media that
Truman made it unequivocally clear that the United States was prepared to use
force to support U.N. efforts to preserve peace.[27]

The administration embraced truce talks as a way of deflecting
criticism that its "moral vacillation" in Palestine threatened postwar peace. The
Times was unimpressed. What good was a truce, the paper wanted to know,
"if there was not the threat of force to back it up." *Times*' editors worried that
such "half measures" in Palestine would doom the United Nations to the same

fate that befell the League of Nations. The administration's persistence in pushing a truce exploded in its face. Marshall's off the record assurance to reporters on April 29 that Jewish and Arab representatives had agreed on thirteen of fourteen points needed in achieving a truce appeared in print the following day and brought an immediate denial from Moshe Shertok, representing the Jewish Agency. Shertok told reporters Marshall "seriously misunderstood the state of negotiations." The two sides, Shertok claimed, were still very far apart.[28]

Privately, Zionists were in no mood to negotiate. The Jewish army, which received its weapons through Czechoslovakia, began a major offensive during the third week of April. By the first of May the Haganah appeared well on its way to securing all the territory given the Jewish state under terms of the partition plan. While the British Foreign Office and the American State Department blamed one another for "the general collapse of Arab forces in Palestine," Shertok told a joint meeting of the American section of the Jewish Agency and the American Zionist Emergency Council that statehood was within their grasp. Shertok saw victory on the battlefield and resentment over America's abandonment of partition creating a surge in public opinion supporting immediate partition. Through the agency's Washington representative, Eliahu Epstein, the time seemed right to meet with U.S. officials to discuss recognition of the Jewish state. In the meantime, Shertok urged that public pressure be maintained to make certain there be no last minute surprises.[29]

Signals from the White House indicated there would be none. On April 30, President Truman appointed General John Hilldring as his assistant secretary of state for Palestinian affairs. Since Hilldring was outspoken in his support for partition, the press interpreted the appointment as Truman's final capitulation on trusteeship and the end of Henderson's control over Palestine policy. The British government reached the same conclusion, largely on the basis of reading American press reports. Forrestal, speaking privately to a reporter from *The Times* of London, confirmed the impression. The reporter told British officials in Washington that Forrestal feared "efforts to resist partition were doomed."[30]

That was the conclusion a United Nations Truce Commission reached after touring Palestine. It reported normal activities had come to a standstill as each side braced for all out war. Arab leaders were now prisoners of previous claims they made through the press. They privately told the State Department they were not anxious to fight but the force of public opinion within their own countries made it necessary. Prince Faisal of Saudi Arabia and Fawzi Bey, representing the Egyptian government, both reported there was little they could do to stem the appetite for war. Arab governments would have to do what they were going to do, or lose face. The U.S. representative in Jerusalem confirmed this impression. Both sides, he reported, had escalated the conflict through the media into a "war of nerves" that appeared to leave them little alternative but to act.[31]

With only days left before the formal end of the British mandate and the expected outbreak of major fighting, twenty-four American, British and Australian reporters prepared to cover a bit of history. Gene Currivan of the *New York Times*, joined by Kenneth Bilby of the *New York Herald-Tribune*, I. F. Stone, of New York's *P.M.* and the *Boston Globe*, Dan DeLuce and Carter Davidson of the Associated Press, Simon Eliav of United Press, Farnsworth Fowle of CBS, John Donovan of NBC, Arthur Holtzman of Mutual Broadcasting, Quentin Reynolds from *Collier's*, Robert Capa from *Life* magazine and Asher Schwartz from the Jewish Telegraph Agency were living out of the Pantiles Hotel in downtown Jerusalem, easily within reach of Jewish and Arab sniper fire. Currivan reported the Jewish victory at Jaffa forced hundreds of Arabs to flee and was a prelude to a major battle of the whole of the northern half of the country. Davidson Taylor, vice president of CBS, met with Jewish Agency officials to make certain that transmissions from the Holy Land would continue uninterrupted. He told Secretary Marshall that the Jewish army had assured him it would "track down and capture whatever facilities were needed" from the British.[32]

Daniel Bishop of the *St. Louis Star-Times* drew an editorial cartoon of a bomb marked "Palestine" on which little men of the United Nations were nervously perched. The end of the British mandate lit the bomb's fuse. Below, a cutline read, "The argument's about to end." The *Chicago Sun-Times* saw the same story. Before Jerusalem's ancient Wailing Wall, a soldier of peace slumped sadly, casting a diminishing shadow across the wall. The *New York Times* reported that "Judea" was certain to be attacked by outside Arab armies, and it asked what the United States and the world community was prepared to do about it.[33]

A LIGHT IN A REFRIGERATOR

In the hours leading up to the formal declaration of a Jewish state in Palestine and the beginning of a major war in the region, a *New York Times* editorial read, "At zero hour, Palestine will belong to the people of Palestine, while remaining on the heart and conscience of the world." The observation captures how completely the State Department failed in making the case that partition threatened vital security interests of the United States. H. V. Kaltenborn continued to feed NBC listeners Foggy Bottom's line that the Soviets "were already sending agents to Palestine in the guise of Jewish refugees" hoping "to further bedevil the situation there." But the possibility of Soviet designs on the region struck many in the media as all the more reason the United States should support the United Nations and its partition plan.[34]

Reluctantly, the State Department got the message by May 10 that there would be partition whether they liked it or not. The negotiations between the department and the White House in the four days leading to Israeli independence reflect the acute self-consciousness of both sides over how their conduct would be perceived in the press. At the United Nations, Ambassador Austin sought some face-saving proposal "to convince public opinion" that the administration had done all it could to avoid bloodshed. His deputy Philip C. Jessup told Dean Rusk he was worried the press was interpreting the breaking off of truce talks as a sign a deal had been struck with the Soviets for the immediate partitioning of Palestine. Rusk answered that the point to be made to the press was that the United States had never abandoned partition in the first place. The President had made up his mind, Rusk told Jessup, that a Jewish state "was going to get an open shot at establishing itself."[35]

Truman's public equivocation, however, continued. By May 6 he told reporters he hoped the Jews and Arabs of Palestine might yet agree to a truce. What he did not know was that Moshe Shertok, the Jewish Agency negotiator, had broken off talks in New York. He was returning to Palestine. The agency now saw no reason to compromise. The failure of Arab forces to defend their blockade of the Jerusalem-Tel Aviv Road broke their siege of Jewish positions in Jerusalem. It intensified public pressure on Truman to back the "winning side" in Palestine. Joseph Harsch ridiculed Arab readiness to fight. Arab propaganda had "cooked up" a holy war, he told his CBS listeners, as phoney as "a Cecil B. DeMille Hollywood production." The American media would be well-served to stop "falling for such stories." Walter Lippmann wrote that Washington should make its peace with a Jewish state to facilitate its "foothold" in the Eastern Mediterranean. Joseph Alsop came to the same conclusion. That is why he could not understand "the uncertainty of purpose and the lack of will" in the White House. Truman's vacillation, he wrote, "is impossible to defend."[36]

Looking back on the controversy, Loy Henderson thought Truman was caught between the forces of the press, Congress, public opinion and his own political party, as well as his worry "about the long term effects of supporting a Jewish state." Clark Clifford, in hindsight, agrees with this analysis and adds Truman's fear that public support for a Jewish state would "create a crisis with Marshall." Clifford notes that Truman "needed" Marshall as "the indispensable symbol of continuity" in an administration known for discontinuity in Cold War policymaking. Truman's position was so precarious, Clifford observes, that he feared the loss of Marshall "could virtually seal the dissolution" of his administration and "send the Western alliance into disarray."[37]

While Henderson had been the chief architect of the administration's Palestine policy, he was studious in getting Marshall's consent for department initiatives. Austin proposed the trusteeship plan under Marshall's direct authorization and Marshall's sense was that Truman had later opposed the plan because of the heat he was taking in the press. If Marshall thought Truman motivated by the media on Palestine, Marshall's opponents found him remarkably ill-informed on developments there. Part of the reason was that Marshall was out of the country for 24 days in April and left the handling of day to day policy decisions on Palestine to his subordinates. After a 75 minute meeting with Marshall, Shertok thought it "a pity" he knew so little of the facts of the case and was flabbergasted Marshall seemed totally unaware that neighboring Arab states had sent troops to Palestine to fight a Jewish state. On the eve of independence Clifford found it "surprising" that Marshall "had never heard" of David Ben-Gurion, the veteran leader of the Jewish Agency who was about to become the new nation's first Prime Minister.[38]

Marshall urged representatives of the Jewish Agency not to take their recent military successes too seriously. He feared that when the Jews declared their state they would be "wiped out" by the Arabs, who were "a warlike people." Then public opinion would "compel" the United States to intervene and "we would be dragged into a military adventure which had no logic in terms of American foreign policy." The agency's Abba Eban thought Marshall came across "like a blue cold light in a refrigerator, pragmatic, unsentimental, empirical." His message to organizers of a Jewish state was "if you survive, you survive; if you don't, it's not my business." Eban remembered, "You did feel a sort of chill."[39]

Clifford felt that chill on the afternoon of May 12. Truman had called State Department and White House officials to the Oval Office to consider a request by the Jewish Agency to recognize a Jewish state when it was formally declared on May 14. Truman favored the proposal and Clifford saw the meeting as Truman's way of determining Marshall's level of opposition to it. Marshall reiterated the warning he had made to Jewish authorities about "the grave risk they were running" in declaring their state. They should not, he told the President, "expect any help from us." Clifford objected, charging the President had been damaged by the State Department's "delaying tactics." He urged Truman to give prompt recognition to the Jewish state "before the Soviet Union did so" and to announce his decision the following day at a news conference. Marshall exploded. Clifford's advice, he charged, was based on "domestic political considerations." His face reddening in anger, he demanded to know why Clifford was even at the meeting. Truman reportedly replied, "Well, General, he's here because I asked him to be here."[40]

Undersecretary Lovett supported Marshall's position. Recognizing a Jewish state prematurely would be "buying a pig in a poke" and would be interpreted in the nation's press as a "very transparent attempt to win the Jewish vote." Marshall, repeating the department's logic, warned Truman that "the great dignity of the office of the President would be greatly diminished" in "a transparent dodge to win a few votes." Turning to Truman he said, "If you follow Clifford's advice and if I were to vote in the election, I would vote against you."[41]

Marshall's statement, which approximated a threat to resign, "stunned everyone in the room," and broke off the meeting with the question of recognition still up in the air. When Truman was asked the following day at his news conference whether the United States was preparing to recognize the Jewish state, he said only, "We will cross that bridge when we come to it." Marshall had been so agitated that he directed the official State Department record of the meeting contain a verbatim account of his remarks. Lovett, hoping to avoid a rupture between Marshall and the White House, interceded. He was convinced that once Marshall cooled off, he would be amenable to accepting the President's position. So was Ross, who thought that in the end Marshall would be "a good soldier" and support his President. Marshall's "self-righteousness" irritated Clifford. It reflected the State Department's characteristic arrogance that there was no "meritorious alternative" to their opposition to a Jewish state that did not contain "an unworthy motive."[42]

RECOGNIZING THE INEVITABLE

When Clifford met with Lovett over lunch on May 14, 1948, six hours before the declaration of an independent Jewish state would take effect, Marshall had still not agreed to early recognition. Lovett continued to press for a delay. Clifford, driven by a desire to "restore" the President's reputation "in support of a partitioned Palestine," told Lovett, "the President doesn't care whether Marshall supports recognition now or never. If you can simply get him to say that he will not oppose this, that's all the President would need." Clifford strengthened his case by showing Lovett a letter drafted by Eliahu Epstein of the Jewish Agency formally requesting recognition and a draft Presidential reply. Clifford had not mentioned to either Epstein or Lovett that the letter had been his idea and was intended to put pressure on Lovett to "deliver" Marshall. Their meeting ended with Lovett's promise to talk to Marshall again.[43]

Truman was heartened by Clifford's report. He saw Lovett "trying to lead Marshall and his colleagues out of the bunker a step at a time." As the two men met, half a world away in Jerusalem, the Associated Press' Carter Davidson lashed an American flag to a dented antennae atop the roof of the Pantiles Hotel, hoping to discourage crossfire between Arab snipers on the walls of the Old City and Haganah forces to the west. Twenty-four reporters, stationed at the hotel, reported 5,000 men from Iraq and 4,500 from Transjordan were preparing to link up with Arab Legion forces in Hebron, Ramallah and Nablus, as well as Syrian and Lebanese forces marching from the north to make their fight for the Holy Land. The radio was reporting the farewell address of British High Commissioner Sir Alan Cunningham. The British mandate over Palestine was ending after twenty-seven years, Cunningham announced. Palestine's future would be up to its inhabitants. Cunningham then boarded a cruiser in Haifa Bay and set sail for Cyprus, retracing the passage *Exodus* passengers had made ten months before.[44]

As Cunningham's yacht was leaving Palestine's territorial waters, members of the Jewish National Council and the world press gathered in Tel Aviv's Museum Hall, a small, stuffy auditorium, sweltering in the late spring heat to hear David Ben-Gurion proclaim the establishment of the State of Israel. The location of the ceremony had been kept a secret for fear of a terrorist attack. It was four o'clock local time, eight hours before the British mandate officially ended. The Jewish Agency decided to move up the announcement to ensure it was not prevented by war. Ralph Ellinger, an engineer radio station WMCA sent from New York to record the event, was so nervous he forgot to turn on his machine. The first three minutes of the address were missed. After the speech was completed, Ben-Gurion added a sentence "trusting in almighty God" for his American listeners.[45]

At four o'clock Washington time, Lovett called Clifford. "I have talked to the General," he told him. "He cannot support the President's position, but he has agreed he will not oppose it." Lovett asked that recognition be deferred until the United Nations adjourned its emergency meeting on Palestine at ten that evening. Clifford said he would check with the President, waited three minutes, and then called Lovett back saying delay was out of the question. At five forty-five Clifford called Rusk in New York and asked him to inform Austin that in fifteen minutes the White House was going to announce its recognition of Israel. After objecting, Rusk did. Austin was so "stunned by the news" he left the floor of the General Assembly, while in the midst of trying to drum up votes for a truce, and drove home without informing the American delegation that there had been a switch back to partition. Aides thought that he had "simply gone to the bathroom."[46]

One minute after six, Washington time, Associated Press moved a story filed by Carter Davidson in Jerusalem and Arieh Dissentchik and Ezriel Carlebach in Tel Aviv. Arab armies under the command of King Abdallah were reportedly crossing into Palestine from the east, with Egyptian armed forces beginning their rush up the Sinai Peninsula. At that moment, Clifford was hurrying past reporters lounging on the worn sofas in the lobby of the West Wing of the White House. When he arrived at Charlie Ross' office he handed him a slip of paper. At six-eleven, Ross read to reporters in the White House press room the following statement: "This Government has been informed that a Jewish state has been proclaimed in Palestine, and recognition has been requested by the Provisional Government thereof." The statement continued: "The United States recognizes the provisional government as the de facto authority of the new State of Israel."[47]

Thomas Hamilton of the *New York Times* reported that when the news of Truman's recognition reached the floor of the U.N. General Assembly "the first reaction was that someone was making a terrible joke." Certainly, that was the reaction of John Rogers of the *New York Herald-Tribune*. When the Colombian delegate confirmed the story through an Associated Press report in the U.N. press room, Soviet delegate Andrei Gromyko charged the American action reflected "a policy devoid of principle." The Syrian delegate had "no words to express my feelings of betrayal." The Lebanese Ambassador hoped the world press would record the "treachery" of the United States. Egypt's delegate thought the American "charade an unworthy mockery of the United Nations" designed to kill the organization. Cuba's delegate had to be physically restrained when he tried to march to the dais to withdraw his nation from the United Nations. An aide to the American delegation ran to Secretary General Trygve Lie's office, and there in a wastebasket, found the ticker-tape account of Truman's statement. Lie, obviously very much satisfied, had gone off to dine.[48]

Truman had his revenge. Career diplomats had publicly humiliated him in switching to trusteeship; now he made life difficult for them by switching back to partition and recognizing Israel. Marshall received an emergency call. The U.S. delegation to the United Nations was threatening to resign en masse. He ordered Rusk to prevent them from doing anything that might be interpreted as undermining the President and the decision he had made. All hands stayed at their posts. Marshall stayed at his and likely voted for Harry Truman as President that fall. By that time, Loy Henderson had been moved out of his job and was named Ambassador to India. Yet, it hardly diminished his respect for Truman, nor what his boss, Robert Lovett, thought of the man at the center of the storm. Both understood that Truman was bound, in the final analysis, by what public opinion would permit. Marshall, who hated the politics of diplomacy, supported the President's decision because of his respect for the Presidency. His only revenge was refusing to talk to Clifford for the rest of his life and knowing that future historians would one day read his angry warnings about the danger of "domestic political considerations" when confronted with an "international" problem.[49]

THE MORAL OF THE STORY

Secretary Marshall was, of course, quite wrong when he said the domestic political environment was not properly a part of foreign policymaking. Clifford observed that attempting to win public consent was a necessary part of all major policy initiatives in the Truman White House. Truman noted that foreign policies, once begun, could not be sustained for long in the absence of public support. His logic was not lost on Loy Henderson, who realized that postwar policymaking could not proceed as it had in the decades before the outbreak of the Second World War. The "Gentlemen's Club" in the State Department now had to compete with an increasingly restless American mass media, a highly attentive citizenry and a fiercely combative President in the development of the nation's foreign policy. This understanding was why Henderson, joined by James Forrestal, had made the mass media, and particularly the *New York Times*, a major target in the effort to construct conventional wisdom in the Cold War consideration of Palestine. Henderson saw his failure to persuade the press and public opinion on the merits of State Department planning as pivotal in the defeat of those plans.[50]

The depth of that defeat was signalled in media reaction to Truman's early recognition of Israel. While much was made of the abrupt turn in administration policy and the shock it provoked at Lake Success, headlines heralded the creation of the world's "newest sovereignty" and Truman's swift support for it. H. V. Kaltenborn continued to argue that "only the Soviet Union stood to gain" by America's "shifting and opportunistic policy." But pointing up administration inconsistencies was an old story. The creation of a new nation, mandated by the United Nations, was a new story, and it dominated media coverage. In an eight column, three line front page banner, the *New York Times* commemorated the birth of Israel and described the immediate threat to its fragile existence. Editorially, the *Times* warned that Israel's uncertain future would continue to depend on world public opinion as much as its own wits. Mutual Radio's Cecil Brown saw Truman's wavering as a deadly warning. Israel had become a reality, he told his nationwide listeners, "not because big powers were honorable, kept their promises, or were wild about justice." The new Jewish state had come into being "because the world still prefers to depend on the force of arms rather than understanding or decency. So the Jewish state was created by the power of guns."[51]

Key members of the Jewish Agency and its propaganda enterprises thought Brown's analysis only half right. They recognized that without success on the battlefield, there would have been no Jewish state. But they also understood that without the backing of the United Nations, they would not have had the international legitimacy to prosecute their cause. Abba Eban, the agency's point man at the United Nations, noted that if trusteeship had been voted, recognition of Jewish independence would "involve defiance of an international decision." Chaim Weizmann, who wrote an impassioned plea to Truman two days before recognition, put it more simply. The expiration of the British Mandate provided "a moment of opportunity for the Jewish nation, which, if missed, might be irrevocably lost." Agency veteran Golda Meir observed that declaring the state on May 14, 1948 was a "deadly gamble."

Defeating trusteeship and winning Truman's support proved the gamble "brilliantly and surprisingly successful." AZEC's Abba Hillel Silver and Israel's first Foreign Minister Moshe Shertok recognized that maintaining November's U.N. decision was "of incalculable significance to our cause" and was greatly facilitated by linking the fate of the United Nations in the public and media mind to the future of the Jewish state.[52]

The Jewish press was exultant. "Two thousand years statelessness ends!" proclaimed one. "Greetings to you, State of Israel!" cried another. The realization of "a dream," claimed a third. Farnsworth Fowle of CBS broke the news to Jewish Agency officials in Jerusalem that Truman had recognized Israel. Ben-Gurion was awakened from a sound sleep and told about it. Israel's first Prime Minister threw a coat over his pajamas and was driven at five in the morning to a radio center in Tel Aviv, where he broadcast an appeal to a thirty station American network linked through a ham radio operator in New Jersey. He thanked the United Nations and Truman for their support and asked for help in defeating the Arab states that made war on Israel. As he spoke, enemy planes could be heard bombing Tel Aviv.[53]

To many in the American media that bombing was an attempt to "strangle" the U.N.'s first born "in her crib," and it constituted an attack "on the authority of international agreement." As U.N. Special Committee on Palestine member Jorge Garcia-Granados put it, "We who considered the problems of Palestine knew Israel must live. It must live! Its existence was the first step toward the achievement of security and peace." This investment of moral capital in Israel's survival found instant expression in the American media, which drew immediate parallels between Israel's struggle for survival and that of America. Quentin Reynolds of *Collier's*, appearing on Israeli radio May 16, portrayed the infant state as a symbol "for all who have fought for freedom." He imagined a heavenly conversation in which Thomas Jefferson tells Tom Paine, "there is something familiar," in the sound of the new nation's declaration of independence. Paine answers, "Maybe we helped them a little and should feel a bit proud." That evening, Reynolds and fellow reporters gathered at press headquarters in Tel Aviv's Armon Hotel, joined their Israeli colleagues in a toast, "to the baby." Editors at the *New York Times* thought the press and the American people could take some satisfaction in sustaining a policy so firmly in the national interest.[54]

In the year and a half leading up to the creation of the state of Israel, great powers engaged in rhetorical warfare aimed at getting their way in a region seen as crucial to their postwar plans. Within the Truman administration, a parallel fight was fought, which spread to the front pages and editorial pages of the nation's leading newspapers and over the airwaves of its radio networks. It was a struggle for the minds and hearts of the men and women in the American media, for the readers and listeners they served, and most of all, for the mind and heart of Harry Truman. The fight was to frame a conventional wisdom in which the future of Palestine was discussed and decided. Up until the United Nations became a major player in the controversy, neither the Holocaust nor the human drama of a million displaced persons persuaded Americans there was any necessity for Jewish statehood. But after November 29, 1947, the stakes changed, not only because the prestige of an organization thought to be the best hope for world peace was on the line but because that peace seemed very much threatened by what was happening in the world.

America's media mirrored these apprehensions, and in the case of the *New York Times*, attempted to lead public opinion to do something about them. "Public opinion was the number problem in the world," *Times* Sunday editor Lester Markel wrote, because when that opinion was unsound "our foreign policy is likely to be unsound and our global stance unsound." And cultivating intelligent public opinion, Markel observed, "is in large part the assignment of the mass media." The November 29 vote at the United Nations finally swung the *Times* into supporting the creation of a Jewish state. And the reversal of American policy on March 19, 1948 made the creation of a Jewish state a positive necessity for the *Times* and a preponderance of major newspapers, news magazines and radio commentators across the country. The way they read the situation, supporting the firm stand of the United Nations in Palestine enhanced prospects for peace in the postwar world. And Americans, by a large majority, agreed.[55]

The force of concerted public and press opinion between March 19 and May 15, 1948 turned out to be a powerful force the administration could not buck, although the State Department tried to and failed. Finally, this public opinion permitted the President, who emotionally supported the Jewish cause in Palestine, to let them have their state and to encourage it with prompt recognition. As he saw it, the force of public opinion allowed him little other course. And in the end, he was just as happy that it had not.[56]

NOTES

1. Margaret Truman, *Harry S. Truman* (New York: William Morrow, 1973), pp. 387-389.

2. Diary of Charles G. Ross, March 29, 1948 entry. Papers of Charles G. Ross. Harry S. Truman Library. Independence, Missouri. Diary of Eben A. Ayers, March 20, 1948 entry. Papers of Eben A. Ayers. Box 16. Folder 5. Truman Library. Also, Oral History Interview: Eben A. Ayers, pp. 73-74. Truman Library. Papers of George Elsey. Foreign Relations: Palestine. Box 60. Truman Library. "Factors Influencing President Truman's Decision to Support Partition and Recognize the State

of Israel," a speech given by Clark Clifford on December 28, 1967, to the American Historical Association meeting in Washington, D. C., pp. 9-12.

3. Ayers diary, March 20, 1948 entry. Ayers Papers. Box 16. Folder 5. Ross diary, March 29, 1948 entry. Ross Papers.

4. On Truman's respect for Marshall, see letter from Dean Rusk to Clark Clifford, dated April 29, 1977, where Rusk states that Truman "considered George Marshall the greatest living American and was strongly inclined to back Marshall's judgment." My thanks to Mr. Rusk for a copy of that letter. Rusk's observation is substantiated by Clifford in "Annals of Government: The Truman Years," in *The New Yorker*, March 25, 1991, pp. 59-71. For Truman's great irritation with "career officers within the State Department," see M. Truman, pp. 386-388. Harry S. Truman, *Memoirs: Years of Trial and Hope* (New York: Doubleday, 1956), p. 163. For hasty efforts at damage control, see Ayers diary, March 20, 1948 entry. Ayers Papers. Box 16. Folder 5. *Foreign Relations of the United States, 1948*, Volume 5 (Washington: Government Printing Office, 1976), p. 750.

5. Ayers diary, March 20, 1948 entry. Box 16. Folder 5. *FRUS 1948*, Volume 5, p. 749.

6. See Elsey Papers. Foreign Relations: Palestine. Box 60. It contains annotated copy of *New York Times*, March 21, 1948, p. 1 article. Also, Cecil Brown Radio Scripts. March 22 and March 20, 1948. Cecil Brown Papers. Box 16. Folder 1. State Historical Society of Wisconsin. Madison, Wisconsin. Joseph Harsch Radio Script. March 21, 1948. Joseph Harsch Papers. Box 12. Folder 2. State Historical Society of Wisconsin. Clifton Utley Radio Script. March 21, 1948. Clifton Utley Papers. Box 50. Folder 2. State Historical Society of Wisconsin. See also, Israel File. Papers of David K. Niles. Box 30. Folder 3. Harry S. Truman Library. Independence, Missouri. And, *Wall Street Journal*, February 26, 1948, p. 1.

7. The Marquis Childs' column appears in the Elsey Papers. Foreign Relations: Palestine. Box 60.

8. *New York Times*, March 22, 1948, p. 1. *Washington Post*, March 22, 1948, p. 1. In "Annals," p. 65, Clifford notes that *Washington Post* publisher Eugene Meyer long opposed a Jewish state. When his son-in-law Philip Graham took over the publishing of the paper on January 1, 1946, that began to change. See Chalmers M. Roberts, *The Washington Post: The First One Hundred Years* (Boston: Houghton Mifflin, 1977), pp. 249, 256 and 277. While an early backer of the Marshall Plan, Graham was reticent about Truman and subscribed to the motto that, "To err is Truman." For Graham's personal political ambition and his desire to transform the *Post* into a player in policymaking, see Tom Kelly, *The Washington Post* (New York: William Morrow, 1983), pp. 98-99.

9. Ayers diary, March 21, 1948 entry. Ayers Papers. Box 16. Folder 5. Ross diary, March 29, 1948 entry. Ross Papers. *New York Times*, March 25, 1948, p. 1. And, *FRUS 1948*, Volume 5, p. 753.

10. *FRUS 1948*, Volume 5, pp. 750 and 753.

11. *New York Times*, March 28, 1948, Section E, p. 3.

12. *Ibid.*, Section E, p. 4 and *New York Times*, March 26, 1948, pp. 7 and 20.

13. Oral History Interview: Raymond P. Brandt, pp. 10 and 18-19. Oral

172 Truman, Palestine, and the Press

History Interview: Robert G. Nixon, pp. 217-218, 445-446, 668-670 and 696. Oral History Interview: Edward T. Folliard, pp. 60 and 73-74. All interviews are in the Harry S. Truman Library. Independence, Missouri.

14. Oral History Interview: Jack L. Bell, pp. 37 and 41. Oral History Interview: Gould Lincoln, p. 26. Oral History Interview: Charles J. Greene, p. 11. Brandt Oral History Interview, p. 40. Oral History Interview: Carleton Kent, pp. 33-34 and 43. Oral History Interview: Robert L. Riggs, pp. 14-15. All interviews are in the Harry S. Truman Library. Independence, Missouri.

15. Brandt Oral History Interview, p. 54. Oral History Interview: Carroll H. Kenworthy, pp. 12-17. Oral History Interview: Robert K. Walsh, p. 60 Ayers Oral History Interview, pp. 75-76. All interviews are available in the Harry S. Truman Library. Independence, Missouri. Also, Francis H. Heller, *The Truman White House: The Administration of the President, 1945-1953* (Lawrence: Regents Press of Kansas, 1980), p. 147.

16. *FRUS 1948*, Volume 5, pp. 754 and 757. Also, Oral History Interview: Loy W. Henderson, pp. 132-135. Clifford, "Factors Influencing," pp. 13-14. And, General File: Palestine. Papers of Eben A. Ayers. Truman Library.

17. Clifford, "Factors Influencing," pp. 13-15. Ayers diary, March 25, 1948 entry. Ayers Papers. Box 16. Folder 5. For a description of Truman's preparations for his meetings with the press see Oral History Interview: George Elsey, p. 77. Truman Library. Compare to Ayers Oral History Interview, pp. 37-40. Full transcripts of press conferences are in Transcriptions. Press Secretary Files. Ayers Papers. Box 63. Truman Library.

18. For a critique of Truman's basic inability to communicate the larger outlines of his policy to the press and the damage this failing did to his intentions of building consensus for his policies see Bell Oral History Interview, p. 37; Oral History Interview: Richard L. Strout, p. 2; Greene Oral History Interview, pp. 6-7; Kenworthy Oral History Interview, pp. 12-15. Riggs Oral History Interview, pp. 15-16. Brandt Oral History Interview, pp. 25-26. Kent Oral History Interview, pp. 10-13. All interviews are available in the Truman Library.

19. Transcriptions. Press Secretary Files. Ayers Papers. Box 63. Truman Library.

20. Trygve Lie, *In the Cause of Peace: Seven Years with the United Nations* (New York: Macmillan, 1954), pp. 170-171.

21. *New York Times*, March 26, 1948, pp. 11 and 20. *FRUS 1948*, Volume 5, pp. 758-759. Abba Hillel Silver, *Vision and Victory: A Collection of Addresses by Dr. Abba Hillel Silver, 1942-1948* (New York: The Zionist Organization of America, 1949), pp. 181-182. The column by Stewart and Joseph Alsop appears in Israel File. Papers of David K. Niles. Box 30. Folder 3. Truman Library.

22. *New York Times*, April 1, 1948, p. 24; April 2, 1948, p. 1 and April 3, 1948, p. 3. Also, Memorandum by Loy Henderson, undated. U.S. State Department Files. 501.BB Pal/3-2448. Box 2148. National Archives. Washington, D. C.

23. Memorandum by Loy Henderson, dated March 26, 1948. U.S. State Department Files. 867N.01/3-2648. National Archives. Washington, D. C. Also, Ayers diary, March 25, 1948 entry. Box 16. Folder 5. Truman Library. And, Clifford, "Factors Influencing," pp. 7 and 18. See also, Henderson Oral History Interview, pp.

158-160. Truman Library. *The Detroit Jewish Chronicle*, March 26, 1948, p. 3. And, File 4-2. Correspondence. Minutes: American Zionist Emergency Council. March 30, 1948. The Temple. Cleveland, Ohio.

24. Ayers diary, April 1, 1948 entry. Box 16. Folder 5. On Truman-Marshall relationship and President's determination not to alienate Marshall, see Clifford, "Annals," pp. 62 and 64. Also, letter from Rusk to Clifford, dated April 29, 1977. See also, Dean Acheson, *Present at the Creation: My Years at the State Department* (New York: W. W. Norton, 1969), p. 735.

25. *New York Times*, March 24, 1948, p. 5; April 2, 1948, p. 1; April 3, 1948, p. 3; April 4, 1948, Section E, p. 4; and April 11, 1948, Section E, pp. 3 and 8.

26. *FRUS 1948*, Volume 5, pp. 840-842.

27. *New York Times*, April 7, 1948, p. 4 and April 9, 1948, p. 22. *New York Herald-Tribune*, April 7, 1948, pp. 1 and 3. *Baltimore Sun*, April 7, 1948, pp. 2 and 4.

28. *New York Times*, April 18, 1948, Section E, pp. 4 and 8. And, *FRUS 1948*, Volume 5, pp. 870-873. See also, Israel File. Nile Papers. Box 30. Folder 2. Truman Library.

29. Jon and David Kimche, *A Clash of Destinies* (New York: Praeger, 1969), pp. 90 and 117-124. Also, Foreign Office. 371/68439. April 12, 1948. E4824. 371/68439. April 13, 1948. E4796. 371/68649. April 19, 1948. E4887 and April 21, 1948. E5020. 371/68544. April 24, 1948. E5124 and E5125. Kew Gardens, England. *FRUS 1948*, Volume 5, pp. 817 and 843. *New York Times*, April 21, 1948, p. 1 and April 22, 1948, p. 1. And, File 4-2. Correspondence. Minutes: American Zionist Emergency Council. April 27, 1948. The Temple. Cleveland, Ohio.

30. Israel File. Niles Papers. Box 30. Folder 3. See also, Press and Radio Conferences. Charles G. Ross and Eben A. Ayers. Ayers Papers. Box 14. According to R. H. Hadlow, a member of the U.K. delegation to the United Nations, Henderson found out about the Hilldring appointment after Jewish sources leaked it to the radio. See memorandum from R. H. Haldow to Philip Mason, dated May 2, 1948. Foreign Office. 371/68554. E6676. Public Record Office. See also, memorandum from U.K. delegation to Foreign Office, citing *New York Times* of April 30, 1948. Foreign Office. 371/68449. E5473. Public Record Office. Also, memorandum from Lord Inverchapel to Foreign Office, dated April 30, 1948. 371/68449. E5592. Public Record Office.

31. *FRUS 1948*, Volume 5, pp. 879 and 888-890.

32. Bernard Postal and Henry W. Levy, *And the Hills Shouted for Joy: The Day Israel Was Born* (New York: David McKay, 1973), pp. 221-243. And, *New York Times*, May 2, 1948, p. 1. Memorandum from McIntyre to Marshall, dated April 30, 1948. U.S. State Department. 867N.6373/1-545. M1390. Roll 27. National Archives. Washington, D. C. Marshall must not have been satisfied with Taylor's report because on May 7, 1948 the State Department requested the Navy set up emergency communication facilities in Jerusalem. See *New York Times*, May 9, 1948, p. 5.

33. *St. Louis Star-Times*, May 1, 1948, p. 18. *Chicago Sun-Times*, May 1, 1948, p. 3. *New York Times*, May 2, 1948, Section E, pp. 1, 2 and 8.

34. *New York Times*, May 14, 1948, p. 1. H. V. Kaltenborn Radio Script. May 14, 1948. H. V. Kaltenborn Papers. Box 185. Folder 1. State Historical Society

of Wisconsin. Madison, Wisconsin. Brown Radio Scripts. May 10 and May 12, 1948. Brown Papers. Box 16. Folder 3. See also, Walter Lippmann's column on Soviet designs on the Near East, appears in the May 9, 1948 edition of the *New York Herald-Tribune*. The article is in the Arthur Creech-Jones Papers. Box 31. Folder 4. Rhodes House Library. Oxford, England. And, Israel File. Niles Papers. Box 30. Folder 4. Truman Library.

35. *FRUS 1948*, Volume 5, pp. 943-953 and 965-969. Also, letter from Dean Rusk to author, dated May 15, 1987.

36. Transcripts. Press Secretary Files. Ayers Papers. Box 63. Truman Library. *FRUS 1948*, Volume 5, pp. 903-916, 918-920 and 926-930. Also, Brown Radio Script. May 3, 1948. Brown Papers. Box 16. Folder 2. Harsch Radio Script. May 7, 1948. Box 12. Folder 2.

37. Henderson Oral History Interview, pp. 134-135. Clifford, "Annals," pp. 62-64.

38. Memorandum from Marshall to Austin, dated March 16, 1948. 501.BB Pal/3-1748. Memorandum from Marshall to Charles E. Bohlen, dated March 22, 1948. 501.BB Pal/3-2248. National Archives. Memorandum from Moshe Shertok to Jewish Agency, dated March 26, 1948. Code 30.02/2414/22. See particularly pp. 2 and 10 of that memo. Israel State Archives. Jerusalem, Israel. See also, Clifford, "Annals," p. 62. And, Forrest C. Pogue, *George C. Marshall: Statseman* (New York: Viking, 1987), pp. 368-369.

39. Leonard Mosley, *Marshall: Hero of Our Times* (New York: Hearst Press, 1982), pp. 418-419. Pogue, pp. 370-371. See also, Shertok memorandum to Jewish Agency, dated March 26, 1948. Code 30.02/2414/22. For background, see Mark A. Stoler, *George C. Marshall: Soldier-Statesman of the American Century* (Boston: Twayne, 1989), his chapter on "Creating a New Foreign Policy, 1947-1949."

40. Clifford, "Annals," pp. 62-63. *FRUS 1948*, Volume 5, pp. 958-969 and 972-974. Also, Oral History Interview: Clark M. Clifford, pp. 99-102. Truman Library.

41. *FRUS 1948*, Volume 5, pp. 972-974. Clifford, "Annals," pp. 63-64.

42. Clifford, "Annals," pp. 64-65. *FRUS 1948*, Volume 5, pp. 972-974. Transcripts. Press Secretary Files. Ayers Papers. Box 63. Truman Library. Clifford, "Factors Influencing," pp. 18-19. Ross diary, March 19, 1948 entry. Ross Papers. Truman Library.

43. Clifford, "Annals," pp. 63 and 67-69. *FRUS 1948,* Volume 5, pp. 989.

44. Clifford, "Annals," p. 68. Postal and Levy, pp. 219 and 222. *FRUS 1948*, Volume 5, pp. 989-992. *New York Times*, May 14, 1948, p. 1.

45. *New York Times*, May 15, 1948, p. 1. Postal and Levy, p. 241.

46. Clifford, "Annals," p. 70. *FRUS 1948*, Volume 5, pp. 994, 996-997 and 1006-1007.

47. Clifford, "Annals," p. 70. *New York Times*, May 15, 1948, p. 1. Ayers diary, May 14, 1948 entry. Ayers Papers. Box 16. Folder 5. Truman Library.

48. *New York Times*, May 15, 1948, p. 1. *New York Herald-Tribune*, May 15, 1948, p. 1. United Nations General Assembly. Documents. A/P.V. 135. Second Special Session. May 14, 1948. Verbatim Record of the 135th Meeting. Flushing Meadow, New York. pp. 90-102, 135-137, 141 and 156. Also, Clifford, "Annals," p.

70. Postal and Levy, p. 275. Abba Eban, *An Autobiography* (New York: Random House, 1977), p. 114.

49. *FRUS 1948*, Volume 5, pp. 994, 996-997 and 1006-1007. Clifford, "Annals," pp. 70-71. Also, Oral History Interview: Robert A. Lovett, pp. 7-21. Henderson Oral History Interview, pp. 104-105. Truman Library. Clifford, "Annals," p. 62.

50. Clifford, "Factors Influencing," p. 19. Henderson Oral History Interview, pp. 104-105 and 134. Manfred Landecker, *The President and Public Opinion* (Washington: Public Affairs Press, 1968), p. 65.

51. Kaltenborn Radio Script. May 14, 1948. Kaltenborn Papers. Box 185. Folder 1. *New York Times*, May 15, 1948, pp. 1 and 14.

52. *New York Times*, May 16, 1948, p. 1. Eban, p. 111. Postal and Levy, p. 282. File 4-2. Correspondence. Minutes: American Zionist Emergency Council. December 11, 1947 and April 27, 1948. Also, Marie Syrkin, *Golda Meir: Woman with a Cause* (London: Victor Gollancz, 1964), p. 207.

53. *The Jewish Advocate* (Boston), May 20, 1948, p. 1. *B'nai Brith Messenger* (Los Angeles), May 21, 1948, p. 1. *The American Hebrew*, May 7, 1948, p. 6 and May 21, 1948, p. 6. And, Postal and Levy, pp. 222 and 230.

54. Eban, p. 111. Jorge Garcia-Granados, *The Birth of Israel: The Drama As I Saw It* (New York: Knopf, 1949), pp. 290-291. Postal and Levy, pp. 246-247. *New York Times*, March 26, 1948, p. 20 and May 15, 1948, p. 14. Bruce J. Evensen, "Surrogate State Department? *Times* Coverage of Palestine, 1948," *Journalism Quarterly* 67, 1990, p. 400.

55. Lester Markel, "The Real Sins of the Press," *Harper's*, December 1962, pp. 85-94. Also, Postal and Levy, p. 278. Charles H. Stember, *Jews in the Mind of America* (New York: Basic Books, 1966), pp. 175-180 and 215-216. Stember points out that between 1945 and 1947, one half of all persons polled indicated they were following developments in Palestine and three-quarters of those polled said they had heard or read something about the situation there. During March, 1948, one half of all persons polled wanted a Jewish state in Palestine encouraged. Only ten percent opposed such a plan. One quarter of those polled took no position.

56. Clifford, "Factors Influencing," p. 13. Clifford, "Annals," p. 71. H. Truman, p. 163.

Conclusion: The Press, the President and Public Opinion: The Palestine Case

The complex relationship of the press, the public and policymaking is not subject to easy generalizations. Part of the difficulty in determining the media's influence in the policymaking process, as V. O. Key has observed, is that while the participation of political parties and individual politicians in the process may be extensive, the place where the media attention intersects the process may be quite narrow. Part of the reason for this, as Bernard Cohen points out, is that on most issues the media are generally playing catch up. Coverage, Cohen notes, often is fragmented and episodic, leaving policymakers and the public little in the way of a coherent, well-balanced view of the world that anticipates future dangers. The reason for these limitations in the pattern of media coverage may lie in the nature of news reporting itself. Reporters concentrate their coverage on distinct events and not on the conditions out of which these events arise, Bernard Roshco notes. As a result, the findings of the media are essentially descriptive and non-analytical.[1]

Because of the perceived unreliability of political reporting, some students of mass media and politics have taken a dim view of the usefulness of public opinion in driving that process. Walter Lippmann believed that public opinion made it difficult to conduct foreign policy intelligently. Too often mistaken, it reached conclusions based on information intended to incite rather than inform. Gabriel Almond argued the public was highly impressionable because it paid little continuing attention to political information. For that reason it was essential that the public not make foreign policy but that it be made for them. Thomas E. Patterson, writing a generation after Almond, shared his misgivings about the participation of the press and the public in political decision-making. His research suggested the former did not supply the latter with the necessary information to participate intelligently in the political process.[2]

Policymakers during the Truman administration viewed public opinion as something to be formed, preferably by foreign policy experts, for the good of the country. Secretary of State James Byrnes may have spoken of "a people's foreign policy," but what he was really talking about was a policy the public could be made to understand, not one the public had a hand in making. Subsequent administrations have expressed a similar interest in establishing the conventional wisdom that guides policymaking. Presidents Gerald Ford and Jimmy Carter told a Columbia University audience in January, 1989, that leading public opinion is a necessary goal of any administration. Carter thought a president's ability to lead public opinion was largely a function of his personal popularity. He suggested that the lower a president's standing in the polls, the less likely it will be that he has the media support needed to convince the public of his interpretation of events. Ford agreed; he saw the White House and the nation's press competing with one another over the interpretations that guide public debate over policy. Ford observed that a president's greatest nightmare is when a national or international issue so careens out of control that he is powerless to insist on his interpretation but must instead be bound by the interpretations of others.[3]

This loss of control is precisely what Montague Kern, Patricia and Ralph Levering found in their study of the Kennedy's administration's difficulties with the press over Vietnam. Kennedy had been remarkably successful in getting his interpretation of the Cuban missile crisis accepted by the press and public opinion, in part because the event occurred with such suddenness. Under these circumstances, the authors found, the press and the American public naturally rally around the nation's leader and allow him to manage the crisis through their implied consent. But the lingering war in Vietnam presented a different kind of issue. The prolonged dispute surrounding the wisdom of American participation in that war enabled the press to locate alternative sources of equal legitimacy that disagreed with Kennedy's interpretation of events. The result was the airing of these differences in the press and a struggle between administration supporters and opponents for public endorsement of their positions.[4]

The findings of Kern, Levering and Levering are consistent with the work of other mass media researchers who have found that the relationship between policymakers, the press and the public is dependent on a variety of circumstances that affect the influence of one upon the other. Jack McLeod describes this relationship as reciprocal and mutually reinforcing. Who is influencing whom at any moment on an issue is subject to change as circumstances change. Research over the last ten years has analyzed what those circumstances are and has found that what an audience knows, or thinks it knows about a certain issue, is an important measure of its willingness to accept alternative interpretations it may read in the press.[5]

The issue of whether or not the U.S. government should support the creation of a Jewish state in Palestine was one that had been discussed at length in the nation's press long before it came to a vote on November 29, 1947, at the United Nations. Between 1945 and 1947 over one half of all persons polled said they had been following developments in Palestine and four in five said they had heard something or read something about the situation there. Between January and March, 1948, public tracking of international events soared from barely thirty percent to nearly eighty percent of all persons polled. More than two-thirds of all respondents favored an enlarged army, navy and air force, and a substantial majority supported an increase in taxes to pay for it. Seven in ten favored Truman's March 17, 1948 call for a return to the military draft. More than one-half saw a major war with the Soviet Union within a year. Three in four favored a tougher policy toward the Soviets, and only one in twenty believed the United States and the Soviet Union would be able to get together and work their problems out.[6]

Widespread public anxiety in March 1948 over the future of East-West relations coincided with increasing attentiveness to efforts by the United Nations to preserve world peace. Over eighty percent of all Americans in that month indicated to pollsters either a great interest or some interest in the U.N. management of international crises. This finding coincides with poll data from 1942 through 1948 showing seven in ten Americans consistently favored an active United States role in world affairs.[7]

These results suggest that any administration initiative on Palestine, if it expected to have public support, needed to take into consideration prevailing interpretations on East-West tensions and the U.N. role in preserving order in the postwar world. The argument the State Department and the White House constructed after March 19, 1948 to justify their switch from partition to trusteeship attempted to do precisely that. But the administration effort failed because it could not overcome the impression in the press and in the public that it had made the wrong decision for the wrong reasons, acting out of cowardice in a time requiring clarity of purpose and consistency in motive. One newspaper said it best: what Truman needed was "a good dose of moral guts!"[8]

A mythology has grown up around Harry Truman as a strong-minded national leader at whose desk the buck stopped. It is an image of a man who confidently set the nation's course with a general disdain for the vicissitudes of public opinion and his critics in the press. No one has worked in his public statements to cultivate this impression more than the former President himself. "A President ought not to worry whether a decision he knows he has to make will prove to be popular," Truman was quoted as saying the year he left office. The important thing, he explained, was to make a decision on the basis of what a president knew to be right without regard to how it might play in the press. "The man who keeps his ear to the ground to find out what is popular will be in trouble," Truman predicted. As far as Truman was concerned, that was the trouble with the media. Newspapermen were "all a bunch of lazy cusses," he told Merle Miller. "One of them writes something, and others rewrite it, and rewrite it, and they keep right on doing it without ever stopping to find out if the first fellow was telling the truth or not."[9]

Truman's aides added to the legend of a dynamic President dominant over contrary opinion. "I was not aware that public opinion polls had any influence on the President," said Edward A. Locke, a special assistant to Truman. "The President did what he thought was best for the country. His reactions were extraordinarily representative of the reactions of the country as a whole." Remarked Truman press aide Roger Tubby, "Remember that President Truman was an extraordinarily good politician, and any President who is a good politician will be ahead of the polls. He ordinarily sensed what was right and sensed what the people wanted before the polls were taken."[10]

Some Cold War analysts have cited these sources in making their case that Truman's strength as a national leader made him less susceptible to the force of public and press opinion than other presidents.[11] But as this research has attempted to show, Truman's political fortunes in the early spring of 1948 were in considerable jeopardy, in large part, because of the perception in much of the media and the public that Truman lacked the leadership necessary to take the nation through the international crisis it faced. The President's changing position on partition contributed to the impression that his administration lacked both a coherent view in foreign policy and the will to carry it out.

The media could have accepted the administration argument in March, 1948 that trusteeship did not represent an abandonment of the principle of partition but rather was a humanitarian gesture designed to avoid further bloodshed in Palestine. Indeed, that is how Truman appears to have genuinely seen it. But the administration could not overcome the larger frames of reference it had helped create; namely, that the future of Palestine was bound up in East-West relations and the fate of the United Nations. This logic was not lost on the President's chief counsel, Clark Clifford, who warned that "shilly-shallying appeasement of the Arabs" would result in the United States "being held in contempt" throughout the world and would inevitably lead to the very loss in prestige that furthered Soviet ambitions in the postwar world.[12]

Contributing to the administration's difficulties was a press that had entered the postwar period increasingly determined to play a role in policymaking. Some old-timers, like Edward Folliard, who began his work on the *Washington Post* in 1923, continued to believe that the essence of good reporting was to be objective or at least try to be. Folliard thought his job was "to give readers the facts and assume that the reader could make his own judgments; if the reader wanted any help, he could read the editorial page. That's the owner's page. That's where the owner has his say and nobody should quarrel with that." But some did not think Folliard's neat formulation went far enough. The Commission on Freedom of the Press, composed of leading educators and bankrolled by Henry Luce, famed magazine mogul, published a statement of principles in 1947 concluding "it is no longer enough to report the fact truthfully. It is now necessary to report the truth about the fact." The Commission's report declared that "a truthful, comprehensive and intelligent account of the day's events" necessarily requires "a context which gives them meaning." Defining the media's role in this way emphasized interpretation as a key contribution to the formation of informed opinion. As *New York Times* Sunday editors Lester Markel put it, "freedom of the press was not a license to print anything" but a recognition that the Cold War required "informed opinion" to serve the national interest.[13]

The media's role in the Truman administration's deliberations on Palestine should be seen at several levels. It served as a site at which definitions of what was happening in Palestine were debated by and for the American public. Some of these definitions arose outside the Truman administration, especially from American Zionist groups, which worked tirelessly to put their message before the American people, and other definitions originated from a divided administration. Administration proponents and opponents of partition hoped to make headlines that would aid their cause. The result, as Clifford saw it, was the spectacle of a government that "had no foreign policy" and "did not know where it was going" and of a President and State Department "bewildered," failing "to furnish leadership in world affairs" and "drifting helplessly."[14]

The administration's hasty, improvised and ill-defined efforts to retrieve the situation after the March 19 reversal on partition only heightened press ridicule. When the major players in the controversy failed to quickly embrace a truce, the administration, lacking internal unity and external support, was in no position to argue its case. Media opposition hardened with every passing day and headline. Various players looked to it to deduce the strategies of their opponents and to try to devise publicity campaigns of their own to defeat the opposition. The beginning of the Cold War found a limited number of arguments available to these contenders. It was a time that seemed analogous to the period after Munich, when a continental European power seemed to threaten American institutions. NBC's Clifton Utley noted it had been that threat that twice had taken America into war.[15] Relentlessly, Utley and other interpreters of the President's Palestine policy turned to the past to predict the future. And the future they saw frightened them.

Just as Palestine became imbedded in policy deliberations extending far beyond its borders during the Cold War, so too the interpretations appearing in the media went far beyond the struggles of two peoples for a single land. That the issue of a Jewish state was seen in this way and not some other way was in part the result of how the media chose to portray the competing definitions available to it. In the power of defining what it was seeing, the media helped subtly reshape the events it covered, assuring a definitive battle for Palestine would be waged before the guns of the region raged.

NOTES

1. V. O. Key, *Public Opinion and American Democracy* (New York: Knopf, 1961), pp. 389-391. Bernard C. Cohen, *The Press and Foreign Policy* (Princeton: Princeton University, 1963), pp. 62-63 and 271-272. Bernard Roshco, *Newsmaking* (Chicago: University of Chicago, 1975), pp. 18, 53-57 and 63-64.

2. Walter Lippmann, *The Public Philosophy* (Boston: Little, Brown, 1955), pp. 16-23. Gabriel A. Almond, *The American People and Foreign Policy* (New York: Praeger, 1961), pp. 53-55 and 60. Thomas E. Patterson, *The Mass Media Election: How Americans Choose Their President* (New York: Praeger, 1980), pp. 173-181.

3. James F. Byrnes, *Speaking Frankly* (New York: Harper, 1947), pp. 243-254. Also, Columbia University forum involving former presidents Gerald Ford and Jimmy Carter on January 18, 1989, and telecast that evening on "McNeil-Lehrer Report" on the Public Broadcasting System.

4. Montague Kern, Patricia W. Levering and Ralph B. Levering, *The Kennedy Crises: The Press, the Presidency and Foreign Policy* (Chapel Hill: University of North Carolina, 1984), pp. 114-116, 175-176 and 195-204.

5. Jack M. McLeod, Lee B. Becker and James E. Byrnes, "Another Look at the Agenda Setting Function of the Press," *Communication Research* 1, 1974, pp. 131-166. See also, Dennis McQuail, "The Influence and Effects of Mass Media," in Morris Janowitz and Paul Hirsch, eds., *Reader in Public Opinion and Mass Communication* (New York: Free Press, 1981), pp. 361-385. Also, Joseph Wagner, "Media Do Make a Difference: The Differential Impact of Mass Media in the 1976 Presidential Race," *American Journal of Political Science* 27, 1983, pp. 407-428. F. Christopher Arterton, *Media Politics: The News Strategies of Presidential Campaigns* (Lexington, Mass.: Lexington Books, 1984), pp. 183-184.

6. Charles Herbert Stember, *Jews in the Mind of America* (New York: Basic Books, 1966), pp. 174-180. George H. Gallup, *The Gallup Poll: Public Opinion, 1935-1971* (New York: Random House, 1972), pp. 721 and 759.

7. William A. Caspary, "The Mood Theory: A Study of Public Opinion and Foreign Policy," *American Journal of Political Science* 64, 1970, pp. 537-547.

8. *The Jewish Advocate* (Boston), March 11, 1948, p. 2.

9. Harry S. Truman, *Mr. Citizen* (New York: Bernard Geis Associates, 1953), p. 263. Merle Miller, *Plain Speaking: An Oral Biography of Harry S. Truman* (New York: Putnam, 1973), p. 251.

10. Francis H. Heller, *The Truman White House: The Administration of the President, 1945-1953* (Lawrence: Regents Press of Kansas, 1980), pp. 86-87.

11. Manfred Landecker, *The President and Public Opinion* (Washington: Public Affairs Press, 1968), pp. 63-67. Michael Leigh, *Mobilizing Consent: Public Opinion and American Foreign Policy, 1943-1947* (Westport: Greenwood Press, 1976), xv-xvi. Thomas G. Paterson, "Presidential Foreign Policy, Public Opinion and Congress: The Truman Years," *Diplomatic History* 3, 1979, pp. 1-3 and 17-18.

12. *Foreign Relations of the United States 1948*, Volume 5 (Washington: Government Printing Office, 1976), pp. 690-695.

13. Oral History Interview: Edward T. Folliard, pp. 73-74. Harry S. Truman Library. Independence, Missouri. The Commission on Freedom of the Press, *A Free and Responsible Press* (Chicago: University of Chicago, 1947), pp. 20-27. Lester Markel, "The Real Sins of the Press," *Harper's*, December, 1962, pp. 85-87.

14. *FRUS 1948*, Volume 5, pp. 692-693.

15. Clifton Utley Radio Script. March 14, 1948. Clifton Utley Papers. Box 50. Folder 2. State Historical Society of Wisconsin. Madison, Wisconsin.

Essay on Sources

Primary sources examined in this study include collections within the Harry S. Truman Library in Independence, Missouri, as well as oral history interviews of many of the reporters who covered the Truman White House, also available at the Truman Library. The files of the American Zionist Emergency Council and the personal papers of American Zionist Abba Hillel Silver were examined at the archives of The Temple, in Cleveland, Ohio. Notebooks and diaries of leading Zionists were analyzed at the American Zionist Archives in Cincinnati, Ohio. Issues of many of the major Jewish newspapers and periodicals were examined in the collections of Hebrew Union College, also in Cincinnati. Other collections in the Jewish press of the Truman period were viewed in the Regenstein Library at the University of Chicago, and collections held at Northwestern University Library in Evanston, Illinois, the University of North Carolina Library at Chapel Hill, the St. Paul Library in St. Paul, Minnesota and the University of Wisconsin Library in Madison.

Also examined at the State Historical Society of Wisconsin, located in Madison, were transcripts of radio newscasts broadcast by leading radio commentators of the Cold War period, including Hans V. Kaltenborn, Joseph Harsch, Cecil Brown and Clifton Utley. The author was able to rely on first-hand accounts of some of these events through correspondence with State Department veteran Dean Rusk, White House Special Counsel Clark Clifford and *New York Times* Middle Eastern correspondent, and future Truman son-in-law, E. Clifton Daniel.

This research began at the Central Zionist Archives and the Israel State Archives in Jerusalem during the winter of 1983-1984 and included material drawn from the Chaim Weizmann Archives in Rehovoth, Israel. Five years later, the research was completed with a trip to the Public Records Office in Kew Gardens, just outside London, and the Rhodes House Library,

Middle East Center and Bodleian Library collections, all in Oxford, England. Of these, the Public Records Office was crucial in following British cabinet decision-making on Palestine, and Rhodes House, with its collection of papers from the estate of Arthur Creech-Jones, was helpful in describing the Colonial Office's handling of the Palestine controversy in the press. Rounding out the picture of British policy in Palestine during the mandatory period were collections at the National Library of Wales in Aberystwyth and the University Library in Bristol, England.

A starting point for research on America's Palestine policy during the Cold War period is the *Foreign Relations of the United States*, particularly the fifth volume in its 1948 series. The studies by Phillip Baram and Aaron David Miller are the most complete in detailing State Department thinking on Palestine in the period leading up to the Cold War. The work by Robert Schulzinger is the best source for an analysis of the training and outlook of the men who made policy within the department. The researcher is particularly encouraged to analyze the papers of Charles Ross, Eben Ayers and George Elsey at the Truman Library for an insight into the White House reading of the daily press. There one finds the intersection of the line the Truman administration tried to get out on Palestine and what actually appeared in the press. The *New York Times* front page is a daily diary of the struggle to "make things mean" by several contending parties. Out of that conflict, this study was born.

Bibliography

UNPUBLISHED SOURCE MATERIALS

Harry S. Truman Library, Independence, Missouri.
       Eben A. Ayers Papers
       Clark M. Clifford Papers
       Matthew Connelly Papers
       George M. Elsey Papers
       Henry F. Grady Papers
       Eddie Jacobson Papers
       James H. McGrath Papers
       Philleo Nash Papers
       David K. Niles Papers
       Charles G. Ross Papers
       Francis Russell Papers
       John W. Snyder Papers
       Harry S. Truman Papers

       Oral History Interviews:
       Eben A. Ayers
       Jack L. Bell
       Raymond P. Brandt
       Clark M. Clifford
       George M. Elsey
       Abraham Feinberg
       Edward T. Folliard
       James A. Fox
       Charles J. Greene
       Loy W. Henderson
       Carleton Kent
       Carroll H. Kenworthy

Gould Lincoln
W. McNeil Lowry
Robert A. Lovett
Robert G. Nixon
Sarah Peltzman
Robert L. Riggs
Samuel I. Rosenman
Richard L. Strout
Walter Trohan
Robert K. Walsh

United States Government Archives, National Archives,
Washington, D. C.
Department of State, Decimal Files, 1947-1948,
Record Group 59

Department of State, Lot Files, Record Group 59:
Office of European Affairs, 1947-1948
Office of Near Eastern Affairs, 1947-1948
Office of Petroleum Division, 1947-1948
Rusk-McClintock Files, 1947-1948

Modern Military Records, Branch:
Records of the Joint Chiefs of Staff, 1947-1948,
Record Group 218

American Jewish Archives, Cincinnati, Ohio
Leon I. Feuer Papers
Harold P. Manson Papers
Emanuel Neumann Papers
Chaim Weizmann Papers
World Zionist Congress Archives

The Temple, Cleveland, Ohio.
Abba Hillel Silver Papers
American Christian Palestine Committee Archives
American Zionist Emergency Council Archives
Eliahu Ben-Horin Papers
Howard M. LeSourd Papers
Harry S. Shapiro Papers

State Historical Society of Wisconsin, Madison, Wisconsin.
American Council for Judaism Archives
Cecil Brown Papers
Marquis Childs Papers
Joseph Harsch Papers

Hans V. Kaltenborn Papers
Clifton Utley Papers

Southern Historical Collection, University of North Carolina, Chapel Hill, North Carolina.
Jonathan Daniels Papers

Bentley Historical Library, University of Michigan, Ann Arbor, Michigan.
Arthur H. Vandenberg Papers

Manuscript Division, Library of Congress, Washington, D. C.
Herbert Feis Papers
Felix Frankfurter Papers
Loy W. Henderson Papers
William D. Leahy Papers
Breckenridge Long Papers

Franklin D. Roosevelt Library, Hyde Park, New York.
Henry Morgenthau Papers
Eleanor Roosevelt Papers
Franklin D. Roosevelt Papers
Samuel I. Rosenman Papers

The Public Records Office, Kew Gardens, England.
Cabinet Papers:
Cab 128 Cabinet Meetings, 1947-1948
Cab 129 Cabinet Memoranda, 1947-1948
Cab 143 Middle East Committee Reports, 1947-1948

Prime Minister's Office:
Pre. 8 Correspondence and Papers, 1947-1948

Foreign Office:
Foreign Office 370, Library
Foreign Office 371, Political

Colonial Office:
Col. Ofc. 732, Middle East Correspondence
Col. Ofc. 733, Palestine Correspondence

The Rhodes House Library, Oxford, England.
Arthur Creech-Jones Papers
Fabian Society Archives

Middle East Center, St. Anthony's College, Oxford, England.
Richard Crossman Papers

Alan Cunningham Papers

Bodleian Library, Oxford, England.
    Western Manuscripts Collection and Archives

National Library of Wales, Aberystwyth, Wales.
    Palestine Commission Archives

Central Zionist Archives, Jerusalem, Israel
    Jewish Agency Archives
    Provisional Government Archives

Israel State Archives, Jerusalem, Israel

The Weizmann Archives, Rehovoth, Israel
    Chaim Weizmann Papers

CONTEMPORARY NEWSPAPERS AND PERIODICALS

Jewish Organizations:
Committee Reporter (American Jewish Committee), 1947-1948.
Commentary (American Jewish Committee), 1947-1948.
Congress Weekly (American Jewish Congress), 1947-1948.
Jewish Frontier (Labor Zionists), 1947-1948
Jewish Telegraphy Agency Daily News Bulletin, 1946-1948.
New Palestine (Zionist Organization of America), 1946-1948.
The Reconstructionist (Jewish Reconstructionist Foundation), 1948.
Yiddisher Kemfer (Poale Zion-Zeire Zion of America), 1947-1948.

Jewish Press:
American Hebrew (New York)
American Israelite (Cincinnati)
American Jewish Times (Greensboro, North Carolina)
American Jewish World (Minneapolis-St. Paul, Minnesota)
B'nai Brith Messenger (Los Angeles)
Day (New York)
Hadoar (New York)
Israelite (Chicago)
Jewish Advocate (Boston)
Jewish Chronicle (Detroit)
Jewish Chronicle (Kansas City, Missouri)
Jewish Daily Forum (Chicago)
Jewish Daily Forward (New York)
Jewish Exponent (Philadelphia)
Jewish Independent (Cleveland)
Jewish Leader (Pittsburgh)

Jewish News (Detroit)
Jewish Post (Paterson, New Jersey)
Jewish Spectator (New York)
Jewish Tribune (San Francisco)
Jewish Weekly Times (Brookline, Massachusetts)
Menorah Journal (New York)
National Jewish Ledger (Washington, D. C.)
National Jewish Post (Indianapolis, Indiana)
Opinion (New York)
Unser Tsait (New York)
Wisconsin Jewish Chronicle (Milwaukee)

Middle East Press:
Al-Ahram (Cairo)
Al-Masri (Cairo)
Al-Musawwar (Cairo)
Musamarat al-Jeib (Cairo)
Roz al-Yusef (Cairo)
Al-Difaa (Haifa)
Journal D'Egypte (Cairo)
Al-Yom (Beirut)
Davar (Jerusalem)
Ha'aretz (Jerusalem)
Ma'ariv (Jerusalem)
Palestine Post (Jerusalem)

United States Press and Peridicals:
America
American Foreign Service Journal
American Heritage
American Historical Review
American Jewish Archives
American Jewish Historical Quarterly
American Jewish History
American Journal of International Law
American Journal of Sociology
American Journalism Historical Quarterly
American Quarterly
American Magazine
American Neptune
American Political Science Review
American Politics Quarterly
American Presbyterian
American Sociological Review
Annals of the American Academy of Political and Social Science
Argosy

Atlanta Constitution
Atlantic Monthly
Baltimore Sun
Boston Globe
Boston Herald
Buffalo Evening News
Business History Review
Business Week
Chicago Daily News
Chicago Sun-Times
Chicago Times
Chicago Tribune
Christian Science Monitor
Christian Century
Christianity and Crisis
Churchman
Cleveland Plain Dealer
Columbia University Forum
Commentary
Communication Research
Critical Studies in Mass Communication
Current History
Daedalus
Detroit Free Press
Diplomatic History
Ethnicity
Experimental Study of Politics
Foreign Affairs
Harper's
Historian
International Studies Quarterly
Jewish Journal of Sociology
Jewish Social Studies
Journal of American History
Journal of Broadcasting
Journal of Church and State
Journal of Communication
Journal of Conflict Resolution
Journal of Contemporary History
Journal of Palestine Studies
Journal of Social History
Journal of Social Studies
Journalism History
Journalism Quarterly
Journalism Monographs
Judaism

Kansas City Star
Louisville Courier-Journal
Memphis Commercial-Appeal
Mid-America
Middle East Journal
Middle Eastern Studies
Midwest Journal of Political Science
Midwest Quarterly
Mississippi Valley Historical Review
Nation
Nation's Business
Near East Report
New Orleans Times-Picayune
New Republic
New York Daily Mirror
New York Daily News
New York Herald-Tribune
New York Post
New York Times
New York Times Magazine
New Yorker
Newsweek
Perspectives in American History
Philadelphia Bulletin
Philadelphia Inquirer
Political Communication Review
Political Science Reviewer
P.M.
Presidential Studies Quarterly
P.S.
Public Opinion Quarterly
Richmond Times-Dispatch
St. Louis Post-Dispatch
St. Louis Star-Times
St. Paul Pioneer Press
San Francisco Chronicle
Saturday Review
Social Science Quarterly
Society for Historians of Foreign Relations Newsletter
South Atlantic Quarterly
The Review of Politics
Time
U. S. News and World Report
Variety
Vogue
Wall Street Journal

Washington Daily News
Washington Evening Star
Washington Post
Western Political Science Quarterly
Wisconsin Magazine of History

British Press and Periodicals:
British Journal of Political Science
The Daily Telegraph
The Economist
The Evening News
Great Britain and the East
The Listener
London Daily Express
London Evening Standard
The Mail
Manchester Guardian
News Chronicle
New Statesman
The Observer
The Star
The Sunday Times
Time and Tide
The Times (of London)

French Press and Periodicals:
Franc-Tireur
Le Figaro

DISSERTATIONS, PAPERS

Abuelkeshk, Abdelkarim. "A Portrayal of the Arab-Israeli Conflict in Three U.S. Journals of Opinion, 1948-1982." University of Wisconsin-Madison, 1985.
Alsaeed, Ibrahim H. "The Origins and Meaning of America's Special Relationship with Israel." University of Houston, 1988.
Bain, Kenneth R. "Roll on, Zion: The United States and the Palestine Question, 1945-1947." University of Texas-Austin, 1977.
Clifford, Clark M. "Factors Influencing President Truman's Decision to Support Partition and Recognize the State of Israel," a paper given to the American Historical Association on December 28, 1976 in Washington, D. C.
Doshe, Michael A. "American Periodicals and the Palestine Triangle, 1936-1947." Mississippi State University, 1966.
Godfried, Nathan. "An American Policy for the Third World: A Case Study of the United States and the Arab East, 1942-1948." University of Wisconsin-Madison, 1980.

Gold, Isadore Jay. "The United States and Saudi Arabia, 1933-1953: Post-Imperial Diplomacy and the Legacy of British Power." Columbia University, 1984.

Hammons, Terry B. "'A Wild Ass of a Man': American Images of Arabs to 1948." University of Oklahoma, 1978.

Haron, Miriam J. "Anglo-American Relations and the Question of Palestine, 1945-1947." Fordham University, 1979.

Hathaway, Robert. "The Paradoxes of Partnership: Britain and America, 1944-1947." University of North Carolina-Chapel Hill, 1976.

Kobland, Clifford E., Liping Du and Joongrok Kwon, "A Sharing of Values: The *New York Times* and American Ideology," a paper given at the Association for Education in Journalism and Mass Communication convention, on August 11, 1990, in Minneapolis, Minnesota.

Kramer, Arnold. "Soviet Bloc Relations with Israel." University of Wisconsin, 1970.

Leith, D. M. "American Christian Support for Jewish Palestine."Senior Thesis. Princeton University, 1957.

Liebovich, Louis. "Failed White House Press Relations in the Early Months of the Truman Administration," a paper given at the Midwest Journalism Historians Convention, University of Illinois at Champaign-Urbana, April 11, 1987.

McLeod, Jack M., Se-Wen Sun, Hsu-Hsien Chi and Zhongdang Pan, "Metaphor and the Media: What Shapes Public Understanding of the War Against Drugs?" a paper given at the Association for Education in Journalism and Mass Communication convention, on August 11, 1990, in Minneapolis, Minnesota.

Oder, Irwin. "The United States and the Palestine Mandate, 1920-1948: A Study on the Impact of Interest Groups on Foreign Policy." Columbia University, 1956.

Rosenberg, Jerry Phillipp. "Berlin and Israel, 1948: Foreign Policy Decision Making During the Truman Administration."University of Illinois, 1977.

Rubin, Barry M. "American Perceptions and Great Power Politics in the Middle East, 1941-1947." Georgetown University, 1978.

Rubenberg, Cheryl A. "United States-Israeli Relations, 1947-1974: A Study in the Convergence and Divurgence of Interests." University of Miami, 1979.

Sachar, David B. "David K. Niles and United States Policy Toward Palestine." Honors Thesis. Harvard University, 1959.

Sheldon, Neuringer M. "American Jewry and United States Immigration Policy, 1881-1953." University of Wisconsin, 1969.

Stevenson, Robert L. and William L. Gonzenbach, "Media Use, Political Activity and the 'Climate of Opinion,'" a paper given at the Association for Education in Journalism and Mass Communication convention, on August 11, 1990, in Minneapolis, Minnesota.

Williams, Herbert Lee. "Truman and the Press, April 12, 1945---January 20, 1953." University of Missouri, 1954.

Yotvat, Schlomo. "British and American Attitudes and Dipsutes Concerning the Palestine Question, 1942-1947." University of Wisconsin-Madison, 1983.

Zindani, Abdul Wahed Aziz. "Arab Politics in the United Nations."Notre Dame University, 1976.

INTERVIEWS AND CORRESPONDENCE

> Clark M. Clifford, April 1987
> E. Clifton Daniel, April 1988
> Dean Rusk, May 1987

PUBLISHED SOURCE MATERIALS

U.S. Public Documents:
> Public Papers of the President of the United States: Harry S. Truman, 1945-
> 1948. Washington, D. C., 1961.

U.S. State Department. *Bulletins*, 1946-1948.
> Department of State Press Releases, 1946-1948.
> Department of State, Treaties and Other International Acts, Series 1629.
> Foreign Relations of the United States, Diplomatic Papers, 1939-1948.

U.S. Congress. *Congressional Record*, 1943-1948.
> Senate Reports, Eightieth Congress, First Session.
> Senate Reports, Eightieth Congress, Second Session.
> House Reports, Eightieth Congress, First Session.
> House Reports, Eightieth Congress, Second Session.
> Public Laws, Eightieth Congress, First Session.
> Public Laws, Eightieth Congress, Second Session.

U.S. Congress. *Congressional Digest*, 1947-1948.
> "Assistance to Greece and Turkey, Hearings before the Committee on Foreign
> Relations, U. S. Senate, Eigtieth Congress, on S. 938, a Bill to
> Provide for Assistance to Greece and Turkey. March 24, 25, 27
> and 31, 1947."
> "Greek-Turkish Aid Bill. Answers Submitted by the Department of State
> Relating to S. 938. Committee on Foreign Relations. March 28,
> 1947.

U.N. Public Documents:
> United Nations General Assembly, *Documents*, 1947-1948.
> United Nations Security Council, *Documents*, 1947-1948.
> United Nations Security Council, Official Records, 2nd year, 1947.
> United Nations Weekly Bulletin, 1947-1948.
> "Report of the U.N. Special Committee on Palestine," *United Nations:
> Yearbook of the United Nations*, 1947-1948.
> "First Monthly Report of United Nations Palestine Commission to President of
> the Security Council. January 30, 1948."
> "Security Council Verbatim Record of the 258th Meeting."United Nations
> Security Council Meeting of March 2, 1948. Lake Success, New
> York.

"Summary Record of the 126th Meeting of the United Nations General Assembly" on April 26, 1948. Lake Success, New York.

"Verbatim Record of the 135th Meeting of the United Nations General Assembly," Second Special Session. May 14, 1948. Flushing Meadow, New York.

U.K. Public Documents:

Hansard. House of Commons Official Reports.

Parliamentary Debates of 1946-1948, 5th series.

Miscellaneous Documents:

Adler, Cyrus and Aaron M. Margalith. *With Firmness in the Right: American Diplomatic Efforts Affecting Jews, 1840-1945* (New York: American Jewish Committee, 1946).

American Jewish Year Book 5707 (1946-1947). (Philadelphia: Jewish Publication Society of America, 1946).

American Jewish Year Book 5708 (1947-1948). (Philadelphia: Jewish Publication Society of America, 1947).

American Jewish Year Book 5709 (1948-1949). (Philadelphia: Jewish Publication Society of America, 1948).

Cohen, Michael J., ed., *The Rise of Israel: A Documentary Record from the Nineteenth Century to 1948*, volumes 30, 31, 34-39 (New York: Garland, 1987).

Dennett, Raymond and Robert K. Turner, eds., *Documents on American Foreign Relations*, Volume 9, 1947 (Princeton: Princeton University, 1949).

Dennett, Raymond and Robert K. Turner, eds., *Documents on American Foreign Relations*, Volume 10, 1948 (Princeton: Princeton University, 1950).

Etzold, Thomas H. and John Lewis Gaddis, eds., *Containment: Documents on American Policy and Strategy, 1945-1950* (New York: Columbia University, 1978).

Fink, Reuben, ed., *America and Palestine* (New York: Arno Press, 1977).

Hurewitz, Jacob C., ed., *Diplomacy in the Near and Middle East: A Documentary Record, 1914-1956* (Princeton: Princeton University, D. Van Nordstrand, 1956).

Hurewitz, Jacob C., ed., *The Middle East and North Africa in World Politics: A Documentary Record, 1914-1945* (New Haven: Yale University, 1979).

Jewish Agency for Palestine, *The Jewish Plan for Palestine: Memoranda and Statements* (Jerusalem: The Jewish Agency for Palestine, 1947).

John, Robert and Sami Hadawi, eds., *The Palestine Diary*, Volume 2, 1945-1948 (New York: New World, 1970).

Kennedy, William J., ed., *Secret History of the Oil Companies in the Middle East* (Salisbury, N. C.: Documentary Publications, 1979).

LeFeber, Walter, ed., *America in the Cold War: Twenty Years of Revolutions and Response, 1947-1967* (New York: John Wiley, 1969).

Learsi, Rufus, ed., *The Jews in America: A History* (New York: KTAV Publishing House, 1972).

Lippy, Charles H., ed., *Religious Periodicals of the United States: Academic and Scholarly Journals* (New York: Greenwood Press, 1986).

Marty, Martin; John G. Deedy, Jr., David Wolf Silverman and Robert Lekachman, eds., *The Religious Press in America*, (New York: Holt, Rinehart and Winston, 1963).

Meyer, Isadore S., ed., *Early History of Zionism in America*, (New York: Arno Press, 1977).

Miller, Sally M., ed., *The Ethnic Press in the United States: A Historical Analysis and Handbook* (New York: Greenwood Press, 1987).

Mosteller, Frederick; Herbert Hyman, Philip J. McCarthy, Eli S. Marks and David B. Truman, *The Pre-Election Polls of 1948: Report to the Committee on Analysis of Pre-Election Polls and Forecasts* (New York: Social Science Research Council, 1949).

Nelson, Anna K., ed., *The State Department Policy Planning Staff Papers*, three volumes (New York: Garland, 1983).

Porter, Kirk H. and Donald P. Johnson. *National Party Platforms* (Urbana: University of Illinois, 1956).

Robinson, Jacob, ed., *Palestine and the United Nations: Prelude to Solution* (Washington: Public Affairs Press, 1947).

Scammon, Richard M. *America at the Polls: A Handbook of American Presidential Elections Statistics, 1920-1964* (New York: Arno Press, 1976).

Sklare, Marshall, ed., *The Jews: Social Patterns of an American Group* (Glencoe: Free Press, 1958).

ADDRESSES, CONFERENCES, BROADCASTS

Bulletin of the 22nd World Zionist Congress, held in Basle, Switzerland. December, 1946.

Resolution Adopted by Extraordinary Zionist Conference, held in Washington, D. C. February 17, 1947.

"American Attitudes on U. S. Policy Towards Russia," a nationwide survey conducted by Survey Research Center, University of Michigan. February 19, 1947.

Address by Rabbi Abba Hillel Silver to members of the United Nations Security Council. March 5, 1947.

Transcripts. "Action for Palestine Week," a series of radio spot announcements produced by the American Zionist Emergency Council in cooperation with various Hollywood celebrities, and airing nationwide the week of May 4, 1947.

Address by Rabbi Abba Hillel Silver to members of the United Nations Security Council. April 28, 1947.

Transcript. Broadcast by Sumner Welles over radio station W.O.L.-AM (New York) on Sunday, June 8, 1947, from 7:45 p.m. to 8:00 p.m. E. S. T.

Address by Howard M. LeSourd of the American Christians for Palestine Committee to the Commonwealth Club of San Francisco. July 1, 1947.

Report of Harry L. Shapiro, executive director of the American Zionist Emergency Council, to the convention of the Zionist Organization of America. July 4, 1947.

Message by Frank W. Buxton, member of the Anglo-American Committee of Inquiry, to the mass demonstration protesting British assault on the Jewish vessel, *Exodus '47*. Speech given in New York City's Madison Square Park. July 24, 1947.

Address by Rabbi Abba Hillel Silver to members of the United Nations General Assembly on the report of the United Nations Special Committee on Palestine. October 2, 1947.

Report of the Central Intelligence Agency, "Review of the World Situation," prepared for a meeting of the National Security Council. November 14, 1947.

Address by Rabbi Abba Hillel Silver to members of the Zionist Organization of America in New York City. December 29, 1947.

University of Chicago Roundtable. "Should a U. N. Army Enforce Partition on Palestine?" A radio discussion by British Colonial Secretary Arthur Creech-Jones; former member of the Anglo-American Committee of Inquiry Bartley Crum; co-founder of American Christians for Palestine Committee Reinhold Niebuhr; Professor of Turkish languages at Princeton University Walter Wright; and Professor of Egyptology at University of Chicago John Wilson, broadcast on NBC February 22, 1948.

Reaction to report on Palestine presented by the United States to members of the United Nations Security Council in Flushing Meadow, New York. March 19, 1948.

Transcript. Broadcast speech by David Ben-Gurion, in behalf of the Provisional State Council, in Tel-Aviv, Israel, declaring the creation of the state of Israel. May 14, 1948.

AUTOBIOGRAPHIES, BIOGRAPHIES, MEMOIRS, DIARIES

Acheson, Dean. *Present at the Creation: My Years in the State Department* (New York: W. W. Norton, 1969).

Acheson, Dean. *A Citizen Looks at Congress* (Westport: Greenwood Press, 1974).

Adler, Cyrus. *Jacob Schiff: His Life and Letters*, two volumes (New York: American Jewish Committee).

Allen, George E. *Presidents Who Have Known Me* (New York: Simon and Schuster, 1950).

Alpern, Sara. *Freda Kirchwey: A Woman of the Nation* (Cambridge: Harvard University, 1987).

Baer, George W. *A Question of Trust: The Origins of U. S.-Soviet Diplomatic Relations, The Memoirs of Loy W. Henderson* (Stanford: Hoover Institution Press, 1986).

Baker, Ray Stannard. *Woodrow Wilson and World Settlement*, volumes 7 and 8 (Garden City: Doubleday, 1932).

Begin, Menachem. *The Revolt: Story of the Irgun* (New York: Henry Schumann, 1951.

Ben-Ami, Yitshaq. *Years of Wrath, Days of Glory: Memoirs from the Irgun* (New York: Robert Speller, 1982).

Ben-Gurion, David. *Rebirth and Destiny of Israel* (New York: Philosophical Library, 1954).

Ben-Gurion, David. *Israel: Years of Challenge* (New York: Holt, Rinehart and Winston, 1963).

Bentwich, Norman and Helen. *Mandate Memories: 1918-1948* (London: Hogarth, 1965).

Ben-Zohar, Michael. *The Armed Prophet:: A Biography of Ben-Gurion* (London: Arthur Barker, 1966).

Ben-Zohar, Michael. *Ben-Gurion: A Political Biography*, volume 1 (Tel Aviv: Am Oved Publishers, 1975).

Berle, Beatrice Bishop and Travis Real Jacobs, eds., *Navigating the Rapids, 1918-1971: From the Papers of Adolph A. Berle* (New York: Harcourt, Brace, Jovanovich, 1973).

Bishop, Jim. *F. D. R.'s Last Year: April 1944—April 1945* (New York: William Morrow, 1974).

Blumberg, Harold M. *Weizmann: His Life and Times* (New York: St. Martin's, 1975).

Bohlen, Charles E. *Witness to History, 1929-1969* (New York: W. W. Norton, 1973).

Branstein, Thomas R. *David Ben-Gurion: Memoirs* (New York: World Publishing, 1970).

Byrnes, James F. *Speaking Frankly* (New York: Harper, 1947).

Campbell, Thomas M. and George C. Herring, eds., *The Diaries of Edward R. Stettinius, Jr., 1943-1946* (New York: New Viewpoints, 1975).

Christman, Henry M., ed., *This Is Our Strength: Selected Papers of Golda Meir* (New York: Macmillan, 1962).

Cellar, Emanuel. *You Never Leave Brooklyn* (New York: John Day, 1953).

Cohen, Warren I. *Dean Rusk* (Totowa, N. J.: Cooper Square, 1980).

Crossman, Richard. *A Nation Reborn* (New York: Antheneum, 1960).

Crossman, Richard. *Palestine Mission: A Personal Record* (New York: Harper, 1947).

Crum, Bartley C. *Behind the Silken Curtain: A Personal Account of Anglo-American Diplomacy in Palestine and the Middle East* (New York: Simon and Schuster, 1947).

Dalton, Hugh. *The Fateful Years: Memoirs, 1931-1945* (London: Frederick Muller, 1957).

Dalton, Hugh. *High Tide and After: Memoirs, 1945-1960* (London: Frederick Muller, 1962).

Daniels, Jonathan. *The Man of Independence* (Philadelphia: J. B. Lippincott, 1950).

Daniels, Josephus. *The Wilson Era: Years of War and After, 1917-1923* (Chapel Hill: University of North Carolina, 1946).

Ducovny, Amram. *David Ben-Gurion in His Own Words* (New York: Fleet Press, 1968).

Dulles, John Foster. *War Or Peace* (New York: Macmillan, 1950).

Eban, Abba. *Abba Eban: An Autobiography* (New York: Random House, 1977).

Eddy, William A. *F. D. R. Meets Ibn Saud* (New York: American Friends of the Middle East, 1954).

Elath, Eliahu. *Zionism at the United Nations: A Diary of the First Days* (Philadelphia: The Jewish Publication Society of America, 1976).

Elath, Eliahu. *The Struggle for Statehood: Washington, 1945-1948*, Volume 2 (Tel Aviv: Am Oved, 1982).

Epstein, Elias M. *Jerusalem Correspondent, 1918-1958* (Jerusalem: The Jerusalem Post Press, 1964).

Ernst, Morris. *So Far So Good* (New York: Harper, 1948).

Ferrell, Robert H., ed., *Off the Record: The Private Papers of Harry S. Truman* (New York: Harper and Row, 1980).

Ferrell, Robert H., *Harry S. Truman and the Modern American Presidency* (Boston: Little, Brown, 1982).

Ferrell, Robert H., ed., *Dear Bess: The Letters from Harry to Bess Truman, 1910-1959* (New York: W. W. Norton, 1983).

Freedman, Max, ed., *Roosevelt and Frankfurter: Their Correspondence, 1928-1945* (Boston: Little, Brown, 1967).

Gallup, George H. *The Gallup Poll: Public Opinion, 1935-1971* (New York: Random House, 1972).

Garcia-Granados, Jorge. *The Birth of Israel: The Drama as I Saw It* (New York: Knopf, 1948).

Goldmann, Nahum. *Memories: The Authobiography of Nahum Goldmann* (New York: Holt, Rinehart and Wisnton, 1969).

Gosnell, Harold F. *Truman's Crises: A Political Biography of Harry S. Truman* (Westport: Greenwood Press, 1980).

Grauel, John S. *Grauel* (Freehold, N. J.: Ivory House, 1982).

Grew, Joseph C. *Turbulent Era*, two volumes (Boston: Houghton Mifflin, 1952).

Hand, Samuel. *Counsel and Advise: A Political Biography of Samuel I. Rosenman* (New York: Garland, 1979).

Haynes, Richard F. *The Awesome Power: Harry S. Truman as Commander-in-Chief* (Baton Rouge: Louisiana State University, 1973).

Hecht, Ben. *A Child of the Century* (New York: Simon and Schuster, 1954).

Helm, William Pickett. *Harry S. Truman: A Political Biography* (New York: Duell, Sloan and Pearce, 1947).

Hillman, William. *Mr. President* (New York: Farrar, Straus and Young, 1952).

Hull, Cordell. *The Memoirs of Cordell Hull*, two volumes (New York: Macmillan, 1948).

Israel, Fred L., ed., *The War Diaries of Breckenridge Long, 1933-1944* (Lincoln: University of Nebraska, 1966).

Jenkins, Roy. *Truman* (New York: Harper and Row, 1986).

Johnson, Gerald W. *An Honorable Titan* (New York: Harper, 1946).

Jones, Joseph M. *The Fifteen Weeks* (New York: Viking Press, 1955).

Kennan, George F. *Memoirs: 1925-1950* (Boston: Little, Brown, 1967).

Krock, Arthur. *Memoirs: Sixty Years on the Firing Line* (New York: Funk and Wagnalls, 1968).

Kurzman, Dan. *Ben-Gurion: Prophet of Fire* (New York: Simon and Schuster, 1983).

Lansing, Robert. *The Peace Negotiations: A Personal Narrative* (Boston: Houghton Mifflin, 1921).

Lash, Joseph P. ed., *From the Diaries of Felix Frankfurter* (New York: W. W. Norton, 1975).

Leahy, William D. "Diary." Unpublished. Library of Congress. Washington, D. C.

Lie, Trygve. *In the Cause of Peace: Seven Years with the United Nations* (New York: Macmillan, 1954).

Litvinoff, Barnet. *Ben-Gurion of Israel* (London: Weidenfeld and Nicolson, 1954).

Litvinoff, Barnet. *Weizmann: Last of the Patriarchs* (London: Hodder and Stoughton, 1976).

Litvinoff, Barnet. *The Essential Chaim Weizmann: The Man, the Statesman, the Scientist* (New York: Holmes and Meier, 1982).

Litvinoff, Barnet, ed., *The Letters and Papers of Chaim Weizmann*, two volumes (New Brunswick: Transaction Books, 1984).

Loewenheim, Francis; Langley Harold and Jonas Manfred, eds., *Roosevelt and Churchill: Their Secret Wartime Correspondence* (London: Berrie and Jankins, 1975).

MacDonald, James G. *My Mission to Israel, 1948-1951* (New York: Simon and Schuster, 1951).

Malkin, Aahuvia and Eli Shealtiel, eds., *Making of Policy: The Diaries of Moshe Sharrett*, volume 5 (Jerusalem: Ha-Sifria, Ha-Zionith, 1979).

Martin, Kingsley. *Harold Laski: A Biographical Memoir* (London: Victor Gallancz, 1953).

Mason, Alpheus T. *Brandeis: A Free Man's Life* (New York: Viking Press, 1946).

Mazuzan, George. *Warren R. Austin at the United Nations, 1946-1953* (Kent: Kent State University, 1977).

McCagg, William O. *Stalin Embattled, 1943-1948* (Detroit: Wayne State University, 1978).

McCoy, Donald R. *The Presidency of Harry S. Truman* (Lawrence: University of Kansas, 1984).

McNaughton, Frank and Walter Hehmeyer. *This Man Truman* (New York: McGraw-Hill, 1945).

McNaughton, Frank and Walter Hehmeyer. *Harry S. Truman, President* (New York: Whittlesey House, 1948).

Meinherzhagen, Col. Richard. *Middle East Diary, 1919-1956* (London: Cresset, 1959).

Meir, Golda. *My Life* (New York: Putnam, 1975).

Miller, Merle. *Plain Speaking: An Oral Biography of Harry S. Truman* (New York: Berkeley Books, 1974).

Millis, Walter, ed., *The Forrestal Diaries* (New York: Viking Press, 1951).

Mosley, Leonard. *Marshall: Hero of Our Times* (New York: Hearst Books, 1982).

Neumann, Emanuel. *In the Arena: An Autobiographical Memoir* (New York: Herzl Press, 1976).

Patai, Raphael. *Nahum Goldmann: His Mission to the Gentiles* (Tuscaloosa: University of Alabama, 1987).

Pearlman, Moshe. *Ben-Gurion Looks Back* (New York: Simon and Schuster, 1965).

Perkins, Francis. *The Roosevelt I Knew* (New York: Viking Press, 1946).

Phillips, William. *Ventures in Diplomacy* (Boston: Beacon Press, 1952).

Poen, Monte M. *Letters Home from Harry Truman* (New York: Putnam, 1984).

Pogue, Forrest C. *George C. Marshall: Statesman, 1945-1959* (New York: Viking Press, 1987).

Pruessen, Ronald R. *John Foster Dulles: The Road to Power* (New York: Free Press, 1982).

Proskauer, Joseph M. *A Segment of My Times* (New York: Farrar, Straus, 1950).

Raphael, Marc Lee. *Abba Hillel Silver: A Profile in American Judaism* (New York: Holmes and Meier, 1989).

Rogow, Arnold A. *James Forrestal: A Study of Personality, Politics and Policy* (New York: Macmillan, 1963).

Roosevelt, Elliott. *As He Saw It* (New York: Duell, Sloan and Pearce, 1946).

Rose, Norman A. *Lewis Namier and Zionism* (London: Oxford University, 1980).

Rose, Norman A. *Chaim Weizmann: A Biography* (New York: Viking Press, 1986).

Rosenman, Samuel I., ed., *The Public Papers and Addresses of Franklin D. Roosevelt*, volume 4 (New York: Harper and Row, 1950).

Rosten, Leo. *The Washington Correspondents* (New York: Harcourt, Brace, 1937).

Ruddy, T. Michael. *The Cautious Diplomat: Charles E. Bohlen and the Soviet Union, 1927-1969* (Kent: Kent State University, 1986).

Sherwood, Robert E. *Roosevelt and Hopkins: An Intimate History* (New York: Harper, 1949).

Shihor, Samuel. *Hollow Glory: The Last Days of Chaim Weizmann, First President of Israel* (New York: Thomas Yoseloff, 1960).

Silver, Abba Hillel. *The World Crisis and Jewish Survival: A Group of Essays* (New York: Richard R. Smith, 1941).

Silver, Abba Hillel. *Vision and Victory: A Collection of Addresses by Dr. Abba Hillel Silver, 1942-1948* (New York: The Zionist Organization of America, 1949).

Smith, Walter Bedell. *My Three Years in Moscow* (Philadelphia: J. B. Lippincott, 1950).

St. John, Robert. *Ben-Gurion: The Biography of an Extraordinary Man* (Garden City: Doubleday, 1954).

Steinberg, Alfred. *The Man from Missouri: The Life and Times of Harry S. Truman* (New York: Putnam, 1962).

Stoler, Mark A. *George C. Marshall: Soldier-Statesman of the American Century* (Boston: Twayne, 1989).

Sulzberger, Cyrus. *A Long Row of Candles: Memoirs and Diaries, 1934-1954* (New York: Macmillan, 1969).

Syrkin, Marie. *Golda Meir: Woman with a Cause* (London: Victor Gollancz, 1964).

Syrkin, Marie, ed., *A Land of Our Own: An Oral Biography by Golda Meir* (New York: Putnam, 1973).

Tompkins, C. David. *Senator Arthur Vandenberg* (East Lansing: Michigan State University, 1970).

Truman, Harry S. *Mr. Citizen* (New York: Bernard Geis Associates, 1953).

Truman, Harry S. *Memoirs: Year of Decisions* (Garden City: Doubleday, 1955).

Truman, Harry S. *Memoirs: Years of Trail and Hope* (Garden City: Doubleday, 1956).

Truman, Margaret. *Harry S. Truman* (New York: William Morrow, 1973).

Truman, Margaret. *Letters from Father* (New York: Arbor House, 1981).

Urofsky, Melvin I., ed., *Letters of Louis D. Brandeis*, volume 5 (Albany: State University of New York, 1978).

Vandenberg, Arthur H. and Joe Alex Morris, eds., *The Private Papers of Senator Vandenberg* (Boston: Houghton Mifflin, 1952).

Victor, Edward, ed., *Meyer Weisgal at Seventy: An Anthology* (London: Weidenfeld and Nicholson, 1966).

Weisgal, Meyer and Joel Carmichael, eds., *Chaim Weizmann: A Biography by Several Hands* (New York: Antheneum, 1963).

Weisgal, Meyer. *So Far* (New York: Random House, 1971).

Weizmann, Chaim. *Trial and Error* (New York: Harper, 1949).

Weizmann, Vera. *The Impossible Takes Longer* (New York: Harper and Row, 1967).

Williams, Francis. *Ernest Bevin: Portrait of a Great Englishman* (London: Hutchinson, 1952).

Williams, Francis. *A Prime Minister Remembers: The War and Post War Memoirs of Earl Attlee* (London: Heinemann, 1961).

Wilson, Evan M. *Decision on Palestine—How the U. S. Came to Recognize Israel* (Stanford: Hoover Institution Press, 1979).

Wise, Stephen. *Challenging Years* (New York: Putnam, 1949).

BOOKS AND PAMPHLETS

Adler, Frank J. *Roots in a Moving Stream: The Centennial History of Congregation B'nai Jehudah of Kansas City, 1870-1970* (Kansas City: The Temple, Congregation B'nai Jehudah, 1972).

Adler, Selig. *The Isolationist Impulse* (New York: Abelard-Schuman, 1957).

Albion, Robert G. and Robert H. Connery. *Forrestal and the Navy* (New York: Columbia University, 1962).

Allen, Robert S. and William V. Shannon, *The Truman Merry-Go-Round* (New York: Vanguard, 1950).

Almond, Gabriel A. *The American People and Foreign Policy* (New York: Prager, 1961).

Almond, Gabriel A. and James C. Coleman, eds., *The Politics of Developing Areas* (Princeton: Princeton University, 1960).

Alperovitz, Gar. *Atomic Diplomacy: Hiroshima and Potsdam* (New York: Simon and Schuster, 1965).

Alsop, Joseph and Stewart. *The Reporter's Trade* (New York: Reynall, 1958).

Amitzur, Ilan. *America, Britain and Palestine: The Origin and Development of America's Intervention in Britain's Palestine Policy, 1938-1947* (Jerusalem: Yad Ben-Avi, 1979).

Anderson, Irving H. *Aramco, the United States and Saudi Arabia: A Study in the Dynamics of Foreign Oil Policy, 1933-1950* (Princeton: Princeton University, 1981).

Anderson, Patrick. *The President's Men* (Garden City: Doubleday, 1968).

Argyris, Chris. *Personality and Organization* (New York: Harper's, 1957).

Argyris, Chris. *Some Causes of Organizational Effectiveness Within the Department of State* (Washington: Center for International Systems Research, 1967).

Arkes, Hadley. *Bureaucracy, the Marshall Plan and the National Interest* (Princeton: Princeton University, 1972).

Aaronson, James. *The Press and the Cold War* (New York: Monthly Press Review, 1990).

Bagdikian, Ben H. *The Information Machines: Their Impact on Men and the Media* (New York: Harper and Row, 1971).

Bailey, Thomas A. *The Marshall Plan Summer: An Eyewitness Report on Europe and the Russians in 1947* (Stanford: Hoover Institution Press, 1977).

Bain, Kenneth. *The March to Zion: United States Policy and the Founding of Israel* (College Station: A & M University, 1979).

Baram, Philiip. *The Department of State in the Middle East, 1919-1945* (Philadelphia: University of Pennsylvania, 1978).

Barber, James David. *The Presidential Character: Predicting Performance in the White House* (Englewood Cliffs: Prentice Hall, 1977).

Bauer, Yehuda. *Flight and Rescue: Bricha* (New York: Random House, 1970).

Bauer, Yehuda. *Diplomacy and Underground in Zionism, 1939-1945* (Philadelphia: Jewish Publication Society of America, 1970).

Becker, William H. and Samuel F. Wells, Jr., eds., *Economics and World Power: An Assessment of American Diplomacy since 1789* (New York: Columbia University, 1984).

Beling, Willard A., ed., *The Middle East: Quest for American Policy* (Albany: State University of New York at Albany, 1973).

Bell, J. Bowyer. *On Revolt: Strategies of National Liberation* (Cambridge: Harvard University, 1976).

Bell, J. Bowyer. *Terror Out of Zion: Irgun Zvai Leumi, Lehi and the Palestine Underground, 1929-1949* (New York: St. Martin's, 1977).

Beloff, Max. *Imperial Sunset: Britain's Liberal Empire, 1897-1921* (New York: Knopf, 1970).

Bemis, Samuel F. and Robert H. Ferrell, eds., *The American Secretaries of State and Their Diplomacy* (New York: Cooper Square, 1972).

Bendiner, Robert. *The Riddle of the State Department* (New York: Farrar and Rinehart, 1942).

Berding, Andrew H. *Foreign Affairs and You* (Garden City: Doubleday, 1962).

Berelson, Bernard and Gary A. Steiner. *Human Behaviour: An Inventory of Scientific Findings* (New York: Harcourt, Brace and World, 1964).

Berger, Meyer. *The Story of the New York Times, 1851-1951* (New York: Simon and Schuster, 1951).

Berger, Morroe. *The Arab World Today* (New York: Doubleday, 1954).

Berger, Peter and Thomas Luckmann. *The Social Construction of Reality* (Garden City: Doubleday-Anchor, 1967).

Bernstein, Barton J. *Politics and the Policies of the Truman Administration* (Chicago: Quadrangle Press, 1970).

Berry, Nicholas O. *Foreign Policy and the Press: An Analysis of the New York Times' Coverage of U. S. Foreign Policy* (Westport: Greenwood Press, 1990).

Bethell, Nicholas. *The Palestine Triangle: The Struggle for the Holy Land, 1935-1948* (New York: Putnam, 1979).

Biddle, Francis. *The World's Best Hope: A Discussion of the Role of the United States in the Modern World* (Chicago: University of Chicago, 1949).

Biggs-Davison, John A. *The Uncertain Ally* (London: Christopher Johnson, 1957).

Blancke, W. Wendell. *The Foreign Service of the United States* (New York: Praeger, 1969).

Bloomfield, Jon. *Passive Revolution: Politics and the Czechoslovakian Working Class, 1945-1948* (New York: St. Martin's, 1979).

Blum, John Morton. *V Was for Victory: Politics and American Culture during World War II* (New York: Harcourt, Brace, Jovanovich, 1976).

Bohlen, Charles E. *The Transformation of American Foreign Policy* (New York: W. W. Norton, 1969).

Boll, Michael M. *National Security Planning: Roosevelt Through Reagan* (Lexington: University Press of Kentucky, 1988).

Boorstin, Daniel J. *The Image* (New York: Antheneum, 1962).

Boulding, Kenneth E. *The Image* (Ann Arbor: University of Michigan, 1956).

Browder, Robert. *The Origins of Soviet-American Diplomacy* (Princeton: Princeton University, 1953).

Brown, Cecil. *Suez to Singapore* (New York: Random House, 1942).

Bryson, Thomas A. *American Diplomatic Relations with the Middle East, 1784-1975: A Survey* (Metuchen, N. J.: Scarecrow Press, 1977).

Cantrill, Hadley. *Public Opinion, 1935-1946* (Princeton: Princeton University, 1951).

Case, Shirley. *The Millennial Hope* (Chicago: University of Chicago, 1918).

Cater, Douglas. *Fourth Branch of Government* (Boston: Houghton Mifflin, 1959).

Chatham House Study. *British Security* (London: Oxford University, 1946).

Childs, J. Rives. *American Foreign Service* (New York: Henry Holt, 1948).

Childs, Marquis. *Witness to Power* (New York: McGraw-Hill, 1975).

Churchill, Winston. *The Second World War*, Volume 6 (London: Cassell, 1953.

Clark, Elmer T. *The Small Sects in America* (New York: Agingdon-Cokesbury, 1949).

Cochran, Bert. *Harry Truman and the Crisis Presidency* (New York: Funk and Wagnalls, 1973).

Cohen, Bernard C. *The Influence of Non-Governmental Groups on Foreign Policy-Making* (Boston: World Peace Foundation, 1959).

Cohen, Bernard C. *The Press and Foreign Policy* (Princeton: Princeton University, 1963).

Cohen, Gavriel. *The British Cabinet and Palestine, April—July, 1943* (Tel Aviv: Hakibbutz Hameuchad, 1976).

Cohen, Michael J. *Palestine: Retreat from the Mandate, the Making of British Policy, 1936-1945* (London: Elek, 1978).

Cohen, Michael J. *Palestine and the Great Powers, 1945-1948* (Princeton: Princeton University, 1982).

Cohen, Michael J. *Palestine to Israel: From Mandate to Independence* (London: Frank Cass, 1988).

Cohen, Michael J. *Truman and Israel* (Berkeley: University of California, 1990).

Cohen, Naomi. *Not Free to Desist: The American Jewish Committee* (Philadelphia: Jewish Publication Society, 1972).

Commission on Freedom of the Press, *A Free and Responsible Press* (Chicago: University of Chicago, 1947).

Condit, Kenneth W. *The History of the Joint Chiefs of Staff and National Policy*, Volume 2 (Wilmington: Michael Glazier, 1979).

Cornwell, Elmer E. *Presidential Leadership of Public Opinion* (Bloomington: Indiana University, 1966).

Corwin, Erwin S. *Total War and the Constitution* (Freeport, N. Y.: Books for Libraries Press, 1970).

Craig, Gordon A. and Alexander L. George, *Force and Statecraft: Diplomatic Problems of Our Time* (New York: Oxford University, 1983).

Cronin, Thomas E. *The State of the Presidency* (Boston: Little, Brown, 1980).

Curtiss, Richard A. *A Changing Image: Americans Perspectives of the Arab-Israeli Dispute* (Washington: American Education Trust, 1982).

Dahl, Robert A. *Congress and Foreign Policy* (New York: Harcourt, Brace, 1950).

Dahl, Robert and Charles Lindbloom. *Politics, Economy and Welfare: Planning Politico-Economic Systems Resolved into Basic Social Processes* (Chicago: University of Chicago, 1956).

Davis, Elmer. *The History of the New York Times* (New York: New York Times, 1921).

Davis, Lynn Etheridge. *The Cold War Begins* (Princeton: Princeton University, 1974).

Davis, Moshe. *Israel: Its Role in Civilization* (New York: Harper, 1956).

Davis, Moshe. *Christian Protagonists for Jewish Restoration* (New York: Arno Press, 1977).

DeConde, Alexander. *A History of American Foreign Policy* (New York: Scribner's, 1971).

Deibel, Terry L. and John Lewis Gaddis, *Containing the Soviet Union: A Critique of U.S. Policy* (Washington: Pergamon-Brassey, 1987).

DeNovo, John A. *American Interests and Politics in the Middle East, 1900-1939* (Minneapolis: University of Minnesota, 1963).

Dennis, Everette E., ed., *Beyond the Cold War: Soviet and American Media Images* (Newbury, Cal.: Sage, 1991).

Denton, Jr., Robert E. and Dan F. Hahn, *Presidential Communication: Description and Analysis* (Westport: Praeger, 1986).

de Rivera, Joseph. *The Psychological Dimension of Foreign Policy* (Columbus: Charles E. Merrill, 1968).

DeSantis, Hugh. *The Diplomacy of Silence: The American Foreign Service, the Soviet Union and the Cold War, 1933-1947* (Chicago: University of Chicago, 1980).

Deutsch, Karl. *Political Communication at the International Level* (Princeton: Princeton University, 1953).

Dilks, David, ed., *Retreat from Power: Studies in Britain's Foreign Policy of the Twentieth Century*, volume 2 (London: Macmillan, 1981).

Dinnerstein, Leonard. *America and the Survivors of the Holocaust* (New York: Columbia University, 1982).

Divine, Robert A. *Second Chance: The Triumph of Internationalism in America during World War II* (New York: Antheneum, 1967).

Divine, Robert A. *Foreign Policy and U. S. Presidential Elections*, Volume 1, 1940-1948 (New York: New Viewpoints, 1974).

Donovan, Robert. *Conflict and Crisis: The Presidency of Harry S. Truman, 1945-1948* (New York: W. W. Norton, 1977).

Dunar, Andrew J. *The Truman Scandals and the Politics of Morality* (Columbia: University of Missouri, 1984).

Duncan, Hugh Dalziel. *Symbols and Social Theory* (New York: Oxford University, 1969).

Edelman, Murray. *The Symbolic Use of Politics* (Urbana: University of Illinois, 1964).

Edinin, Ben. *Jewish Community Life in America* (New York: Hebrew Publications, 1947).

Edwards, George C. *The Public Presidency: The Pursuit of Popular Support* (New York: St. Martin's, 1983).

Edwards, George C. and Stephen J. Wayne. *Presidential Leadership: Politics and Policy Making* (New York: St. Martin's, 1985).

Elder, Robert E. *The Policy Machine: The Department of State and American Foreign Policy* (Syracuse: Syracuse University, 1960).

Ellul, Jacques. *Propaganda: The Formation of Men's Attitudes* (New York: Knopf, 1965).

Ellul, Jacques. *The Political Illusion* (New York: Knopf, 1967).

Farrell, John C. and Asa P. Smith, eds., *Image and Reality in World Politics* (New York: Columbia University, 1968).

Feingold, Henry. *The Politics of Rescue: The Roosevelt Administration and the Holocaust, 1938-1945* (New Brunswick: Rutgers University, 1970).

Feis, Herbert. *The Birth of Israel: The Touseled Diplomatic Bed* (New York: W. W. Norton, 1969).

Feis, Herbert. *From Trust to Terror: The Onset of the Cold War, 1945-1950* (New York: W. W. Norton, 1970).

Fishman, Hertzel. *American Protestantism and a Jewish State* (Detroit: Wayne State University, 1973).

Fernau, Frederick W. *Moslems on the March* (New York: Knopf, 1954).

Folkerts, Jean and Dwight L. Teeter, Jr. *Voices of a Nation: A History of Media in the United States* (New York: Macmillan, 1989).

Forbath, Peter and Carey Winfrey. *The Adversaries: The President and the Press* (Cleveland: Regal Books, 1974).

Freeland, Richard M. *The Truman Doctrine and the Origins of McCarthyism: Foreign Policy, Domestic Politics, and Internal Security, 1946-1948* (New York: Knopf, 1972).

Friedman, Lee M. *Jewish Pioneers and Patriots* (New York: Macmillan, 1943).

Friedrich, Carl J. *American Policy Toward Palestine* (Washington: American Council on Public Affairs, 1944).

Froom, Leroy E. *The Prophetic Faith of Our Fathers* (Washington: Review and Herald, 1950).

Frost, Richard, ed., *The British Commonwealth and World Society* (London: Oxford University, 1947).

Gaddis, John Lewis. *The United States and the Origins of the Cold War* (New York: Columbia University, 1972).

Gaddis, John Lewis. *Strategies of Containment: A Critical Appraisal of Postwar American National Security Policy* (New York: Oxford University, 1982).

Ganin, Zvi. *Truman, American Jewry and Israel, 1945-1948* (New York: Holmes and Meier, 1979).

Gardner, Lloyd C. *Economic Aspects of New Deal Diplomacy* (Madison: University of Wisconsin, 1964).

Gardner, Lloyd C. *Architects of Illusion: Men and Ideas in American Foreign Policy, 1941-1949* (Chicago: Quadrangle Press, 1970).

Gardner, Lloyd C. *Imperial America: American Foreign Policy since 1898* (New York: Harcourt, Brace, 1976).

Gardner, Richard N. *Sterling Dollar Diplomacy: Anglo-American Collaboration in the Reconstruction of Multilateral Trade* (Oxford: Clarendon Press, 1956).

Gati, Charles, ed., *Caging the Bear: Containment and the Cold War* (Indianapolis: Bobbs-Merrill, 1972).

George, Alexander L. *Presidential Decisionmaking in Foreign Policy: The Effective Use of Information and Advice* (Boulder: Westview Press, 1980).

Gerson, Louis L. *The Hyphenate in Recent American Politics and Diplomacy* (Lawrence: University of Kansas, 1964).

Ghareeb, Edmund, ed., *Split Vision: The Portrayal of Arabs in the American Media* (Washington: American-Arab Affairs Council, 1983).

Gibb, H. A. R. *Modern Trends in Islam* (Chicago: University of Chicago, 1947).

Gilbert, Martin. *Exile and Return: The Emergence of Jewish Statehood* (London: Weidenfeld and Nicolson, 1978).

Gildersleeve, Virginia C. *Many a Good Crusade* (New York: Macmillan, 1954).

Glick, Edward B. *Latin America and the Palestine Problem* (New York: Theodore Herzl Foundation, 1958).

Glick, Edward B. *The Triangular Connection: America, Israel and American Jews* (London: George Allen & Unwin, 1982).

Glubb, Brigadier Jon Bagot. *The Story of the Arab Legion* (London: Hodder & Stoughton, 1950).

Gordon, Milton M. *Assimilation in American Life: The Role of Race, Religion and National Origins* (New York: Oxford University, 1964).

Goldman, Eric F. *The Crucial Decade and After, America 1945-1960* (New York: Vintage Books, 1960).

Gorni, Joseph. *Partnership and Conflict: Chaim Weizmann and the Jewish Labour Movement in Palestine* (Tel Aviv: Hakibbutz Hameuchad, 1976).

Graber, Doris A. *Mass Media and American Politics* (Washington: Congressional Quarterly, 1980).

Graber, Doris A., ed., *The President and the Public* (Philadelphia: Institute for the Study of Human Issues, 1982).

Grose, Peter. *Israel in the Mind of America* (New York: Knopf, 1983).

Grossman, Michael Baruch and Martha Joynt Kumar. *Portraying the President: The White House and the News Media* (Baltimore: Johns Hopkins, 1981).

Gruber, Ruth. *Destination Palestine: The Story of the Haganah Ship Exodus 1947* (New York: Current Books, 1948).

Grunebaum, Gustave von. *Modern Islam: The Search for Cultural Identity* (New York: Vintage Press, 1964).

Gurevitch, Michael; Tony Bennett, James Curran and Janet Woollacott. *Culture, Society and the Media* (London: Metheun, 1982).

Hacker, Louis M. and Mark D. Hirsch. *Proskauer: His Life and Times* (University, Alabama: University of Alabama, 1978).

Haines, Gerald K. and J. Samuel Walker, eds., *American Foreign Relations: A Historiographical Review* (Westport: Greenwood Press, 1981).

Halperin, Morton. *Bureaucratic Politics and Foreign Policy* (Washington: Brookings Institute, 1974).

Halperin, Samuel. *The Political World of American Zionism* (Detroit: Wayne State University, 1961).

Halpern, Ben. *The American Jew: A Zionist Analysis* (New York: Theodore Herzl Foundation, 1956).

Halpern, Ben. *The Idea of a Jewish State* (Cambridge: Harvard University, 1961).

Hamady, Sania. *Temperament and Character of the Arabs* (New York: Twayne, 1960).

Hancock, William K. *Survey of British Commonwealth: Problems of Nationality, 1918-1936* (London: Oxford University, 1937).

Handlin, Oscar. *The Uprooted* (New York: Grosset and Dunlap, 1951).

Harr, John E. *The Anatomy of the Foreign Service* (New York: Carnegie Endowment for International Peace, 1965).

Hatchey, Thomas, ed., *Confidential Dispatches: Analyses of America by the British Ambassador, 1939-1945* (Evanston: Northwestern University, 1974).

Hathaway, Robert. *Ambiguous Partnership: Britain and America, 1944-1947* (New York: Columbia University, 1981).

Heald, Morrell and Lawrence S. Kaplan, eds., *Culture and Diplomacy: The American Experience* (Westport: Greenwood Press, 1977).

Heimert, Alan. *Religion and the American Mind* (Cambridge: Harvard University, 1968).

Heller, Francis H. *The Truman White House: The Administration of the President, 1945-1953* ((Lawrence: Regents Press of Kansas, 1980).

Henderson, Loy W. *Foreign Policies: Their Formation and Enforcement* (Washington: U. S. Government Printing Office, 1946).

Herberg, Will. *Protestant, Catholic, Jew: An Essay in American Religious Sociology* (Garden City: Doubleday, 1955).

Hero, Jr., Alfred O. *American Religious Groups View Foreign Policy: Trends in Rank and File Opinion, 1937-1969* (Durham: Duke University, 1973).

Higham, John. *Send These To Me: Jews and Other Immigrants in America* (New York: Antheneum, 1975).

Hilsman, Roger. *The Politics of Policy Making in Defense and Foreign Affairs: Conceptual Models and Bureaucratic Politics* (Englewood Cliffs: Prentice Hall, 1987).

Hiro, Philip. *Inside the Middle East* (New York: McGraw-Hill, 1982).

Hofstadter, Richard. *The Paranoid Style in American Politics and Other Essays* (New York: Knopf, 1967).

Hogan, Michael J. *The Marshall Plan: America, Britain and the Reconstruction of Western Europe, 1947-1952* (Cambridge: Cambridge University, 1987).

Holly, David C. *Exodus 1947* (Boston: Little, Brown, 1969).

Horowitz, David. *State in the Making* (New York: Knopf, 1953).

Howe, Irving. *World of Our Fathers* (New York: Harcourt, Brace, Jovanovich, 1976).

Hughes, Barry M. *The Domestic Context of American Foreign Policy* (San Francisco: W. H. Freeman, 1978).

Hughes, Emmet John. *The Living Presidency: The Resources and Dilemmas of the American Presidential Office* (Baltimore: Penguin, 1973).

Hurewitz, Jacob C. *The Struggle for Palestine* (New York: W. W. Norton, 1950).

Iatrides, John O. *Revolt in Athens: The Greek Communist "Second Round," 1944-1945* (Princeton: Princeton University, 1972).

Isaacs, Stephen D. *Jews and American Politics* (New York: Doubleday, 1974).

Isaacson, Walter and Evan Thomas. *The Wise Men: Six Friends and the World They Made: Acheson, Bohlen, Harriman, Kennan, Lovett, McCloy* (New York: Simon and Schuster, 1986).

Jablon, Howard. *Crossroads of Decision: The State Department and Foreign Policy, 1933-1937* (Lexington: University Press of Kentucky, 1983).

Jervis, Robert. *The Logic of Images in International Relations* (Princeton: Princeton University, 1970).

Jervis, Robert. *Perception and Misperception in International Politics* (Princeton: Princeton University, 1976).

Jessup, Philip. *The Birth of Nations* (New York: Columbia University, 1974).

Johnson, Walter. *1600 Pennsylvania Avenue: Presidents and the People since 1929* (Boston: Little, Brown, 1963).

Joseph, Samuel. *Jewish Immigration to the United States from 1881-1910* (New York: Columbia University, 1914).

Kaltenborn, Hans V. *I Broadcast the Crisis* (New York: Random House, 1938).

Kaltenborn, Hans V. *Kaltenborn Edits the War News* (New York: Dutton, 1942).

Kaltenborn, Hans V. *Europe Now: A First Hand Report* (New York: Didier, 1945).

Katzburg, Nathaniel. *The Palestine Problem in British Policy, 1940-1945* (Jerusalem, Yad Ben Zvi, 1976).

Kedourie, Elie. *The Chatham House Version and Other Middle Eastern Studies* (London: Weidenfeld and Nicolson, 1970).

Kedourie, Elie and Sylvia G. Haim, eds., *Palestine and Israel in the Nineteenth and Twentieth Centuries* (New York: Frank Cass, 1982).

Kedourie, Elie and Sylvia G. Haim, eds., *Zionism and Arabism in Palestine and Israel* (London: Frank Cass, 1982).

Kelly, Tom. *The Imperial Post* (New York: William Morrow, 1983).

Kern, Montague; Patricia W. Levering and Ralph B. Levering. *The Kennedy Crises: The Press, The Presidency and Foreign Policy* (Chapel Hill: University of North Carolina, 1984).

Key, Jr., V. O. *Politics, Parties and Pressure Groups* (New York: Thomas Y. Crowell, 1963).

Key, Jr., V. O. *Public Opinion and American Democracy* (New York: Knopf, 1961).

Kimche, Jon. *Seven Fallen Pillars: The Middle East, 1945-1952* (London: Secker and Warburg, 1953).

Kimche, Jon and David. *The Secret Roads: The "Illegal" Migration of a People, 1938-1948* (London: Secker and Warburg, 1954).

Kimche, Jon and David. *A Clash of Destinies* (New York: Praeger, 1960).

Kimche, Jon. *The Second Arab Awakening* (New York: Holt, Rinehart, 1970).

Kirk, George. *Survey of International Affairs: The Middle East in the War*, two volumes (London: Oxford University, 1954).

Kirkendall, Richard S. *The Truman Period as a Research Tool: A Reappraisal* (Columbia: University of Missouri, 1974).

Kobler, Franz. *The Vision Was There* (London: Lincoln-Prager, 1956).

Kolko, Gabriel. *The Politics of War: The World and United States Foreign Policy, 1943-1945* (New York: Random House, 1968).

Kolko, Joyce and Gabriel. *The Limits of Power: The World and United States Foreign Policy, 1945-1954* (New York: Harper and Row, 1972).

Krammer, Arnold. *Forgotten Friendship: Israel and Soviet Bloc, 1947-1953* (Urbana: University of Illinois, 1974).

Krasner, Stephen. *Defending the National Interest: Raw Materials, Investments and U. S. Foreign Policy* (Princeton: Princeton University, 1978).

Kraus, Sidney and Denise Davis. *The Effects of Mass Communication on Political Behaviour* (State College: Penn State University, 1976).

Kraus, Sidney, ed., *Mass Communication and Political Information Processing* (Hillsdale, N. J.: Lawrence Erlbaum, 1990).

Kuniholm, Bruce R. *The Origins of the Cold War in the Near East: Great Power Conflict and Diplomacy in Iran, Turkey and Greece* (Princeton: Princeton University, 1980).

Lacey, Michael J., ed., *The Truman Presidency* (New York: Cambridge University, 1989).

Laffin, John. *The Arab Mind Reconsidered: A Need for Understanding* (New York: Taplinger, 1975).

Landecker, Manfred. *The President and Public Opinion* (Washington: Public Affairs Press, 1968).

Lane, Robert E. *Political Ideology: Why the American Common Man Believes What He Does* (New York: Free Press, 1962).

Laqueur, Walter. *A History of Zionism* (New York: Holt, Rinehart and Winston, 1972).

Lasswell, Harold D. and Abraham Kaplan. *Power and Society: A Framework for Political Inquiry* (New Haven: Yale University, 1970).

Lasswell, Harold D.; Daniel Lerner and Ithiel de Sola Pool. *The Comparative Study of Symbols* (Stanford: Stanford University, 1952).

Lazarsfeld, Paul F.; Bernard Berelseon and Hazel Gaudet. *The People's Choice: How the Voter Makes Up His Mind in a Presidential Campaign* (New York: Duell, Sloan and Pearce, 1944).

Learsi, Rufus. *Fulfillment: The Epic Story of Zionism* (Cleveland: World Publishing, 1951).

Leatherdale, Clive. *Britain and Saudi Arabia, 1925-1939: The Imperial Oasis* (London: Frank Cass, 1983).

LaFeber, Walter. *America, Russia and the Cold War* (New York: John Wiley, 1976).

Lee, Richard. *Politics and the Press* (Washington: Acropolis Books, 1970).

Leigh, Michael. *Mobilizing Consent: Public Opinion and American Foreign Policy, 1937-1947* (Westport: Greenwood Press, 1976).

Lenczowski, George. *The Middle East in World Affairs* (Ithaca: Cornell University, 1952).

Levanstrosser, William F., ed., *Harry S. Truman: The Man from Independence* (New York: Greenwood Press, 1986).

Levering, Ralph B. *The Public and American Foreign Policy, 1918-1978* (New York: William Morrow, 1978).

Liebovich, Louis. *The Press and the Origins of the Cold War, 1944-1947* (Westport: Praeger, 1988).

Lilienthal, Alfred M. *What Price Israel* (Chicago: Henry Regenery, 1953).

Lilienthal, Alfred M. *The Zionist Connection: What Price Peace?* (New York: Middle East Perspectives, 1978).

Linsky, Martin. *Impact: How the Press Affects Federal Policymaking* (New York: W. W. Norton, 1986).

Lippmann, Walter. *Public Opinion* (New York: Free Press, 1922).

Lippmann, Walter. *The Public Philosophy* (Boston: Little, Brown, 1955).

Lipsky, Louis. *Thirty Years of American Zionism* (New York: Nesher Publishing, 1927).

Litvinoff, Barnet. *To the House of Their Fathers: A History of Zionism* (New York: Praeger, 1965).

Lorch, Netanel. *Israel's War of Independence, 1947-1949* (Hartford: Hartmore House, 1968).

Louis, William Roger. *Imperialism at Bay: The United States and the Decolonization of the British Empire, 1941-1945* (New York: Oxford University, 1978).

Louis, William Roger. *The British Empire in the Middle East, 1945-1951: Arab Nationalism, the United States, and Postwar Imperialism* (Oxford: Clarendon Press, 1984).

Lowdermilk, Walter Clay. *Palestine: Land of Promise* (New York: Harper, 1944).

Lundestad, Geir. *The American Non-Policy Towards Eastern Europe, 1943-1947* (New York: Columbia University, 1978).

Manis, Jerome G. and Bernard N. Maltzer, eds., *Symbolic Interaction* (Boston: Allyn and Bacon, 1967).

Manuel, Frank E. *The Realities of American-Palestinian Relations* (Washington: Public Affairs Press, 1949).

Ma'oz, Moshe. *The Image of the Jew in Arab Literature and Communication Media* (Jerusalem: Hebrew University of Jerusalem, 1976).

Markel, Lester, ed., *Public Opinion and Foreign Policy* (New York: Harper, 1949).

Mastny, Vojtech. *Russia's Road to the Cold War* (New York: Columbia University, 1979).

Mazuzan, George T. *Warren R. Austin at the United Nations, 1946-1953* (Kent: Kent State University, 1977).

McCamy, James L. *The Administration of American Foreign Policy* (New York: Knopf, 1950).

McCoy, Donald R. and Richard T. Ruetten. *Quest and Response: Minority Rights and the Truman Administration* (Lawrence: University of Kansas, 1973).

McLean, Joseph E. *The Public Service and University Education* (Princeton: Princeton University, 1949).

McLellan, David S. *Dean Acheson: The State Department Years* (New York: Dodd, Mead, 1976).

McWilliams, Carey. *A Mask of Privilege: Anti-Semitism in America* (Boston: Little, Brown, 1948).

Medhurst, Martin J. *Cold War Rhetoric: Strategy, Metaphor and Ideology* (Westport, Conn.: Greenwood Press, 1990).

Mee, Jr., Charles L. *The Marshall Plan: The Launching of Pax Americana* (New York: Simon and Schuster, 1984).

Messer, Robert. *The End of an Alliance: James F. Byrnes, Roosevelt, Truman and the Origins of the Cold War* (Chapel Hill: University of North Carolina, 1982).

Miller, Aaron David. *Search for Security: Saudi Arabian Oil and American Foreign Policy, 1939-1949* (Chapel Hill: University of North Carolina, 1982).

Monroe, Elizabeth. *Britain's Moment in the Middle East, 1914-1956* (London: Methuen, 1963).

Montague, Ashley. *Man's Most Dangerous Myth: The Fallacy of Race* (New York: Columbia University, 1945).

Morse, Arthur. *While Six Million Died: A Chronicle of American Apathy* (New York: Random House, 1968).

Mosse, George L. *The Crisis of German Ideology: Intellectual Origins of the Third Reich* (New York: Grosset and Dunlap, 1964).

Mousa, Issam Sulieman. *The Arab Image in the U. S. Press* (New York: Peter Lang, 1984).

Nacos, Brigette Lebens. *The Press, Presidents and Crises* (New York: Columbia University, 1990).

Nagai, Yonosuke and Akira Iriye, eds., *The Origins of the Cold War in Asia* (New York: Columbia University, 1977).

Nash, Gerald D. *United States Oil Policy, 1890-1964: Business and Government in Twentieth Century America* (Pittsburgh: University of Pittsburgh, 1968).

Nathan, Robert R.; Oscar Gass and Daniel Creamer. *Palestine: Problems and Promise, An Economic Study* (Washington: Public Affairs Press, 1946).

Nathan, James A. and James K. Oliver. *Foreign Policy Making and the American Political System* (Boston: Little, Brown, 1987).

Needler, Martin C. *Understanding Foreign Policy* (New York: Holt, Rinehart and Winston, 1966).

Neustadt, Richard E. *Presidential Power: The Politics of Leadership* (New York: John Wiley, 1960).

Neustadt, Richard E. *Presidential Power: The Politics of Leadership from F. D. R. to Carter* (New York: John Wiley, 1980).

New York Times Staff. *The Newspaper: Its Making and Meaning* (New York: Scribner's, 1945).

Niebuhr, H. Richard. *The Kingdom of God in America* (Chicago: Willett, Clark, 1937).

Nimmo, Dan M. *Popular Images of Politics: a Taxonomy* (Englewood Cliffs, Prentice Hall, 1974).

Nusbeibeh, Hazem Zaki. *The Ideas of Arab Nationalism* (Ithaca: Cornell University, 1956).

Nutting, Anthony. *The Arabs: A Narrative History from Mohammed to the Present* (New York: Clarkson N. Potter, 1964).

O'Ballance, Edgar. *The Arab-Israeli War, 1948* (New York: Praeger, 1967).

Oneal, John R. *Foreign Policy Making in Times of Crisis* (Columbus: Ohio State University, 1982).

Orren, Elhannan. *Settlement Amid Struggles: The Pre-State Strategy of Settlement, 1936-1947* (Jerusalem: Yad Izhak Ben Avi, 1978).

Painter, David S. *Oil and the American Century: The Political Economy of United States Foreign Oil Policy, 1941-1954* (Baltimore: Johns Hopkins University, 1973).

Pappe, Ilan. *Britain and the Arab-Israeli Conflict, 1948-1951* (New York: St. Martin's, 1988).

Paterson, Thomas G., ed., *Containment and the Cold War: American Foreign Policy since 1945* (Reading, Mass.: Addison-Wesley, 1973).

Pearlman, Moshe. *The Army of Israel* (New York: Philosophical Library, 1950).

Peters, Joan. *From Time Immemorial* (New York: Harper and Row, 1984).

Phillips, Cabell. *The Truman Presidency* (Baltimore: Penguin Books, 1969).

Piper, Donald C. and Ronald J. Terchek *Interaction: Foreign Policy and Public Policy* (Washington: American Enterprise Institute, 1983).

Piscatori, James P., ed., *Islam in the Political Process* (Cambridge: Cambridge University, 1983).

Polland, Robert A. *Economic Security and the Origins of the Cold War, 1945-1950* (New York: Columbia University, 1985).

Polk, William R. *The United States and the Arab World* (Cambridge: Harvard Univbersity, 1975).

Porath, Yesoshua. *The Emergence of the Palestinian-Arab Movement, 1918-1929* (London: Frank Cass, 1973).

Porath, Yesoshua. *The Palestinian-Arab Movement: 1929-1939* (London: Frank Cass, 1977).

Postal, Bernard and Henry W. Levy. *And the Hills Shouted for Joy: The Day Israel Was Born* (New York: David McKay, 1973).

Pragai, Michael J. *Faith and Fulfillment: Christians and the Return to the Promised Land* (London: Vallentine, Mitchell, 1985).

Problems of Journalism (Washington: American Society of Newspaper Editors), Volume 16, 1938; Volume 19, 1941; Volume 20, 1942; Volume 21, 1943; Volume 22, 1944; Volume 25, 1947; and Volume 28, 1950.

Purvis, Hoyt, ed., *The President and the Press* (Austin: Lyndon Baines Johnson School of Public Affairs, 1976).

Rausch, David A. *Zionism within Early American Fundamentalism, 1878-1918* (New York: Edward Mellen, 1979).

Redding, John M. *Inside the Democratic Party* (Indianapolis: Bobbs-Merrill, 1958).

Reynolds, David. *The Creation of the Anglo-American Alliance, 1937-1941: A Study in Competitive Cooperation* (Chapel Hill: University of North Carolina, 1981).

Rischin, Moses. *The Promised Land: New York's Jews, 1870-1914* (Cambridge: Harvard University, 1962).

Roberts, Chalmers M. *The Washington Post: The First 100 Years* (Boston: Houghton Mifflin, 1977).

Robinson, Eugene E. *Powers of the President in Foreign Affairs* (San Francisco: Commonwealth Club of California, 1966).

Rodinson, Maxime. *The Arabs* (Chicago: University of Chicago, 1981).

Rose, Norman A. *The Gentile Zionists—A Study in Anglo-Zionist Diplomacy, 1929-1939* (London: Frank Cass, 1973).

Rosenblatt, Bernard A. *Two Generations of Zionism: Historical Recollections of an American Zionist* (New York: Shengold Publishers, 1967)

Roshco, Bernard. *Newsmaking* (Chicago: University of Chicago, 1975).

Rossiter, Clinton. *The American Presidency* (New York: Harcourt, Brace, 1956).

Rourke, John. *Congress and the Presidency in U. S. Foreign Policymaking: A Study of Interaction and Influence, 1945-1982* (Boulder: Westview Press, 1983).

Rubin, Barry. *The Arab States and the Palestine Conflict* (Syracuse: Syracuse University, 1981).

Sachar, Abram. *The Redemption of the Unwanted: The Post Holocaust Years* (New York: St. Martin's, 1983).

Sachar, Howard M. *Europe Leaves the Middle East, 1936-1954* (New York: Knopf, 1972).

Sandeen, Ernest R. *The Roots of Fundamnetalism: British and American Millennarianism, 1800-1930* (Chicago: University of Chicago, 1970).

Sanders, Ronald. *The Downtown Jews: Portrait of an American Generation* (New York: Harper and Row, 1969).

Sanders, Ronald. *Shores of Refuge: A Hundred Years of Jewish Immigration* (New York: Henry Holt, 1988).

Sanford, Charles L. *The Quest for Paradise* (Urbana: University of Illinois, 1961).

Schechtman, Joseph B. *The United States and the Jewish State Movement, the Crucial Decade, 1939-1949* (New York: Herzl Press, 1966).

Schudson, Michael. *Discovering the News: A Social History of American Newspapers* (New York: Basic Books, 1978).

Schulzinger, Robert D. *The Making of the Diplomatic Mind: The Training, Outlook and Style of U. S. Foreign Service Officers, 1908-1931* (Middletown: Wesleyan University, 1975).

Schulzinger, Robert D. *The Wise Men of Foreign Affairs: The History of the Committee on Foreign Relations* (New York: Columbia University, 1984).

Shapiro, Yonathan. *Leadership of the American Zionist Organization, 1897-1930* (Urbana: University of Illinois, 1971).

Sharrett, Moshe. *At the Threshhold of Statehood* (Tel Aviv: Am Oved, 1964).

Shoup, Lawrence H. and William Minter. *Imperial Brain Trust: The Council on Foreign Relations and United States Foreign Policy* (New York: Monthly Review Press, 1977).

Sigal, Leon V. *Reporters and Officials: The Organization and Politics of Newsmaking* (Lexington: Heath, 1973).

Silver, Abba Hillel. *The Democratic Impulse in Jewish History* (New York: Block Publishing, 1928).

Silver, Daniel, ed., *In the Harvest of Time* (New York: Macmillan, 1963).

Silverberg, Robert. *If I Forget Thee, O Jerusalem* (New York: William Morrow, 1970).

Sklare, Marshall. *Conservative Judaism: An American Religious Movement* (Glencoe: Free Press, 1955).

Slutsky, Yehuda. *History of the Haganah*, Volume 3 (Tel Aviv: Am Oved, 1972).

Smith, Gaddis. *American Diplomacy in the Second World War, 1941-1945* (New York: John Wiley, 1965).

Smith, Howard K. *The State of Europe* (New York: Knopf, 1949).

Snetsinger, John. *Truman, the Jewish Vote, and the Creation of Israel* (Stanford: Hoover Institution Press, 1974).

Snyder, Richard C. and Edgar S. Furniss, Jr. *American Foreign Policy: Formulation, Principles and Programs* (New York: Rinehart, 1954).

Soltes, Mordecai. *The Yiddish Press: An Americanizing Agency* (New York: Columbia University, 1923).

Speiser, Ephraim A. *The United States and the Near East* (Cambridge: Harvard University, 1947).

Steele, Richard W. *Propaganda in an Open Society: The Roosevelt Administration and the Media, 1933-1941* (Westport: Greenwood Press, 1985).

Stember, Charles Herbert. *Jews in the Mind of America* (New York: Basic Books, 1966).

Stevens, Richard. *American Zionism and United States Foreign Policy, 1942-1947* (New York: Pageant Press, 1962).

Stoff, Michael B. *Oil, War and American Society* (New Haven: Yale University, 1980).

Stone, I. F. *Underground to Palestine* (New York: Pantheon, 1946).

Stuart, Graham H. *The Department of State* (New York: Macmillan, 1949).

Stuart, Graham H. *American Diplomatic and Consular Practice* (New York: Appleton-Century-Crofts, 1952).

Sweet, William H. *Religion in the Development of American Culture* (New York: Scribner's, 1952).

Taubman, Eilliam *Stalin's American Policy: From Entente to Detente to Cold War* (New York: W. W. Norton, 1982).

Tebbel, John and Sarah Miles Watts. *The Press and the Presidency: From George Washington to Ronald Reagan* (New York: Oxford University, 1985).

Theoharis, Athan G. *The Truman Presidency: The Origins of the Imperial Presidency and the National Security State* (Stanordville, N. Y.: Earl E. Coleman, 1979).

Thompson, Kenneth W., ed., *Ten Presidents and the Press* (Washington: University Press of America, 1983).

Truman, David B. *The Governmental Process: Political Interests and Public Opinion* (New York: Knopf, 1951).

Tucker, Nancy Bernkopf. *Patterns in the Dust: Chinese-American Relations and the Recognition Controversy, 1949-1950* (New York: Columbia University, 1983).

Turner, Kathleen J. *Lyndon Johnson's Dual War: Vietnam and the Press* (Chicago: University of Chicago, 1985).

Ulam, Adam. *The Rivals: America and Russia since World War II* (New York: Viking Press, 1971).

Ullmann, Walter. *The United States in Prague, 1945-1948* (New York: Columbia University, 1978).

Urofsky, Melvin I. *American Zionism from Herzl to the Holocaust* (Garden City: Doubleday, 1975).

Vaughn, Stephen, ed., *The Vital Past: Writings on the Uses of History* (New York: Pantheon, 1985).

Vietor, Richard H. K. *Energy Policy in America since 1945: A Study in Business-Government Relations* (Cambridge: Cambridge University, 1984).

Voss, Carl Hermann. *The Palestine Problem Today: Israel and Its Neighbors* (Boston: Beacon Press, 1953).

Wallas, Graham. *Human Nature in Politics* (Lincoln: University of Nebraska, 1962).

Wasserstein, Bernard. *Britain and the Jews of Europe, 1939-1945* (London: Clarendon Press, 1979).

Weil, Martin. *A Pretty Good Club: The Founding Fathers of the United States Foreign Service* (New York: W. W. Norton, 1978).

Welles, Sumner. *Where Are We Headed?* (New York: Harper, 1946).

Welles, Sumner. *We Need Not Fail* (Boston: Houghton Mifflin, 1948).

Westerfield, H. Bradford. *Foreign Policy and Party Politics: From Pearl Harbor to Korea* (New Haven: Yale University, 1955).

Wischnitzer, Mark. *To Dwell in Safety: The Story of Jewish Immigration since 1800* (Philadelphia: Jewish Publication Society of America, 1948).

Wildavsky, Aaron, ed., *Perspectives on the Presidency* (Boston: Little, Brown, 1975).

Wilkins, Mira. *The Maturing of Multinational Enterprise: America Business Abroad from 1914 to 1970* (Cambridge: Harvard University, 1974).

Williams, William A. *The Tragedy of American Diplomacy* (Cleveland: World Publishing, 1959).

Wilson, Maj. R. D. *Cordon and Search: With the Sixth Airborne Division in Palestine* (London: Aldershot, Gale and Polden, 1949).

Wimmer, Roger D. and Joseph R. Dominick, eds., *Mass Media Research: An Introduction* (Belmont, Cal.: Wadsworth, 1987).

Wittner, Lawrence S. *American Intervention in Greece, 1943-1949* (New York: Columbia University, 1982).

Woodhouse, Christopher M. *The Struggle for Greece, 1941-1949* (London: Hart-Davis, MacGibbon, 1976).

Woodward, Sir Llewellyn. *British Foreign Policy in the Second World War*, Volume 4 (London: Her Majesty's Stationery Office, 1975).

Yergin, Donald. *Shattered Peace: The Origins of the Cold War and the National Security State* (Boston: Houghton Mifflin, 1977).

Yost, Charles W. *The Insecurity of Nations* (New York: Prager, 1968).

ARTICLES

Adler, Les K. and Thomas G. Paterson. "Red Fascism: The Merger of Nazi Germany and Soviet Russia in the American Image of Totalitarianism," *American Historical Review* 75, 1970, pp. 1046-1064.

Adler, Selig. "Franklin D. Roosevelt and Zionism—The Wartime Record," *Judaism* 83, 1972, pp. 265-276.

Allen, George V. "The Utility of a Trained and Permanent Foreign Service," *American Foreign Service Journal* 13, 1936, pp. 5-7 and 32-36.

Almond, Gabriel. "Public Opinion and the Development of Space Technology," *Public Opinion Quarterly* 24, 1960, pp. 552-559.

"America and the Holy Land: A Colloquim," *American Jewish Historical Quarterly* 62, 1972, pp. 5-62.

Angell, Robert C. "Social Values of Soviet and American Elites: Content Analysis of Elite Media," *Journal of Conflict Resolution* 8, 1964, pp. 330-341.

Atkinson, Brooks. "America's Global Planner," *New York Times Magazine*, July 13, 1947, pp. 9 and 32-33.

Baird, Joseph H. "Professionalized Diplomacy," *American Foreign Service Journal* 16, 1939, pp. 542-543.

Balutis, Alan P. "The Presidency and the Press," *Presidential Studies Quarterly* 7, Fall 1977, pp. 244-251.

Baughman, James L. "The Self-Publicist from the Pedernales, Lyndon Johnson and the Press," *Diplomatic History* 12, 1988, pp. 103-110.

Ben-Horin, Eliahu. "The Soviet Wooing of Palestine," *Harper's*, May 1944, pp. 413-418.

Ben-Horin, Eliahu. "Palestine: Realities and Illusions," *Atlantic Monthly*, April 1947, pp. 74 and 77.

Benson, Lee. "An Approach to the Scientific Study of Past Public Opinion," *Public Opinion Quarterly* 31, 1967, pp. 522-567.

Berelson, Bernard and P. J. Salter. "Magazine Assigned Stereotyping," *Public Opinion Quarterly* 10, 1946, pp. 168-190.

Bickerton, Ian J. "President Truman's Recognition of Israel," *American Jewish Historical Quarterly* 58, 1968, pp. 173-240.

Bierbrier, Doreen. "The American Zionist Emergency Council: An Analysis of a Pressure Group," *American Jewish Historical Quarterly* 60, 1970, pp. 82-105.

Blankenburg, William B. and Ruth Walden. "Objectivity, Interpretation and Economy in Reporting," *Journalism Quarterly* 54, 1977, pp. 591-595.

Boyer, John H. "How Editors View Objectivity," *Journalism Quarterly* 58, 1981, pp. 24-28.

Brody, David. "American Jewry, the Refugees and Immigration Restriction, 1932-1942," *Publications of the American Jewish Historical Society* 65, 1956, pp. 219-247.

Brown, Alexander C. "Exodus 1947: An Interim Report on the Career of the Steamer President Warfield," *American Neptune*, April 1948, pp. 127-131.

Brown, Ira V. "Watcher for the Second Coming: The Millennarian Tradition in America," *Mississippi Valley Historical Review* 39, 1952, pp. 441-458.

Buckley, Gary J. "American Public Opinion and the Origins of the Cold War: A Speculative Reassessment," *Mid-America* 60, 1978, pp. 35-42.

Burton, William. "Protestant America and the Rebirth of Israel," *Jewish Social Studies* 26, October 1964, pp. 203-214.

Canham, Erwin D. "The Newspaper's Obligation in War Time," *Journalism Quarterly* 20, 1943, pp. 315-317.

Cargo, William I. "The Creation of the U.N. Special Committee on Palestine," Department of State *Bulletin* 17, July 6, 1947, pp. 3-17.

Carroll, Raymond L. "Harry S. Truman's 1948 Election: The Inadvertent Broadcast Campaign," *Journal of Broadcasting and Electronic Media* 31, Spring 1987, pp. 120-132.

Carynnyk, Marco. "The Famine the *Times* Couldn't Find," *Commentary* 76, November 1983, pp. 356-358.

Caspary, William R. "The Mood Theory: A Study of Public Opinion and Foreign Policy," *American Political Science Review* 64, 1970, pp. 536-547.

Clifford, Clark M., "Recognizing Israel," *American Heritage* 28, April 1977, pp. 4-11.

Clifford, Clark M. "Annals of Government: Serving the President, The Truman Years," *New Yorker*, March 25, 1991, pp. 40-71.

Cohen, Michael J. "American Influence on British Policy in the Middle East During World War II: First Attempts at Coordinating Allied Policy on Palestine," *American Jewish Historical Quarterly* 67, September 1977, pp. 50-70.

Cohen, Michael J. "The Moyne Assasination, November 1944: A Political Analysis," *Middle Eastern Studies* 15, 1979, pp. 358-373.

Cornwell, Elmer E. "The Presidential Press Conference: A Case Study in Institutionalization," *Midwest Journal of Political Science* 4, November 1960, pp. 378-392.

Dann, Uriel. "The U.S. and Recognition of Trans-Jordan, 1946-1948," *Asian and African Studies* 11, Autumn 1976, pp. 213-240.

Darnton, Robert. "Writing News and Telling Stories," *Daedalus* 104, Spring 1975, pp. 175-194.

Divine, Robert A. "The Cold War and the Election of 1948," *Journal of American History* 59, June 1972, pp. 90-110.

Dobkowski, Michael N. "American Anti-Semitism: A Reinterpretation," *American Quarterly* 39, Summer 1977, pp. 166-181.

Drew, S. Nelson. "Expecting the Approach of Danger: The Missle Gap as a Study of Executive-Congressional Competition in Building Consensus on National Security Issues," *Presidential Studies Quarterly* 19, 1989, pp. 317-335.

Eagleton, Clyde. "Palestine and the Constitutional Law of the United Nations," *American Journal of International Law* 42, April 1948, pp. 397-399.

Elath, Eliahu. "Truman and the Zionist Struggle," *Molad* 16, September 1970, pp. 364-368.

Erskine, Hazel Gaudet. "The Cold War: Report from the Polls," *Public Opinion Quarterly* 25, Summer 1961, pp. 300-315.

Evensen, Bruce J. "Surrogate State Department? *Times* Coverage of Palestine, 1948," *Journalism Quarterly* 67, 1990, pp. 391 400.

Fedler, Fred; Mike Meeske and Joe Hall. "*Time* Magazine Revisited," *Journalism Quarterly* 56, 1979, pp. 353-359.

Feingold, Henry. "Roosevelt and the Holocaust: Reflections on New Deal Humanitarianism," *Judaism* 18, Summer 1964, pp. 259-276.

Feldblum, Esther. "On the Eve of a Jewish State, American Catholic Response," *America Jewish Historical Quarterly* 64, December 1974, pp. 99-119.

Feuer, Leon I. "Abba Hillel Silver: A Personal Memoir," *American Jewish Archives* 19, November 1967, pp. 107-126.

Feuer, Leon I. "More on Abba Hillel Silver," *American Jewish Archives* 20, November 1968, pp. 127-128.

Feuer, Leon I. "The Birth of the Jewish Lobby---A Reminiscence," *American Jewish Archives* 28, November 1976, pp. 107-118.

Fierst, Herbert A. "Lest We Forget: Tribute to Hilldring," *Near East Report* 18, January 30, 1974, p. 116.

Fitzsimmons, M. A. "Britain and the Middle East, 1944-1950," *The Review of Politics* 23, January 1959, pp. 21-30.

Frank, M. Z. "Silver and Ben-Gurion," *Hadoar* 47, November 11, 1966, pp. 19-20.

Gaddis, John Lewis. "Was the Truman Doctrine a Real Turning Point?" *Foreign Affairs* 52, January 1974, pp. 386-392.

Gaddis, John Lewis. "The Corporatist Synthesis: A Skeptical View," *Diplomatic History* 10, 1986, pp. 357-362.

Gal, Alon. "The Mission Motif in American Zionism," *American Jewish History* 75, 1986, pp. 363-385.

Ganin, Zvi. "The Limits of American Jewish Political Power: America's Retreat from Partition, November 1947-March 1949," *Jewish Social Studies* 39, Winter 1977, pp. 1-36.

Glazer, Steven. "The Palestinian Exodus in 1948," *Journal of Palestine Studies* 60, Summer 1980, pp. 96-118.

Glick, Edward Bernard. "Latin America and the Establishment of Israel," *Middle Eastern Studies* 9, January 1958, pp. 11-16.

Grabill, Joseph L. "Protestant Diplomacy and Arab Nationalism," *Journal of Palestine Studies* 64, Summer 1986, pp. 113-124.

Griffith, Robert. "Truman and the Historians: The Reconstruction of Postwar American Foreign Policy," *Wisconsin Magazine of History* 59, 1975, pp. 20-50.

Grosset, Ed. "Should Congress Admit 400,000 D.P.'s Outside of U.S. Immigration Quotas?" *Congressional Digest* 24, January 1948, pp. 21 and 23.

Gustafson, Merlin. "Religion and Politics in the Truma Administration," *Rocky Mountain Social Science Journal* 3, 1966, pp. 125-134.

Gustafson, Merlin. "Truman and Religion: The Religion of the President," *Journal of Church and State* 10, Autumn 1968, pp. 379-387.

Gustafson, Merlin. "Harry Truman as a Man of Faith," *Christian Century* 90, January 17, 1973, pp. 75-78.

Gustafson, Merlin. "The Religious Role of the President," *Midwest Journal of Political Science* 14, 1980, pp. 708-722.

Haddad, H. S. "The Biblical Bases of Zionist Colonialism," *Journal of Palestine Studies* 3, Summer 1974, pp. 94-113.

Halperin, Samuel and Irwin Oder. "The United States in Search of a Policy: Franklin D. Roosevelt and Palestine," *The Review of Politics* 24, 1962, pp. 320-341.

Hamby, Alonzo L. "The Accidental Presidency: Truman Vs. Dewey, The 1948 Election," *Wilson Quarterly*, Spring 1988, pp. 49-57.

Haron, Miriam. "The British Decision to Give the Palestine Question to the United Nations," *Middle Eastern Studies* 17, April 1981, pp. 241-248.

Hamilton, Thomas J. "Partition of Palestine," *Foreign Policy Records* 23, February 15, 1948, pp. 286-295.

Heller, Joseph. "Neither Masada Nor Vichy: Diplomacy and Resistance in Zionist Politics, 1945-1947," *The International History Review* 3, October 1981, pp. 540-564.

Henderson, Loy W. "American Political and Strategic Interests in the Middle East and Southeast Europe," Department of State, *Bulletin* 18, November 23, 1947, pp. 996-1000.

Hess, Gary R. "The Iranian Crisis of 1945-1946 and the Cold War," *Political Science Quarterly* 89, March 1974, pp. 128-132.

Hitchens, Harold L. "Influences on the Congressional Decision to Pass the Marshall Plan," *Western Political Quarterly* 21, March 1988, pp. 51-68.

Hogan, Michael J. "The Search for a 'Creative Peace': The United States, European Unity, and the Origins of the Marshall Plan," *Diplomatic History* 6, 1982, pp. 267-277.

Hopkins, Frank Snowden. "Psychological Tensions in the Foreign Service," *American Foreign Service Journal* 24, March 1947, pp. 10-11 and 40-46.

Hopkins, Mark W. "Lenin, Stalin, Khrushchev: Three Concepts of the Press," *Journalism Quarterly* 42, 1965, pp. 523-531.

Hudson, Darryl J. "Vandenberg Reconsidered: Senate Resolution 239 and American Foreign Policy," *Diplomatic History* 1, 1977, pp. 46-64.

Huff, Earl D. "A Study of a Successful Interest Group: The American Jewish Movement," *Western Political Science Quarterly* 25, March 1972, pp. 109-124.

Jackson, Scott. "Prologue to the Marshall Plan: The Origins of the American Commitment for a European Recovery Program," *Journal of American History* 65, March 1977, pp. 1043-1068.

Jacobson, Edward. "Two Presidents and a Haberdasher, 1948," *American Jewish Archives* 20, April 1968, pp. 3-15.

Kahn, Alfred E. "Palestine: A Problem in Economic Evaluation," *The American Economic Review* 34, September 1944, pp. 538-560.

Kaufman, Menachem. "A Trust Betrayed: The American Trusteeship Proposal for Palestine in 1948," *The Jewish Journal of Sociology* 25, June 1983, pp. 5-32.

Kochavi, Arieh J. "Anglo-American Discord: Jewish Refugees and United Nations Relief and Rehabilitation Administration Policy, 1945-1947," *Diplomatic History* 14, 1990, pp. 529-551.

Kolinsky, M. "The Efforts of the Truman Administration to Resolve the Arab-Israeli Conflict," *Middle Eastern Studies* 20, January 1984, pp. 81-93.

Kramer, Arnold. "Soviet Activities in the Partition of Palestine, 1947-1948," *Journal of Palestine Studies* 2, Winter 1973, pp. 102-119.

Lammers, William W. "Presidential Press Conference Schedule: Who Hides and When?" *Political Science Quarterly* 96, Summer 1981, pp. 261-278.

Lazarowitz, Arlene. "From Diplomatic History to Foreign Relations:Teaching United States Foreign Policy," *The Society for Historians of American Foreign Relations Newsletter* 21, June 1990, pp. 9-20.

Leffler, Melvyn P. "From the Truman Doctrine to the Carter Doctrine: Lessons and Dilemmas of the Cold War," *Diplomatic History* 7, 1983, pp. 245-252.

Leffler, Melvyn P. "The American Conception of National Security and the Beginnings of the Cold War, 1945-1948," *American Historical Review* 89, 1984, pp. 364-381.

Leigh, Michael. "Is There a Revisionist Thesis on the Origins of the Cold War," *Political Science Quarterly* 89, March 1974, pp. 101-116.

Leloup, Lance T. and Steven A. Shull. "Congress Vs. the Executive: The 'Two Presidencies' Reconsidered," *Social Science Quarterly* 59, 1979, p. 707.

Levering, Ralph B. "Public Opinion, Foreign Policy and American Politics since the 1960's," *Diplomatic History* 13, 1989, pp. 383-394.

Lorenz, Jr., A. L. "Truman and the Press Conference," *Journalism Quarterly* 43, 1966, pp. 671-679.

Lubell, Samuel. "Sputnik and Public Opinion," *Columbia University Forum* 1, Winter 1957, pp. 18-21.

Maddux, Thomas R. "American News Media and Soviet Diplomacy, 1934-1941," *Journalism Quarterly* 58, 1981, pp. 29-37.

Magnes, Judah L. "Toward Peace in Palestine," *Foreign Affairs* 21, January 1943, pp. 239-249.

Maier, Charles S. "Revisionism and the Interpretation of Cold War Origins," *Perspectives in American History* 4, 1970, pp. 313-347.

Manheim, Jarol B. "The Honeymoon's Over: The News Conference and the Development of Presidential Style," *Journal of Politics* 41, February 1979, pp. 55-74.

Manheim, Jarol B. and William W. Lammers. "The News Conference and Presidential Leadership of Public Opinion: Does the Tail Wag the Dog?" *Presidential Studies Quarterly* 11, 1981, pp. 177-188.

Margalit, Elkana. "The Debate in the Labor Movement on Bi nationalism," *Zionism* 4, 1975, pp. 183-258.

Markel, Lester. "The Real Sins of the Press," *Harper's*, December 1962, pp. 85-94.

Marshall, George C. "Should Congress Admit 400,000 D.P.'s?" *Congressional Digest* 27, January 1948, pp. 20 and 22.

McCoy, Donald R. "Trends in Viewing Herbert Hoover, Franklin D. Roosevelt, Harry Truman and Dwight D. Eisenhower," *Midwest Quarterly* 20, Winter 1979, pp. 117-136.

McCoy, Donald R. "Harry S. Truman: Personality, Politics and Presidency," *Presidential Studies Quarterly* 12, 1982, pp. 216-225.

Mee, Jr., Charles L.; Averell Harriman and Elie Abel, "Who Started the Cold War?" *American Heritage* 28, August 1977, pp. 8-23.

Melanson, Richard A. "Revisionism Subdued: Robert James Maddox and the Origins of the Cold War," *Political Science Reviewer* 7, 1977, pp. 229-271.

Merrill, John C. "How *Time* Stereotyped Three U.S. Presidents," *Journalism Quarterly* 42, 1965, pp. 563-570.

Miller, James E. "Taking Off the Gloves: The United States and the Italian Elections of 1948," *Diplomatic History* 7, 1983, pp. 35-55.

Monroe, Alan, "Consistency Between Public Preferences and National Policy Decisions," *American Politics Quarterly* 7, January 1979, pp. 3-19.

Morris, Benny. "The Causes and Character of the Arab Exodus from Palestine: The Israel Defense Forces Intelligence Branch Analysis of June, 1948," *Middle Eastern Studies* 22, January 1986, pp. 5-19.

Nachmani, Amikam. "Britain's Post-War Relations with America in the Middle East," *Journal of Contemporary History* 18, January 1983, pp. 117-139.

Neumann, Emanuel. "Abba Hillel Silver: History Maker," *The American Zionist*, February 5, 1953, pp. 5-11.

Niebuhr, Reinhold. "Jews After the War, Part I," *The Nation*, February 21, 1942, pp. 214-216.

Niebuhr, Reinhold. "Jews After the War, Part II." *The Nation*, February 28, 1942, pp. 253-255.

Ovendale, Ritchie. "The Palestine Story of the British Labour Government, 1945-1946," *International Affairs* 55, July 1979, pp. 409-431.

Pappe, Ilan. "Moshe Sharrett, David Ben-Gurion and the Palestinian Operation, 1948-1956," *Studies in Zionism* 7, Spring 1986, pp. 77-96.

Parzen, Herbert. "President Truman and the Palestine Quandry: His Initial Experience, April---December 1945," *Jewish Social Studies* 35, January 1973, pp. 42-72.

Parzen, Herbert. "The Roosevelt Palestine Policy, 1943-1945: An Exercise in Dual Diplomacy," *American Jewish Archives* 26, April 1974, pp. 31-64.

Paterson, Thomas G. "Presidential Foreign Policy, Public Opinion and Congress: The Truman Years," *Diplomatic History* 3, 1979, pp. 1-18.

Patterson, David S. "What's Wrong (and Right) with American Diplomatic History: A Diagnosis and Perscription," *The Society for Historians of American Foreign Relations Newsletter* 9, September 1978, pp. 1-14.

Peck, Sara. "The Campaign to Change American Response to the Holocaust, 1943-1945," *Journal of Contemporary History* 15, April 1980, pp. 367-400.

Pentkower, Monty N. "Ben-Gurion, Silver and the 1941 U.P.A. National Conference for Palestine: A Turning Point in American Zionist History," *American Jewish History* 69, September 1979, pp. 66-78.

Plesur, Milton. "The Relations Between the United States and Palestine," *Judaism* 3, 1954, pp. 469-479.

Podet, Allen H. "Anti-Zionism in a Key United States Diplomat: Loy Henderson at the End of World War II," *American Jewish Archives* 30, November 1978, pp. 155-187.

Polenberg, Robert. "Historians and the Liberal Presidency: Recent Appraisals of Roosevelt and Truman," *South Atlantic Quarterly* 75, November 1976, pp. 20-35.

Pollard, Robert A. "Economic Security and the Origins of the Cold War: Bretton Woods, the Marshall Plan, and American Rearmament, 1944-1950," *Diplomatic History* 9, 1985, pp. 271-283.

Quester, George H. "Origins of the Cold War: Some Clues from Public Opinion,"
    Public Opinion Quarterly 93, 1978, pp. 647-663.
Randall, Stephen J. "Harold Ickes and U. S. Foreign Petroleum Policy Planning, 1939-
    1945," *Business History Review* 58, 1983, pp. 367-387.
Ritzer, Stanley. "I Ran the Blockade to Palestine: The True Story of the Exodus,"
    Argosy, February 1960, pp. 19-21 and 78-80.
Roosevelt, Kermit. "The Partition of Palestine: A Lesson in Pressure Politics," *The
    Middle East Journal* 2, January 1948, pp. 1-16.
Roosevelt, Kermit. "Triple Play in the Middle East," *Harper's*, April 1948, pp. 359-
    369.
Rovere, Richard. "The Unassailable Vandenberg," *Harper's*, May 1948, pp. 394-403.
Russell, Francis H. "The Function of Public Opinion Analysis in the Formation of
    Foreign Policy," Department of State *Bulletin* 20, March 6, 1949, pp. 275-277.
Schneider, William; Michael D. Berman and Mark Schultz. "Bloc Voting
    Reconsidered: Is There a Jewish Vote?" *Ethnicity* 1, 1974, pp. 345-392.
Scott, Andrew M. "The Department of State: Formal Organization and Informal
    Culture," *International Studies Quarterly* 13, March 1969, pp. 1-19.
Scott, Andrew M. "Environmental Change and Organizational Adaptation: The
    Problem of the State Department," *International Studies Quarterly* 14, March
    1970, pp. 85-95.
Shafir, Shlomo. "Taylor and McDonald: Two Divurgent Views on Zionism and the
    Emerging Jewish State," *Jewish Social Studies* 39, 1977, pp. 323-346.
Sigelman, Lee. "Gauging the Public Response to Presidential Leadership," *Presidential
    Studies Quarterly* 10, 1980, pp. 427-433.
Sigelman, Lee and Dixie Mercer McNeil, "White House Decision Making Under
    Stress: A Case Analysis," *American Journal of Political Science* 24, 1980, pp.
    652-673.
Sigelman, Lee and Carol K. Sigelman, "Presidential Leadership of Public Opinion:
    From 'Benevolent Leader' to 'Kiss of Death'?" *Experimental Study of Politics*
    7, Summer 1981, pp. 1-22.
Silver, Abba Hillel. "Why the Jews Should Have Palestine," *American Magazine*,
    December 1947, pp. 34 and 130.
Slonim, Shlomo. "The 1948 American Arms Embargo to Palestine," *Political Science
    Quarterly* 94, 1979, pp. 495-514.
Smith, Geoffrey S. "Harry, We Hardly Knew You: Revisionism, Politics and
    Diplomacy, 1945-1954," *American Political Science Review* 70, 1976, pp. 560-
    582.
Steele, Richard W. "The Pulse of the People: Franklin D. Roosevelt and the Gauging
    of American Public Opinion," *Journal of Contemporary History* 9, October
    1974, pp. 195-216.
Steele, Richard W. "News of the Good War: World World II News Management,"
    Journalism Quarterly 62, 1985, pp. 707-717 and 783.
Stolberg, Benjamin. "The Man Behind the *New York Times*," *Atlantic Monthly* 138,
    1926, pp. 721-731.
Stratton, William G. "Should Congress Admit 400,000 D.P.'s Outside of the U.S.
    Immigration Quotas?" *Congressional Digest* 27, January 1948, pp. 22 and 24.

Steinitz, Mark S. "The U.S. Propaganda Effort in Czechoslovakia, 1945-1948,"
    Diplomatic History 6, 1982, pp. 359-385.
Theoharis, Athan. "Ignoring History: Harry S. Truman, the Revisionists and the
    Press," *Chicago Journalism Review*, March 1973, pp. 14-15.
Thompson, Carol L. "Palestine: The Promised Land," *Current History* 12, April 1947,
    p. 353.
Thorne, Christopher. "Chatham House, Whitehall and Fear Eastern Issues, 1941-
    1945," *International Affairs* 54, January 1978, pp. 1-29.
Timewell, H. C. "Exodus 1947 Takes on Her Cargo," *American Neptune* 9, 1949, pp.
    300-301.
Trice, Robert H. "The American Elite Press and the Arab-Israeli Conflict," *Middle
    East Journal* 33, 1979, 310-325.
Wagner, Robert F. "Palestine—A World Reponsibility," *The Nation*, September 15,
    1945, pp. 247-249.
Wala, Michael. "Selling the Marshall Plan at Home: The Committee for the Marshall
    Plan to Aid European Recovery," *Diplomatic History* 10, 1986, pp. 247-265.
Walker, Jack L. "A Critique of the Elitist Theory of Democracy," *American Political
    Science Review* 60, 1966, pp. 285-295.
Washburn, Patrick L. "The Office of Censorship's Attempt to Control Press Coverage
    of the Atomic Bomb during World War II," *Journalism Monographs* 120,
    April 1990, pp. 11-35.
Wasserstein, Bernard. "New Light on the Moyne Murder," *Midstream* 26, March
    1980, pp. 30-38.
Weizmann, Chaim. "Palestine's Role in the Solution of the Jewish Problem," *Foreign
    Affairs* 20, January 1942, pp. 324-338.
Weizmann, Chaim. "The Palestine Papers, 1943-1947," *Journal of Palestine Studies*
    2, Summer 1973, pp. 33-54.
Wilson, Evan M. "The American Interest in the Palestine Question and the
    Establishment of Israel," *The Annals of the American Academy of Political and
    Social Science* 401, May 1972, pp. 64-73.
Wittner, Lawrence. "The Truman Doctrine and the Defense of Freedom," *Diplomatic
    History* 4, 1980, pp. 161-188.

AGENDA-SETTING RESEARCH

Altheide, David. *Creating Reality: How T. V. News Distorts Events* (Beverly Hills:
    Sage, 1976).
Arterton, F. Christopher. *Media Politics: The News Strategies of Presidential
    Campaigns* (Lexington: Lexington Books, 1984).
Ball-Rokeach, Sandra J. "The Origins of Individual Media-System Dependency: A
    Sociological Framework," *Communication Research* 12, 1985, pp. 485-510.
Becker, Lee B. and Jack M. McLeod. "Political Consqeuences of Agenda-Setting,"
    Mass Communication Research 3, 1976, pp. 8-15.
Berelson, Bernard and Morris Janowitz, eds., *Reader in Public Opinion and
    Communication* (New York: Free Press, 1966).

Chaffee, Steven H. and Donna G. Wilson. "Media Rich. Media Poor: Two Studies of Diversity in Agenda-Holding," *Journalism Quarterly* 54, 1977, pp. 46-47.

Cohen, Bernard C. *The Public's Impact on Foreign Policy* (Lanham: University Press of America, 1983).

Cook, Fay Lomax; Tom P. Tyler, Edward G. Goertz, Margaret T. Gordon, David Protess, Donna R. Leff and Harvey L. Molotch. "Media and Agenda-Setting: Effects on the Public, Interest Group Leaders, Policy Makers, and Policy," *Public Opinion Quarterly* 47, 1983, pp. 16-25.

Epstein, Edward Jay. *News from Nowhere* (New York: Vintage Press, 1973).

Gaddy, Gary D. and Enoh Tanjong. "Earthquake Coverage by the Western Press," *Journal of Communication* 36, 1986, pp. 105-112.

Gans, Herbert J. *Deciding What's News: A Study of CBS Evening News, NBC Nightly News, Newsweek and Time* (New York: Random House, 1980).

Gormley, Jr., William Thomas. "Newspaper Agendas and Political Elites," *Journalism Quarterly* 52, 1985, pp. 304-308.

Graber, Doris A. *Processing the News: How People Tame the Information Tide* (New York: Longman, 1984).

Lasswell, Harold D. *Propaganda Techniques in the World War* (New York: Knopf, 1927).

Lazarsfeld, Paul and Frank Stanton, eds., *Radio Research, 1943-1944* (New York: Duell, Sloan and Pearce, 1944).

Leff, Donna R.; David L. Protess and Stephen C. Brooks. "Crusading Journalism: Chaning Public Attitudes and Policy making Agenda," *Public Opinion Quarterly* 50, 1986, pp. 300-315.

McCombs, Maxwell E. and Donald L. Shaw. *Public Opinion Quarterly* 36, 1972, pp. 176-184.

McCombs, Maxwell E. "Agenda-Setting Research: A Bibliographic Essay," *Political Science Review* 1, 1976, pp. 1-7.

McLeod, Jack M.; Lee B. Becker and James E. Byrnes. "Another Look at the Agenda-Setting Funtion of the Press," *Communication Research* 1, 1974, pp. 131-166.

Noelle-Neumann, Elizabeth. *The Spiral of Silence: Public Opinion ---Our Social Skin* (Chicago: University of Chicago, 1984).

Page, Benjamin I. and Robert Y. Shapiro, "Effects of Public Opinion on Policy," *American Political Science Review* 77, March 1983, pp. 175-190.

Patterson, Thomas E. *The Mass Media Election: How Americans Choose Their President* (New York: Praeger, 1980).

Protess, David L.; Donna R. Leff, Stephen C. Brooks and Margaret T. Gordon. "Uncovering Rape: The Watchdog Press and the Limits of Agenda-Setting," *Public Opinion Quarterly* 49, 1985, pp. 19-37.

Rogers, Everett M. and James W. Dearing. "Agenda-Setting Research: Where Has It Been, Where Is It Going?" in James A. Anderson, ed., *Communication Yearbook* (Beverly Hills: Sage, 1987).

Rogers, Everett M.; James W. Dearing and Soonbum Chang, "AID's in the 1980's: The Agenda Setting Process for a Public Issue," *Journalism Monographs* 126, April 1991, pp. 21-44.

Rosenau, James N. *Public Opinion and Foreign Policy* (New York: Random House, 1961).

Rosenau, James N. *National Leadership and Foreign Policy: A Case Study in the Mobilization of Public Support* (Princeton: Princeton University, 1963).

Wagner, Joseph. "Media Do Make a Difference: The Differential Impact of Mass Media in the 1976 Presidential Race," *American Journal of Political Science* 27, 1983, pp. 407-428.

Walker, Jack L. "Setting the Agenda in the U.S. Senate: A Theory of Problem Selection," *British Journal of Political Science* 7, 1977, pp. 433-445.

Index

Abdallah of Transjordan, King, 88, 166

Academy of Political Science, 114

Acheson, Dean, 29, 31, 37, 38, 62, 115

Agenda-Setting, 8, 99

Aiken (South Carolina) *Journal and Review*, 28

Ajax, 78

Akzin, Benjamin, 57

Albania, 106

Allen, Robert S., 11

Almond, Gabriel, 177

Alsop, Joseph, 11, 36, 141, 142, 159, 163

Alsop, Stewart, 11, 141, 142, 159, 163

American Christian Palestine Committee (ACPC), 56-57, 76, 85, 110

American Council for Judaism, 34, 134

The American Hebrew (New York), 59

American Jewish Committee, 64, 134-135

American Jewish Conference, 87

American League for a Free Palestine, 34, 64

American Society of Newspaper Editors, 26

American Zionist Emergency Council (AZEC): Action for Palestine Week, 58-61; acts independently, 55-56; and American Christian Palestine Committee, 56; attempts to discredit Grand Mufti, 109; attitude toward Arthur Krock, 33; attitude toward *New York Times*, 32, 34, 131, 133-135; attitude toward State Department, 136, 138; celebrates partition decision, 117; on the defensive, 132-134; divided, 130; early leadership under Abba Hillel Silver, 51; evaluates success of Zionist campaign, 169; and *Exodus 1947*, 81, 85, 92; grass roots work, 33, 60, 108, 116, 133, 137, 158; isolated, 65, 78; and Joseph Harsch, 134; and Walter Lippmann, 57; as mobilizer of public opinion, 10, 23, 38, 51, 55-60, 64-65, 92, 108, 133, 159; opposed by Chaim Weizmann, 49, 65; optimism about likelihood of Jewish state, 108-109; pessimism about chances for a Jewish state, 139; and press, 92, 133-135; pressure tactics, 55, 57-60, 108, 110; strategy sessions, 31, 55,

About the Author

BRUCE EVENSEN is Assistant Professor in the department of Communication at DePaul University. He has covered the Middle East as a reporter and is the author of several articles that have appeared in scholarly journals.